D0008259

Managing Risks for Corporate Integrity:
How to Survive an Ethical Misconduct Disaster

Lynn Brewer
President and CEO
The Integrity Institute, Inc.

Robert Chandler
Blanche E. Seaver Professor of Communication
Pepperdine University

O.C. Ferrell
Bill Daniels Distinguished Professor of Business Ethics
University of Wyoming

BOWLING GREEN STATE
UNIVERSITY LIBRARY

Australia · Brazil · Canada · Mexico · Singapore · Spain · United Kingdom · United States

THOMSON

Managing Risks for Corporate Integrity:
How to Survive an Ethical Misconduct Disaster

Lynn Brewer • Robert Chandler • O.C. Ferrell

COPYRIGHT © 2006 by Texere, an imprint of Thomson/South-Western, a part of The Thomson Corporation. Thomson and the Star logo are trademarks used herein under license.

Composed by:
Chip Butzko

Printed in the United States of America by RR Donnelley, Crawfordsville

1 2 3 4 5 09 08 07 06
This book is printed on acid-free paper.

ISBN 0-324-20351-9

This publication is designed to provide accurate and authoritative information in regard to the subject matter covered. It is sold with the understanding that the publisher is not engaged in rendering legal, accounting, or other professional services. If expert assistance is required, the services of a competent professional person should be sought. ALL RIGHTS RESERVED.

No part of this work covered by the copyright hereon may be reproduced or used in any form or by any means—graphic, electronic, or mechanical, including photocopying, recording, taping, Web distribution, or information storage and retrieval systems, or in any other manner— without the written permission of the publisher.

The names of all companies or products mentioned herein are used for identification purposes only and may be trademarks or registered trademarks of their respective owners. Texere disclaims any affiliation, association, connection with, sponsorship, or endorsements by such owners.

For permission to use material from this text or product, submit a request online at *http://www. thomsonrights.com.*

A CIP Library of Congress Cataloging in Publication Data Requested.

For more information about our products, contact us at:
Thomson Learning Academic Resource Center 1-800-423-0563

Thomson Higher Education
5191 Natorp Boulevard
Mason, Ohio 45040
USA

ii

Preface

This book is designed to help managers prepare and manage for organizational integrity. The risks of an ethical misconduct disaster (EMD) have never been greater due to the increasing level of regulatory and stakeholder scrutiny. An ethical misconduct disaster is an unexpected organizational crisis that results from employee misconduct, illegal activities, or unethical decisions that disrupts operations and threatens the reputation and possible existence of the organization. This book is a managerial guide to planning, preventing, managing and recovering from misconduct that occurs in all organizations. The question is not if your firm will experience ethical misconduct but when misconduct happens, will you be prepared?

Ethical Continuity

Ethics continuity planning includes strategies, systems and procedures that help ensure that a firm's ethics and compliance programs are in place and operating (with all necessary redundancies, backup checks and balances, safeguards, monitoring, etc.). The development of an ethical organizational culture requires integrity being placed on the strategic agenda beyond required regulatory compliance issues. This book provides direction to guide planning for ethical continuity through decision making; design; development; implementation; assessment and revision of programs.

Facing Ethical Disaster Threats and Risks

There are many reasons to develop the most effective organizational ethics and compliance program possible. Organizations face significant threats from ethical misconduct and illegal behavior from employees and managers. Well-meaning managers often devise schemes that appear legal, but are so ethically flawed they result in scandals and a myriad of legal issues. There is a need to identify these potential risks and uncover the existence of activities or events that relate to misconduct that if left undetected could devastate the company. There must be a plan and infrastructure to determine what is happening and deal with it as soon as possible rather than covering up, ignoring, and assuming that no one will ever find out about ethical and legal lapses. There is a need to discover, disclose, expose, and resolve issues as they occur. All firms have misconduct and discovering and dealing with these events is the only effective way to be successful in today's complex regulatory system. The existence of plaintiff-friendly civil litigation can destroy reputation and draw intense scrutiny to a company, not to mention judgments that can ultimately destroy the company's market capitalization.

Legal and Regulatory Incentives for Ethical Conduct

The Federal Sentencing Guidelines for Organizations (FSGO), which went into effect in 1991, with significant amendments in 2004, generally tie potential penalties for violations of the law to the quality of corporate ethics and compliance programs. The United States Sentencing Commission, which developed the guidelines, recommends strict and severe enforcement of existing regulations and statutory requirements, particularly in cases where companies have failed to take proactive actions to promote ethics and compliance. Judges, courts, and regulatory agencies look for evidence of a proactive commitment to ethics including the existence of strong compliance programs, evidence of voluntary disclosure of misconduct, and evidence of full cooperation in the investigation of misconduct. Failing to find such evidence, the United States Sentencing Commission recommends that judges enforce regulations and sentencing without any mitigation.

The requirements imposed by the Sarbanes-Oxley Act (SOX) are also significant for ethical planning. This legislation has created new requirements for accountability and ethical conduct as a result of the corporate financial scandals in recent years. The major provisions of the SOX include criminal and civil penalties for non-compliance violations, certification of internal auditing by external auditors, and increased disclosure regarding all financial statements, and prison terms up to ten years for retaliation against whistleblowers. In addition, the law mandates codes of ethics for senior financial officers and disclosure of audit committee financial experts.

According to one study, compliance costs as a percentage of profits could be as much as 53% of profits. Pointoflow.com indicates that it costs medium sized companies 30% more to comply with SOX than four years ago when the legislation was passed. Compliance may be costly but non-compliance can be devastating.

The Department of Justice, through the Thompson Memo (Larry Thompson, Deputy Attorney General, 2003 memo to the United States Attorneys) advanced general principles to consider in cases involving corporate wrongdoing. This memo makes it clear that ethics and compliance programs are important to detect types of misconduct most likely to occur in a particular corporation's line of business. Without an effective ethics and compliance program to detect ethical and legal lapses, the firm should not be treated leniently. Also, the prosecutor generally has wide latitude in determining when, whom and whether to prosecute violations of Federal law. United States Attorneys are directed that charging for even minor misconduct may be appropriate when the wrongdoing was pervasive by a large number of employees in a particular role, e.g., sales staff, procurement officers, or was condoned by upper management. Without an effective program to identify whether the misconduct is at the hands of an isolated rogue employee or the entire culture is rotten, there can be serious consequences associated with regulatory issues, enforcement, and sentencing.

The 2004 amendment to the FSGO requires that a business's governing authority be well informed about its ethics program with respect to content, implementation, and effectiveness. This places the responsibility squarely on the shoulders of the firm's leadership, usually the board of directors. The board must ensure that there is a high-ranking manager accountable for the day-to-day operational oversight of the ethics program. The board must provide for adequate authority, resources, and open access to its members or an appropriate subcommittee of the board. The board must ensure that there are confidential mechanisms available so that the organization's employees and agents may report or seek guidance about potential or actual misconduct without fear of retaliation. Finally, the board is required to oversee the discovery of risks and to design, implement, and modify approaches to deal with those risks. If board members do not understand the nature, purpose, and methods available to implement an ethics program, the firm is at risk of inadequate oversight in the event of ethical misconduct that escalates into a scandal.

Developing Organizational RADAR

To guide your journey through this book we present our RADAR model for preparing for and managing an EMD. Using organizational RADAR to identify and deal with the potential for an ethical disaster. The RADAR model includes the need to:

(R)ecognize–Define the issues, threat forecasting, risk assessment, anticipation to recognize
(A)void–Develop proactive ethical leadership and effective ethics/ compliance programs
(D)iscover–Actively communicate and monitor, formal and informal feedback systems
(A)nswer–Ongoing oversight, integrated systems, rapid actions, and program development
(R)ecover–Diligence to restore image, stabilize situation, and resume productivity

An Insiders Look at Enron

The book also includes an insiders view of the Enron ethical disaster. Perhaps the most widely recognized Enron whistleblower to go to the United States Government, explores the ethical misconduct scandal at Enron from an internal perspective to try to better understand the individual and organizational factors and pressures that resulted in such a devastating disaster. Lynn Brewer, as an executive in four different divisions at Enron, provides a front-row seat of Enron's implosion from the inside. Now CEO and founding chairman of The Integrity Institute, Inc., Brewer has written about her personal experiences at Enron in *Confessions of an Enron Executive: A Whistleblower's Story*. In this book she explores both the corruption that destroyed the company, as well as the glue that held the company together – the complacency. The devastation caused by both equally destructive forces will be looked at as we examine the risks of an EMD that can be caused by silence.

Sustaining Positive Corporate Reputation and Image

Reputation is one of an organization's greatest intangible assets with tangible value. Corporate reputation, image, and brands are more important than ever and are among the most critical aspects of sustaining relationships with constituents including investors, customers, financial analysts, media, and government watchdogs. Corporate reputation has substantial business value and is best managed at the strategic level. There are many potential threats to reputation. Reputation can be damaged by poor performance, mismanagement, or ethical misconduct. In the aftermath of the well publicized ethics disasters there has been a dramatic realization in corporate boardrooms that reputations are valuable but fragile corporate assets. It is vital to understand not only the importance of corporate reputation but also the factors that are essential for the creation of, as well as the fundamental threats to a positive reputation.

In recent years, while there has been increasing attention to monitoring, measuring, protecting, and managing the corporate reputation, the critical connection between ethical conduct and reputation has not received the strategic attention that it deserves. The fact that a single negative incident can influence perceptions of a corporation's image and reputation instantly and the ill effects can linger for years afterward demands that organizations must focus on recognizing, avoiding, discovering, answering, and responding to ethical misconduct concerns. Ethics disasters and the related media publicity are a significant threat to positive corporate reputation. Obviously, stakeholders who are most directly affected by negative events will have a corresponding shift in their perceptions of a firm's reputation.

Ethical disasters can depress employee motivation and morale, may lead to high levels of turnover and resignation, and may prove to be a substantial obstacle in recruiting the next generation of top prospects to work for your company. On the other hand, even those indirectly connected to negative events can shift their reputation perceptions. Ethical disasters can devastate how financial analysts, as well as institutional and individual investors perceive a company. A scandal will generally impact the company's reputation both from investor confidence and consumer confidence. A tarnished reputation will also extend to diminish the value of your corporate brand. As investor perceptions and decisions begin to take their toll, shareholder value will drop exposing the company to class action suits which can further the damage. Meanwhile, reputation is also a factor in the consumers' perceptions of product attributes and corporate image features that lead to consumer willingness to purchase goods and services at profitable prices. Turning your critical attention to the issues of avoiding ethical misconduct disasters and sustaining integrity is one of the most strategic investments that senior management can make.

Responding to Ethical Disasters and Scandals

While the ultimate goal is to resolve ethical problems before they become front page headlines, it is also essential that you be completely prepared to respond in the event that your problems find their way into the public sphere. Preparation and planning will enable a prudent company to effectively respond in the event that an ethical lapse cascades into a major ethical disaster. Effective response requires a consistent system of policies and procedures, feedback mechanisms, and an action plan of specific steps to mitigate and manage the disaster. Crisis communication with key constituents including employees, investors, customers, and other stakeholders is essential to respond to an ethics crisis. In particular, it is imperative that your company understands the role and function of the news media as well as being thoroughly prepared to respond to the critical journalists scrutiny. To fully respond a company must have a communication plan that enables your message to reach the various key constituents and persuade, inform, and motivate them as you attempt to salvage and repair your corporate reputation.

Recovering from an Ethical Disaster and Scandal

Corporate integrity is a key part of building a trustworthy reputation and trust is the foundation upon which investors, vendors, employees, and customers base their relationship with your company. However, if a major ethical misconduct disaster has rocked your business, these trusting relationships may have been damaged or broken. How does a company strategically plan to recover from ethics disasters? The grim reality is that sometimes companies simply do not recover from these disasters. Ethical disasters can be fatal for organizations. Ignoring the risks is done at great peril. Inadequate or neglected preparation and planning for ethical lapses decreases the odds of successful continuity of business operations. However strategic planning and management may enable your company to survive and recover from the impact of such scandals.

Every movement of your internal disciplinary process,

entanglement with the legal system, and news reports about the nature of your operations will influence the motivation, morale, and expectations of all of your stakeholders- and it will do so with an intensity that was not present before the crisis occurred. Successful recovery requires careful advance planning, skillful management, and attention to the deliberate processes essential to repair your corporate reputation and image. Recovery will also depend on accurate assessment of underlying cultural norms, ethical decision-making, reward- disciplinary structures, communication content, implicit- explicit rule systems, loss of respect and trust that will need to be restored, and understanding what went wrong and what can be done to prevent a recurrence of the event. Surviving ethical misconduct disasters is possible but it requires strategic planning and skillful management.

Goals for this Book

We hope that this book is useful in managing your risks for corporate integrity. We believe that managing integrity is not only good business and required by statute but it is also the right and professional thing to do. We believe that in the long run, organizational integrity is not only profitable, but it is quite frankly a mission critical aspect of sustained business continuity. The risks of not managing integrity are great and can result in an ethical misconduct disaster that sends executives to prison, costs millions in fines and penalties, costs billions in lost brand, image, and reputation valuation, disrupt productivity, morale, motivation, and recruitment, and leave a corporate train wreck in the spot where a successful enterprise once stood.

On the positive side there is adequate evidence that firms who successfully manage ethical risks, do not have as many ethical problems and those that do occur are far less likely to escalate into ethical misconduct disasters. These firms have excellent relationships with their stakeholders and have long run profitability. Just as important high integrity firms make a significant contribution to society and the well-being of all stakeholders. If this book can encourage, motivate, and empower more strategic organizational integrity continuity efforts then it will have met the goals for which we created it.

Lynn Brewer
Robert C. Chandler
O.C. Ferrell
January 2006

Dedication

*To my husband, Douglas Brewer, for his support and
dedication that allows me to change the world's view of
integrity, and pursue my dreams of measuring it. To my
"parents," Judy and Alan Morris, for their quiet guidance
that has always allowed me to remain steadfast to my
convictions of right and wrong which has made all of
the difference.*

–Lynn Brewer

*To my parents Bob and Mary Ann Chandler who taught me
to value education and knowledge, service to others, and
acting with integrity.*

–Robert Chandler

*To my mother Kathlene Ferrell who provided my first
ethical foundation and my son James Ferrell who
carries on the tradition by resolving legal conflicts as
an attorney.*

–O.C. Ferrell

Table of Contents

Chapter

1

Overview

There is a risk that few organizations to date have focused on–how will our business continuity be impacted by an ethical misconduct disaster? Whether you become the next Coca-Cola, Merck, Wal-Mart or Enron will be determined by how you prepare for and manage the ethical risks that jeopardize your corporate integrity. The purpose of this book is to give you not only an insider's view of Enron and the behaviors that lead up to the implosion, but also to provide you with a better understanding of how to recognize, avoid, discover, answer and recover from an ethical misconduct disaster.

At one time our markets were based upon the trading of goods using a currency of trust. That currency of trust still remains at the core of our capital markets, which often adjust more to perception than fair market value. However, in the case of a breach of trust, how the market responds often depends upon how the corporation has managed the risk of an ethical misconduct disaster and of the goodwill built by the organization's effort to be transparent.

Corporate America, long portrayed as the most efficient and credible business model in the world, is facing an unprecedented ethics crisis after a wave of accounting scandals. The true costs of these ethical disasters are only beginning to become clear; however, as the table below demonstrates, the loss to shareholder value can be significant upon the public learning of ethical misconduct:

SEARS	$ 6 Billion in 1 Day
MARSH	$ 16 Billion in 1 Week
COCA-COLA	$ 15 Billion in 3 Weeks
AIG	$ 70 Billion in 1 Month
TYCO	$ 40 Billion in 2 Months
ENRON	$ 90 Billion in 24 Days

These scandals, including the complete downfall of several well-known corporations such as Enron and Arthur Andersen, have put the discussion of the impact and cost of a disaster relating to ethical misconduct at the top of the senior management agenda, in large part because of the huge penalties now facing companies. According to HealthSouth, they have spent "approximately $440 million in, among other things, stabilizing [their] operations, reconstructing [their] accounting records, producing restated and other financial statements, restructuring the Company finances and restoring HealthSouth's credibility–all responses to the crises created as a direct result of the fraud perpetrated while Richard Scrushy was CEO and Chairman." The result was "a cumulative net reduction in shareholders' equity of $3.9 billion."[1] In addition, the company agreed to pay "$100 million to settle a lawsuit claiming violations of federal securities laws" and "$325 million plus interest as part of a global settlement regarding certain alleged inappropriate Medicare billing practices."

Ethical misconduct, whether illegal or simply unethical, is a serious issue and ethics scandals can be disastrous for individuals, companies, and society. Of course, not every decision that comes under public scrutiny is unethical and, unfortunately, many times the cover-up itself is the source of the unethical behavior. And while not every unethical decision rises to the level of a crisis, many times companies that are unprepared for an impending disaster and the consequences that follow find themselves facing penalties and additional public scrutiny, which can diminish shareholder value and may destroy the company. The purpose of this book is to provide guidance in the preparedness and management of ethical misconduct disasters.

An *ethical misconduct disaster (EMD)*[1b] is an unexpected organizational crisis that results from employee misconduct, illegal activities such as fraud, or unethical decisions and which significantly disrupts operations and threatens or is perceived to threaten the firm's continuity of operations. An EMD can be even more devastating than traditional natural disasters or technological disruptions. It can disrupt routine operations, paralyze employees and reduce productivity, destroy organizational reputations, erode stakeholder confidence, and have the potential to result in incalculable legal and financial costs.

As organizations plan for natural disasters and insure against traditional risks, so too should they prepare for ethical crises. The purpose of this book is to identify, illustrate and define the business problem of an EMD and to present a guide to identify and develop plans to prevent, mitigate, cope with, respond to and survive an EMD. As we shall discuss, an EMD can be managed by organizational initiatives to recognize, avoid, discover, answer and recover from the misconduct. This book provides the detail necessary to understand and implement a systematic approach to avoiding such disasters.

Our goal in this chapter is to provide an understanding about the nature of a corporate EMD and the consequences to the firm and all of its stakeholders. We assess the potential damage of an ethical disaster to both business and society. The costs of an EMD from both a financial and reputation perspective are assessed, as well as the need for planning to avoid an EMD. Additionally, the legal pressure to develop ethics programs and the role of leadership in preventing a disaster are presented from a contingency planning perspective.

Preparing for an Ethical Misconduct Disaster

As we found with Hurricane Katrina, being unprepared can cause a disaster that is far greater than the damage caused from the underlying event. The ethical disaster risks facing organizations today are significant and the reputational damage caused can be far greater for those companies that find themselves unprepared. The key is to recognize that the risks associated with ethical misconduct are real and that if insufficient controls are in place the company can suddenly find itself the subject of an EMD. Although we can't predict an ethical disaster, we can and must prepare for one.

In 2001, the year Enron imploded, the Securities and Exchange Commission received on average 6,400 reports of securities and financial fraud every month from whistleblowers. In 2004, three years after the EMD at Enron and two years after the passage of the Sarbanes-Oxley Act (SOX), those reports had mushroomed to an astounding 40,000 reports per month[2]. With approximately 16,000 public companies traded on the U.S. stock exchanges, one could surmise that even if half of the reports are "false positives" or frivolous reports filed by disgruntled employees, there are still more reports filed every month than there are publicly traded companies.

The Ethics Resource Center *(www.erc.org)* reported in its most recent National Business Ethics Survey that "one in two employees witnessed at least one specific type of misconduct."[3] At least 52 percent of employees observed at least one type of misconduct in the past year, while the percentage of employees willing to report the misconduct dropped by 10 percentage points between 2003 and 2005,[4] which may explain the increase in whistleblowing reports to the SEC. Even with the requirement that public companies have an anonymous and confidential means of reporting misconduct under SOX Section 301, companies are at greater risk, which means they are as likely to learn about the ethical misconduct at the same time as the public.

The worst approach for any company is the false assumption that ethical scandals "can't happen to us." Of course, such sentiment is intrinsically related to the corresponding aftermath statement, "I never thought this would happen to us." The reality is that all of the common justifications for ignoring ethical misconduct are based on unsubstantiated trust in unmanaged human nature and in ignoring the systemic factors that give rise to an EMD.

The goal is to recognize that while we cannot remove the risk of ethical misconduct, great leaders are prepared. As Jeff Immelt, CEO of General Electric stated in his 2002 letter to his shareholders, "One concern that keeps me up at night is that among the 300,000-plus GE employees worldwide, there are a handful who choose to ignore our code of ethics. I would be naïve to assume a few bad apples don't exist in our midst." Perhaps this is why when GE received a letter of inquiry from the SEC in 2005, it had little impact on the overall stock value of the company.

Obviously managing ethics requires more strategic planning and enactment beyond hiring "good, basically moral people." Even systematically hiring only employees with the highest levels of morals and ethics is no sure-fire method for preventing a major scandal, as evidenced by several scandals surrounding the conduct of some priests as well as respected political and corporate icons. Even having a detailed written statement of ethics or specific documented policies does not guarantee the avoidance of such disasters. Take Enron as an example. The 65-page corporate *Code of Ethics,* written in 2000, was intended to help guide employees for "conducting the business affairs…in accordance with all applicable laws and in a moral and honest manner."[5] but was nothing more than lip service, as mid-level employees witnessed senior level executives granted waivers from conflicts of interests such as the sister of Chairman Ken Lay being allowed to provide corporate travel services or the Chief Financial Officer Andrew Fastow being allowed to engage in self-dealing with Enron through his hedge fund. When the words and deeds of leadership do not properly align with the code of conduct, one cannot expect to adequately avoid these scandals by delegating planning and execution to subordinates without proper internal controls.

Organizational standards and expectations must be clarified and such standards must be used in the formation of formal and informal processes and be part of an active and ongoing training program to ensure employee alignment be meshed with the decision-making processes that occur at various levels and functions in the organization, and be included in regular and periodic assessment of employee behavior. All of these efforts should be considerations at the highest levels of management.

As part of the preparation for an EMD, continuity planning should include the strategies, systems, and procedures that help ensure that your firm's ethics programs are in place and operating (including all necessary redundancies, back-up checks and balances, safeguards, monitoring, etc.) and must occur as part of the strategic planning process. It must be integrated with decisions on development, transformation, goal setting, prioritization, and regulatory compliance issues.

Throughout this book our focus will be based upon the premise that the risk for an ethical disaster exists and with good preparation, in the event you are struck by an EMD, you can manage the disaster to reduce the damage caused to your reputation and your ability to sustain your business continuity.

Recognizing an Ethical Misconduct Disaster

It is perhaps important to point out the difference between *ethical lapses*, which are instances where unethical behavior or inappropriate decisions occur and *ethical disasters*, which can emerge in those instances where an ethical lapse escalates into a scandal of devastating dimensions. Ethical lapses occur all too frequently in business, but few rise to the level of ethical disasters. There are recognizable phases of escalation from an unethical decision to disaster, including a questionable or debatable event, recognized ethical issue, organizational discovery, and organizational response—which, without appropriate anticipation and intervention, can inevitably lead to organizational disaster. Misconduct—whether because of its severity, persistence, lack of quick or appropriate response, public scrutiny of the (mis)handling of the event, or the involvement of legal or regulatory structures—may escalate to a level where it truly becomes a disaster for a business. Such disasters go well beyond the mere disruption of routine operations. They result in disastrous consequences that have potentially significant economic consequences or, in some cases, present a threat to the company's very survival.

An EMD can negatively affect an organization, a major business unit, the reputation and image of a brand, and all stakeholders of the organization. It can disrupt business operations, threaten productivity and performance, and result in criminal charges against senior management, top executives, and even mid-level managers. An EMD can also damage, perhaps severely, an organization's financial performance (bankruptcy or dissolution), threaten employees (layoffs and voluntary turnover), result in litigation (civil and criminal), result in regulatory responses (probation, fines, and restitution), and create a media circus that can destroy the public's basic trust in a firm, its reputation, and its image. These scandals can threaten the continuity and very existence of the corporation itself, as in the case of Arthur Andersen, one of the leading accounting firms in the world.

An EMD can be plotted on a continuum with results ranging from minor disruptions with modest costs to the extinction of the company. In the middle range are disasters that may hurt earnings, send managers and executives to prison, generate fines and punitive sanctions, hurt morale, depress sales, and create a long-term drag on operations. Although HealthSouth Corporation's CEO Richard Scrushy was acquitted of participating in a $27 billion accounting fraud, many of his executives plea-bargained deals with the government for more lenient sentences.[6] Moreover, the resulting damage to the firm's reputation was a disaster and their only means of distancing themselves from their former leader was to provide the following comment on the company's website:

> *"As HealthSouth continues its unprecedented recovery from a massive fraud that occurred during the tenure of Richard Scrushy as CEO and Chairman, it is astonishing that he would have the audacity and shamelessness to comment on the current operations or the dedication of our approximately 40,000 employees. As we have stated in the past, Scrushy will not be offered any position within the Company by this management team or this Board of*

Directors. Under no circumstances would we reach out to Scrushy, who by his own defense has claimed a complete lack of knowledge as to the financial workings of the Company during his tenure as CEO and Chairman, despite his claims of possessing valuable expertise."[7]

Of course, not every unethical decision relates to accounting fraud. Many often begin as a marketing effort that only in retrospect is it revealed to be unethical. And clearly not every one becomes a crisis. When Blockbuster introduced its "The End of Late Fees," policy and promotion, a lawsuit brought by the New Jersey Attorney General's office over possible deceptive pricing did not seem to dampen Blockbuster's reputation and stakeholder confidence. The attorney general's office was concerned that some consumers did not understand that they would have to pay the cost of the videocassette or DVD if they failed to return movies to Blockbuster within a stated period of time.[8]

In contrast, Coca-Cola, in 1999, in the months following the allegations of tainted Coke in Belgium, lost $34 billion in market value; profits of the company's European subsidiary fell by more than $205 million.[9] The proposal made by Coke to acquire Orangina was rejected by the European Commission and the CEO lost his job soon after.[10] Although the company laid off a number of high-level executives as a result of the troubles and the general counsel resigned, the troubles for the soft-drink giant did not end there. To add insult to injury, the company came under additional scrutiny when it was discovered that their Dansani "bottled water" was nothing more than tap water. Then it emerged that what the company described as its "highly sophisticated purification process", based on NASA spacecraft technology, was in fact reverse osmosis used in many modest water purification units.[11]

In 2002, Coca-Cola once again ran into troubles when Matthew Whitley, a mid-level accounting executive, filed a whistle-blowing suit against the company alleging retaliation for revealing fraud in a market study performed on behalf of Burger King. In the three weeks after the filing of the lawsuit, and the lack of leadership integrity became public, Coca-Cola lost $15 billion in shareholder value. Subsequently, a number of top level executives were fired; Coke paid $21 million to Burger King to settle its disputes with the fast-food giant, $540,000 to the whistle-blower, and a $9 million pre-tax write off had to be taken. Although Coca-Cola disputes or denies the allegations made both in 1999 and 2002, the net result means that

7

shares of Coca-Cola trade today at the same level they did nearly 10 years ago, possibly because of the unethical decisions that became an EMD.

Businesses that effectively manage ethics can systemically absorb, react and appropriately adjust to most breakdowns in conduct or decisions. In Blockbuster's case, the company modified its promotion from the "End of Late Fees" to "Life after Late Fees" to clarify its return policies for consumers.[12] However, while simple changes to marketing campaigns may work to boost consumer confidence in Coca-Cola products, investor confidence does not appear to be improving.

People make poor choices all the time. Many ethical lapses result from poor choices by employees that have not been trained about the complexity and consequences of their decisions. The key is whether the organization has adequately planned to mitigate the potential results of poor choices through leadership, effective ethics programs, prompt response, disciplinary actions, appropriate disclosure, communication to the workforce and public crisis management communication so that they do not escalate into catastrophes.

Recent revelations about ethical misconduct scandals make the prospects of the "unthinkable ethical disaster" a realistic concern. Ask yourself what ethics issues come to mind when you hear the following names: Martha Stewart, Enron, Merrill Lynch, Sears Holding, Halliburton, Mitsubishi Motors, United Way of America, SmithBarney, Citigroup, Xerox, HealthSouth or the Roman Catholic Church. Senior executives, as well as middle managers, are facing prison sentences as a result of some of these scandals. Although prison sentences used to be relatively mild, today, under the revised Federal Sentencing Guidlines for Organizations (FSGO), corporate executives are seeing prison terms of nearly 30 years. Table 1 provides additional examples of individuals and firms that were involved in an EMD. In a world regulated by SOX, the Securities and Exchange Commission and the Department of Justice, what prudent executive would ignore the risks of an ethical scandal? On the other hand, there are still top executives who believe a good moral background is adequate to prevent ethical lapses. Good character is necessary, but not sufficient, to prevent unintentional misconduct in a world where the rules of the game change often.

| Table 1 Ethical Misconduct Disasters[13] ||
Company	Misconduct
Enron	Accounting fraud, manipulating power prices, overstatement of business prospects to shareholders
Worldcom	Accounting fraud
Arthur Andersen	Obstruction of justice (later overturned by U.S. Supreme Court for poor jury instructions)
Microsoft	Antitrust settlement
Firestone	Product liability
Sunbeam	Inflating earnings through a "bill and hold" accounting scheme to overstate earnings
Waste Management Co.	Overstating earnings
Global Crossing	"Capacity swaps" to inflate earnings
Tyco International	Corporate governance failure, expense abuses and tax evasion by CEO Dennis Kozlowski
Qwest	Accounting fraud and overcharging customers
Columbia HCA	Filed false Medicare claims and kickbacks to doctors
Adelphia	Founder John Rigas sentenced for fraud and conspiracy
Imclone	Founder Sam Waksal serving time for insider trading

Although predicting ethical scandals in American business is not an exact science, one www.*CFO.com* projection forecasts up to 20 major business EMDs every year.[14] Of course, every corporation in the world discovers misconduct, including Warren Buffett's own Berkshire Hathaway.[15] The key is to recognize that in order to effectively manage an EMD, organizations must be prepared. Failure to do so can lead to a disaster that can threaten the business continuity. Given the statistics and the significant increase in whistleblowing reports to the SEC since the implosion of Enron, companies should therefore be prepared for such an unexpected disaster. Managing a potential EMD by quick response and recovery determines which of those companies will avoid being one of the 20 major disasters. Thus, the risk of an EMD must be managed with the same prudence as any other serious threat to business continuity.

The Risks of an Ethical Misconduct Disaster

Reputation is one of an organization's greatest intangible assets. The value of a positive reputation is difficult to quantify, but it is an important intangible asset. A single negative incident can influence perceptions of a corporation's image and reputation instantly and for years afterward. Thus, protecting a firm's reputation is a critical priority. When the United Parcel Service (UPS) lost a cardboard box containing computer tapes with personal information for about 3.9 million Citigroup customers, the reputations of both companies were tarnished. This incident involved the names, social security numbers, account numbers and payment history of all of Citigroup's U.S. customers. This blunder created a major embarrassment for a company that had built its recent reputation around an image of identify-theft protection.[16]

Reputation is not a trait or state in the possession of a company, but exists in the collective minds of the various stakeholders. It is tied to perceptions of the corporate image, brand and (mental) associations in the minds of key stakeholders. Although reputation is certainly an asset, it is one that lies in the perceptions of those to whom the organization is accountable. Such stakeholders include employees, customers, vendors, suppliers, neighbors, investors, regulators and labor unions. The news media, to the extent that it views itself as a public watchdog of the greater society, is both a constituent to whom organizations are accountable as well as an adversary. Its watchdog role suggests that the media will have its own agenda and message to pursue that may not inherently align with the agenda and message that is in your best interest and relied upon to create a sustainable positive reputation for your company. Nonetheless, the news media plays a major role in shaping the perceptions of key stakeholders.

There are other factors, however, that influence the perceptions of corporate reputation. These perceptions are formed and influenced based on an individual's experiences with a company or members of its work force, subjective judgments of corporate actions (or inactions), assessments of responsibility and culpability for negatively perceived events, scrutiny of communication messages received, along with the influence of media scrutiny of an organization's performance and ethics.

Positive reputations develop slowly and incrementally. It takes a series of rich positive experiences and symbolic actions to craft a positive reputation. One such example is Hershey Foods. Milton Hershey established a corporate culture based on integrity and values that endure more than 100 years later. On the other hand, damage to a positive reputation can occur very quickly, and in some cases the positive image cannot be immediately or fully restored. Microsoft's lengthy antitrust battles provide just one example.

There are many potential threats to reputation. Reputation can be damaged by poor performance or ethical misconduct. Poor performance is easier to recover from than ethical misconduct. Obviously, stakeholders who are most directly affected by negative events will have a corresponding shift in their perceptions of a firm's reputation. On the other hand, even those indirectly connected to negative events can shift their reputation attributions. In many cases, those indirectly connected to the negative events may be more influenced by the news media or general public opinion than those who are directly connected to your organization.

A scandal will generally impact the company's reputation both from investor confidence and consumer confidence. As investor perceptions and decisions begin to take their toll, shareholder value will drop exposing the company to class action suits which can further the damage. Meanwhile, reputation is also a factor in the consumers' perceptions of product attributes and corporate image features that lead to consumer willingness to purchase goods and services at profitable prices. Some scandals may lead to boycotts and aggressive campaigns to dampen sales and earnings. Nike experienced such a backlash from its use of offshore subcontractors to manufacture its shoes and clothing. When Nike claimed no responsibility for the subcontractors' poor working conditions and extremely low wages, some consumers demanded greater accountability and responsibility by engaging in boycotts, letter-writing campaigns, public-service announcements, etc. Nike ultimately responded to the growing negative publicity by changing its practices.

Finally, a disaster may invite increased regulatory or legal investigative scrutiny, which further threatens reputation. The increased scrutiny might turn up issues and challenges that might have otherwise gone unnoticed, as was the case at Enron. When the SEC began its investigation and the board of directors appointed William Powers, Dean of the University of Texas Law School, to investigate two special purpose entities, a proverbial Pandora's Box was opened causing the company to restate its earnings, which ultimately lead to the implosion of the company as investors and creditors lost complete confidence in the company. In any instance, this increased attention and scrutiny will consume time, energy, and resources, and divert executives' attention from more important mission critical matters.

Reputation is also inherently intertwined with brand values. This value is tied to general perceptions of the brand manufacturer's character and reputation. Coca Cola, Harley-Davidson and Tide, for example, are valuable global brands worth billions of dollars, but have all found their ethics called into question. On April 14, 2004, Harley-Davidson shares closed at an all-time high of $59.50 only to have them plunge to a 14 month low a year later. By July 2005, the motorcycle maker had received a letter of inquiry from the SEC based upon allegations of "channel stuffing", something that has become a common allegation against many brand leaders.

A positive reputation is one of the most important attributes of any company. Brands such as Coca-Cola, Ford's Explorer and Merck's Vioxx, and hundreds of others have all been damaged by negative publicity associated with questionable conduct. The conduct, when called into question, may indirectly affect a company's overall net worth if brand assets are included in stakeholder judgments and perceptions, as we have seen with many of the pharmaceutical companies. Reputations are measured based on a variety of external factors, including the established criteria of *Fortune's* "Most Admired Companies", which is often leveraged by the company as publicity; however, this is no guarantee of ethical superiority, as we have seen in the case of Freddie Mac and Tenet Healthcare, as well as Enron.

Below is a list of the 2003 "Global Most Admired Companies" according to *Fortune* magazine. The majority have been under investigation in one form or another.

1) Wal-Mart
2) General Electric
3) Microsoft
4) Dell Computer
5) Johnson & Johnson
6) Berkshire Hathaway
7) Procter & Gamble
8) IBM
9) Coca-Cola
10) FedEx
11) Toyota Motor
12) BMW
13) Sony
14) Pfizer
15) Intel
16) United Parcel Service
17) Home Depot
18) Nokia
19) Nestlé
20) PepsiCo
21) Singapore Airlines
22) Cisco Systems
23) L'Oreal
24) Merck
25) Citigroup
26) Honda Motor
27) American International Group (AIG)
28) Target
29) Walt Disney
30) Colgate-Palmolive
31) BP
32) Exxon Mobile
33) Royal Dutch Shell Group
34) Anheuser-Busch
35) Northwestern Mutual Life
36) DuPont
37) Volkswagen
38) Costco Wholesale
39) Caterpillar
40) Walgreen
41) Unilever
42) Lowe's
43) Boeing
44) Michelin
45) Continental Airlines
46) SBC Communications
47) Emerson Electric
48) General Motors
49) TIAA-CREF
50) HSBC Holdings

Compare Coca-Cola's position in 1996 and 1997, when the company was number one on *Fortune's* list of "Most Admired Companies". By 1998, the soft drink giant fell to number three and although it regained position in 1999, coming in at number two, for the next three years Coca-Cola fell off the top ten list. By 2003 *Fortune* magazine was asking "Has Coke Lost its Fizz?[17]" and by May 2004, Coca-Cola couldn't find anyone willing to take over the beleaguered company.

Although an organization does not control its reputation in a direct sense, its actions, choices, behaviors and consequences do influence the reputation that exists in the perceptions of stakeholders. Hence, there are things that are within the direct control of executives that have the potential to influence various stakeholders' perceptions. Managing business continuity with an emphasis on preparing for an EMD is one means of influencing the reputation of a business. A reputation is an intangible thing, but it constitutes a real value for a company. At a time when corporate reputations are all too frequently influenced by scandals, it is an urgent priority to appreciate and understand how costly such harm to a reputation can be.

Yet, many executives do not understand the magnitude of the risk and potential harm of ethical misconduct. Executives must move beyond giving only lip service to ethical concerns and make a strong and strategic commitment to ethical integrity to best ensure the continuity of long-term value and business sustainability. There is a need for proactive commitment to ensuring an ethical culture. The past few years have been an early warning sign of the lurking dangers of ethical lapses. The challenges of sustaining ethical integrity rival the challenges of surviving economic downturns, security threats and all other challenges to business success. Executives need to devote much time and energy to setting ethical conduct objectives, restructuring reward and discipline systems, training employees, discovering problems, answering questions, and recovering from ethical lapses.

The fact is that every organization is vulnerable to an EMD and such risks must be continually and proactively managed. Of course, a false sense of security, perhaps believing the brand is sufficient to sustain the company, is a main factor that prevents companies from creating a plan of action to follow if a disaster occurs. Obviously no company is immune from scandals regardless of their efforts to manage ethics and compliance.

Not all crises are of a company's making, and there are certainly those disgruntled antagonists who will spread false rumors, slander and distort the truth for their own self-interests. For instance, Wendy's fast food restaurant faced a potential crisis, when in early 2005 a woman claimed she found part of a finger in a bowl of chili. The incident quickly made the national news and even became fodder for late-night talk-show hosts. Ultimately, the woman—who seemed to have a penchant for litigation—was arrested for attempted grand theft when it was discovered that her claims were nothing more than falsehood. Wendy's losses exceeded $2.5 million and the company was forced to lay off employees after nervous customers deserted the fast-food giant.[18] Thus, the threat of such scandals and public disasters of all types, including ethical misconduct, necessitate strategic planning.

Likewise, the failure to plan and to rely on the personal values of a company's founder can invite disaster. Take Wal-Mart as an example. The company was contacted by one of this book's authors more than 10 years ago about assisting with the development of an organizational ethics program and was informed by Wal-Mart that the company had "Sam Walton's ethics and values" and that was adequate. Of course, many would argue Sam Walton's values have failed to transcend his death, which is why when ethical misconduct is exposed, such as the hiring of illegal immigrants by a sub-contractor, the stakeholders are far less tolerant. Today it is reported that Wal-Mart receives more than 75,000 whistle-blowing reports internally every year, of which thousands are considered serious for the Company, which is why they must manage their business continuity for a potential EMD.

The Consequences of an Ethical Misconduct Disaster (EMD)

The loss of confidence of both consumers and investors that arises in the aftermath of major ethics scandals has a significant impact on the overall economy. In the 2½ years following the implosion of Enron, our capital markets lost between $4 trillion and $7 trillion, much believed to be attributable to the ethics scandals that have shaken the financial markets by ruining pension plans, costing jobs, wiping out investments, and hindering an already sputtering economy. As such, corporate scandals can weigh heavily on the stock market, the value of the U.S. dollar, and the U.S. economy in general. They can undermine the credibility and trustworthiness of entire industrial sectors of the economy and shake the fundamental basis of trust and confidence of the capitalism market.

The consequences of such scandals directly affect the financial markets and are subsequently and quickly felt in the "real economy" in which workers and consumers live. *The Cost of Corporate Recklessness* related to corporate scandals has been estimated at more than $200 billion. These costs include lost investment savings, jobs, pension losses and tax revenue. The report estimated that more than a million workers lost their jobs at the affected companies. Further, the costs to businesses, stakeholders and management include hundreds of millions in litigation costs; punitive and compensatory fines; tarnished brands, images and reputations; and loss of consumer and investor confidence.[19]

Desperate to reassure nervous investors about their balance sheets during the recent financial scandals, some executives slashed costs, sold divisions or subsidiaries, and used free cash to pay down debt. Although such strategies helped to restore corporate profits in the short run, they often came at the expense of rebuilding inventories, hiring new workers, and investing in new equipment—activities that are directly related to the real economy.

Over the last few years, some crises have grown into a broad cascade of scandals that involved not just individual companies and their corporate officers, but also accounting firms, law firms, and investment and commercial banks. The number of publicly traded companies restating their earnings went from 48 in 1996 to 233 in 2000 to 414 in 2004.[20] In 1996, there were 108 federal securities fraud class action suits; there were 488 in 2001. From November 2001 to November 2002, there were scandals or serious financial problems at Enron, Kmart, Global Crossing, WorldCom, Qwest, Adelphia, Xerox and Tyco. The stock market declined sharply as investors lost confidence; the Standard & Poor's 500 Index lost almost 323 points from mid-March 2002 to mid-July 2002.[21]

The Brookings Institute issued a report entitled "Cooking the Books: The Cost to the Economy," which estimated that the corporate accounting scandals of the early 2000s cost the U.S. economy $35 billion in the first year. The estimate was based on the analysis that the scandals caused about 60 percent of the 28 percent decline in the market from March 19, 2002 until July 19, 2002.[22]

Corporate scandals also affected individual's private portfolios. According to the Brookings Institute report, individuals in their 50s who had a 401(k) lost almost $11,000 on average, or about 12 percent, from their 401(k) portfolios based on a $92,000 portfolio. The report said that individuals in their 40s lost an average of $8,000, or about 13 percent, based on a $63,000 portfolio. Corporate scandals are boosting companies' insurance costs and making it harder for firms to attract board members.[23] All too frequently, organizations experience substantial episodes that qualify as some level of disaster that affects routine operations. In most cases, strategic and risk management planners are caught unprepared for the disruption and aftermath of these EMD events. This is because planners do not consider the costs of an ethical disaster. As we discussed, these apparent disasters seem to come without warning, causing a dramatic drop in shareholder value virtually overnight.

However, the economic consequences of such issues can greatly exceed the direct punitive sanctions imposed by regulatory fines or lawsuits. These consequences often include lost sales and customer loyalty, lost employee and investor confidence, and irreparable damage to company image and reputation. The penalties can be enormous and in some cases exceed the company's assets, causing the company to cease to exist. Although the 100 biggest corporate fraud cases of the 1990s resulted in fines of over $2.34 billion, the fines are getting significantly higher. The $2.25 billion in penalties imposed against WorldCom was more than the penalties imposed in the largest 100 combined.

Ethical behavior, which is seen at the heart of the "corporate recklessness", is a growing concern across society in general and can have a serious impact on the company's ability to operate efficiently if the misconduct is seen as an injustice to society, as seen with Wal-Mart. Yet, despite data that ethical behavior is one of the most important personal attributes of employees, and with overwhelming evidence of the grave impact of a full-blown EMD event, few companies and industries are prepared for an EMD. The reality is that every organization should be concerned with cultivating a sense of positive business ethics and be engaged in active planning to recognize, avoid, discover, answer and recover from an EMD event as the basis for the preparedness.

It is no surprise these issues are encroaching into the workplace on many different fronts. A survey by Golin/Harris International found that 82 percent of the public believes that the crisis of trust in America will stay the same or worsen and two-thirds hold CEOs personally responsible for restoring trust and confidence in business.[24] Times have changed since the days when one could categorically assume that all employees are hired with a fundamental and rigid commitment to recognizing, understanding and acting ethically in every possible situation.

A survey of nearly 25,000 high school students revealed that 62 percent of the students admitted to cheating on an exam at least once; 35 percent confessed to copying documents from the Internet; 27 percent admitted to shoplifting; and 23 percent owned up to cheating in order to win in sports.[25] If today's students are tomorrow's leaders, there is likely to be a correlation between acceptable behavior today and tomorrow, adding to the argument that the leaders of today must be prepared for the ethical risks associated with this downward trend.

Furthermore, a significant percentage of employees say that they know of, but have not reported, instances of misconduct in their organizations. Most employees cite, as reasons for not coming forward about ethical misconduct, a lack of confidentiality policies, fear that existing policies won't protect them, and fear of retaliation.[26] According to the Ethics Resource Center, "nearly half of all employees who report misconduct received positive feedback for having done so"; however, "nearly one in four employees experienced retaliation."[27] Meanwhile, ISR, a leading employee research firm, released a study that revealed potential lapses in ethical behavior on the job. Based on a survey of 154,000 employees at 109 U.S. companies, 83 percent of the employees surveyed at high performing companies believe that their company acts with integrity when dealing with customers, suppliers and the public.[28] Equally important is the other 17 percent that view their company as being at risk with flawed cultures that provide opportunities for misconduct. Discovering unethical subcultures in organizations and preventing misconduct can prevent an EMD. As Warren Buffett said in his interview in May of 2005 on Public Broadcasting Corporation's *Business Nightly News*, "We have 180,000 employees, we know there is somebody doing something wrong today, we just hope it's small and that we catch it. But that is going to happen in any large organization."

Business misconduct, whether illegal or simply alleged, is a serious issue for society. In fact, Alonovo *(www.alonovo.com)* is making a business out of providing comprehensive overviews of a company's social responsibility values and has an agreement with Amazon. com to provide ratings for customers of products bought through Amazon.com. These ratings gauge the company on everything from social responsibility, healthy environment, fair workplace, customer commitment and business ethics. So now customers can vote with their ethical wallets.

Even respected companies such as Intel have been accused of monopolistic bullying. A competitor, Advanced Micro Devices (AMD), claimed in a lawsuit that 38 companies, including Dell and Sony, were strong-arming customers into buying Intel chips rather than those marketed by AMD. The AMD lawsuit seeks billions of dollars and will take years to litigate.[29] In many cases the alleged misconduct can not only have monetary and legal implications but can threaten reputation, investor confidence and customer loyalty.

Even Wal-Mart, with its 1.6 million employees and sales approaching $300 billion, is feeling the pressure. The company has been involved in numerous conflicts involving gender-discrimination litigation, wage and pay disputes, union-busting allegations, as well as the resignation of a top officer over financial improprieties. The company made a multi-million dollar settlement with immigration authorities over the employment of illegal workers, but continues to face dozens of lawsuits attempting to delay construction of super-centers because of community concerns about the firm's impact on the environment, small businesses and quality of life.[30] When all the ethical issues are combined, they add up to a small-sized corporate ethical disaster. Wal-Mart has focused primarily on investors and customers with its ultra-low prices, and rarely on the interests of other stakeholders such as employees, suppliers, communities and society. The claims range from firing whistleblowers to discriminating against women (and most recently black truck drivers) to violating child labor laws, locking workers into stores overnight, mooching off the taxpayers, disregarding local zoning laws, mistreating immigrant janitors, abusing young Bangladeshi women, paying poverty-level wages in the United States, and destroying small-town America. No company is immune—no matter how large—to the damage caused to one's reputation as a result of ethical misconduct as Wal-Mart now acknowledges the impact the stakeholders' efforts have had on the company. Wal-Mart CEO Lee Scott recently called the backlash "one of the most organized, most sophisticated, most expensive corporate campaigns ever launched against a single company."[31]

Many companies—Colombia/HCA, Firestone, Sunbeam,Waste Management, WorldCom, Rite Aid, Mitsubishi Motors, Xerox, Daiwa Bank of Japan, Archer Daniels Midland and Microsoft to name but a few—survived ethical and legal crises, but paid a high price not only financially but also in terms of compromised reputation and declining stakeholder trust. Consider that Qwest spent $7 million a month in 2003 on outside legal counsel to defend the company against allegations of accounting irregularities and fraud.[32]

Krispy Kreme, once a high-flying company, experienced a meltdown when two executives tried to manage earnings to meet Wall Street expectations. The company's stock, which had traded for $105/share in November 2000 before two-for-one stock splits, traded at five dollars/share in January 2006.[33] A poll by Harris Interactive found many scandal-plagued firms at the bottom of its annual survey of perceived corporate reputation, including Enron, Global Crossing, WorldCom, Andersen Worldwide and Adelphia. The survey, which ranks companies according to how respondents rate them on 20 attributes, also found that public perceptions of trust had declined considerably as a result of the accounting scandals of the early 21st century. Joy Sever, a Harris vice president, reported, "The scandals cost many companies their emotional appeal, the strongest driver of reputation."[34]

One study found that publicity about unethical corporate behavior lowers a company's stock prices for at least six months.[35] Another study found that companies perceived by their employees as having a high degree of honesty and integrity had a three-year total return to shareholders of 101 percent, whereas companies perceived as having a low degree of honesty and integrity had a three-year total return to shareholders of just 69 percent.[36]

Despite the high costs of misconduct or even perceived misconduct, a PriceWaterhouseCoopers survey indicates that U.S. companies are failing to identify and manage ethical, social, economic and environmental issues of concern. Although most companies recognize that these issues have the potential to harm corporate reputation and threaten relationships with customers, suppliers and other stakeholders, few are taking steps identify, evaluate and respond to them.[37]

Ethical Misconduct Disaster Recovery Planning

Most organizations have long acknowledged that business continuity planning is an essential priority in order to effectively anticipate, prevent, mitigate and survive natural disasters, data loss, accidents and deliberate malevolent acts. What many are only now discovering is that *ethical continuity planning* is also a duly diligent policy and business priority that focuses on the non-financial performance or structural soundness of the organization's policies and practices for adverting an EMD. Ethical continuity planning involves strategic development, leadership, and plans for an ethical corporate culture and an effective ethical compliance program to prevent misconduct. Ethical issues must be on the strategic agenda. Such planning must go beyond compliance issues and reactive disciplinary policies to actually managing ethics.

Should your company plan to better manage the threat of these contingencies? The answer to this question is always yes! Every company (large and small) faces potential risk from these ethical misconduct and regulatory compliance failure contingencies. Corporations are increasingly being held accountable for their efforts to educate, train and enable employees to act ethically, legally and with integrity in the performance of their duties.

The FSGO, which went into effect in 1991, with significant amendments in 2004, generally ties potential penalties for violations of the law to the quality of corporate self-policing efforts.[38] The United States Sentencing Commission, which developed the guidelines, recommends strict and severe enforcement of existing regulations and statutory requirements, particularly in cases where companies have failed to proactively promote ethics and compliance. Judges, courts, and regulatory agencies look for evidence of voluntary disclosure of misconduct, and evidence of full cooperation in the investigation of misconduct. Failing to find such evidence, the

Commission recommends that judges enforce regulations without any mitigation. Furthermore, the Commission also recommends stern and rigid enforcement in cases where senior executives are involved in misconduct, or where senior executives had ordered employees to obstruct justice. In such cases, executives involved face stiff penalties. Companies that take the prescribed proactive steps, and do not appear to have greater institutional culpability, will receive consideration to avoid onerous penalties should a violation occur.[39] In recent years, almost no firms with an effective ethics program have been sentenced for a major crime. The Open Compliance and Ethics Group found (as shown in the Appendix A) organizations with an ethics and compliance program in place for ten years or more have not experienced any significant reputational damage in the last five years.

Of course, the requirements imposed by SOX are also significant for ethical continuity planning. This legislation has created new requirements for accountability and ethical conduct as a result of the corporate financial scandals in recent years. The major provisions of the SOX include criminal and civil penalties for noncompliance violations, certification of internal auditing by external auditors, and increased disclosure regarding all financial statements. In addition, the law mandates codes of ethics for senior financial officers and disclosure of audit committee financial experts. SOX also details expectations for analyst conflict of interest conduct and treatment of securities analysts by registered securities associations and national securities exchanges.

However, it is important not to merely emphasize legal compliance at the expense of developing an ethical corporate conscience. Training, educating and motivating employees to act in ways consistent with both legal requirements and ethical expectations is at the core of planning to prevent and manage an EMD. Companies themselves do much to establish the climate, the values and the expectations for conduct that employees hold about daily life within the firm. This is achieved explicitly through codes of conduct and statements of values/ethics reported in organizational publications. This is also accomplished implicitly through dress codes, anecdotes about company heroes and villains, treatment of customer complaints, treatment of employee complaints, how meetings are conducted, and in which behaviors and accomplishments get rewarded and recognized compared with which behaviors get criticized, ignored, or punished.

All organizations, regardless of their high standards and

expectations, can find themselves faced with ethical lapses and ethical disasters. Even "good" companies/employees can "go bad." As with all aspects of an organization's culture and style, ethical values and conduct norms evolve and change over time. Perhaps there are elements of production demands or limited financial rewards in some markets that encourage companies to act unethically, but there are many cases of good corporate cultures that have given way to demands to cut corners, cheat, put profit above proper behavior, and break the law. Changes in management or leadership roles can create new opportunities for changed philosophies of operation. Even employee perceptions or misperceptions of management expectations can inadvertently lead to misconduct. Contingency planners should recognize that constant vigilance and attention is required to keep misconduct contingencies from encroaching into the workplace. The formal codes of conduct and statements of company values/ethics must continually be reinforced and "ethical concerns must be regarded as on a par with economic and pragmatic concerns in decision-making."[40]

Effectively managing an EMD requires proactive planning long before the emergence of a scandal. It is, therefore, essential to lay a strong and solid foundation of integrity, ethics and legal compliance to ensure your organization's continuity and survival through the storms of an EMD. The process of EMD Recovery Planning begins with an assessment of the organization's values, development of an ethics program, an ethics audit, and the ability to develop contingency plans for a potential EMD. Every company should not only identify their key values, but also communicate and support a specific value structure in the workplace.

Ethics programs provide an organizational approach to creating an ethical climate as a key component of organizational culture. A key element of an ethics program is company-wide training, involving the communication of values, codes of ethics, enforcement standards as well as continuous improvement efforts. An evaluation or audit of the company's ethics program is necessary on a regular basis to allow for continuous improvement. Contingency planning should be tied to risk assessment and planning for those potential occurrences. Contingency planning also provides ready tools for responding to ethical crises.

Because it is impossible to obtain universal agreement on how to make ethical decisions on a daily basis, there will always be variation in understanding how to resolve ethical dilemmas. Some corporate cultures grant employees considerable flexibility in ethical decision-making. However, in these cultures with less formal policies and procedures and where identification of organizational risk areas is lacking, there are greater chances for employees to make decisions that will result in a potential EMD, which is one of the reasons SOX requires companies to document their internal controls under Section 404.

Organizational members who engage in questionable conduct can cause an EMD. These rogue employees are a risk to the overall integrity of the organization. In the case of prosecutable misconduct, the FSGO provides some opportunity for organizations to receive concessions in fines and sentences for maintaining due diligence in their ethical compliance programs. However, they do not provide a safety net to support the interests of all stakeholders. For example, the corporate reputation, common stock value, employee confidence and customer trust are all at risk if the organization does not shoulder the responsibility for the misconduct.

Even the best of prevention planning and crafting of an underlying fabric of ethics and integrity cannot guarantee that a given business will not endure a scandal or accusations of a scandal. In both instances, the escalation of unethical conduct into a scandal or a malicious false accusation that creates an undeserved scandal or crisis of reputation, it is essential to respond and manage aggressively the crisis event (and recognize it as potentially lethal to the organization).

Contingency planning is tied to risk assessment and planning for those potential occurrences. Contingency planning also provides ready tools for responding to ethical crises.

Ethical Misconduct Disaster Management

As we shall discuss throughout the remainder of this book, an EMD can be managed by organizational initiatives to *recognize, avoid, discover, answer*, and *recover* from the misconduct. Figure 1 provides a model to prepare for and manage an EMD.

Figure 1

Preparing for and Managing an Ethical Misconduct Disaster (EMD): Using Organizational RADAR to Identify and Deal with Ethical Disasters

(R)ecognize–define the issues, threat forecasting, risk assessment, anticipation to recognize

(A)void–develop proactive ethical leadership and effective ethics/compliance programs

(D)iscover–actively communicate and monitor, formal and informal feedback systems

(A)nswer–ongoing oversight, integrated systems, rapid actions and program development

(R)ecover–diligence to restore image, stabilize situation and resume productivity

---

© Lynda Ferrell 2006

Recognize

There must be recognition at the highest levels of senior management that the threat of an EMD is real and that there is a need to develop a strategic approach to manage a potential EMD. Thus, there should be an effort at this level to define the relevant issues; identify potential threats; develop ethics programs, compliance efforts, organizational policies, and senior-level responsibility for ensuring compliance and enforcement; review disciplinary and reward systems; and initiate planning for how to respond to and recover from a potential EMD.

It is also important to conduct a comprehensive risk assessment in an effort to predict what types of ethical lapses might leave your company most vulnerable. It is important to make such analyses as broad as possible in order to anticipate all likely risks and to develop worst-case scenarios. The designation of an ethics officer is a significant step to demonstrate that the issue has been recognized at the strategic level.

Avoid

Avoidance entails developing and demonstrating proactive ethical leadership. This leadership must be consistent and embody the values, ethical principles, and norms that lie at the heart of the organizational culture. Rules governing conduct, compliance information and expectations for how to make ethical decisions and how to handle situations must be disseminated widely across the organization. This information should be communicated in a wide variety of different means, ways, and channels to ensure that it reaches everyone. It is also essential to develop and implement comprehensive ethics and compliance programs.

Discover

Preparing for an EMD requires discovery through active listening through all available communication channels. The implementation of a confidential reporting system and active observation to discover warning signs of potential unethical behavior are important components of any prudent company's preparedness. The monitoring of ethical behavior must include both formal and informal means. These range from simple managing by walking around to a wide variety of formal procedures and mechanisms. There must be consistent and frequent proactive dissemination of information about compliance, ethical expectations, ethical decision making and means to report and monitor activity across the organization. There should also be an ongoing system of dialog and feedback across all levels of the organization about ethics and expectations for ethics.

Answer

A company's answer is its action plan or response to any detected issues that need attention. It is vitally important to answer and respond quickly and appropriately when incidents of misconduct are discovered. It is also important to manage aggressively the organizational response to emerging ethical disasters. The same series of integrated systems that should be in place to detect and discover ethical lapses should also allow for an appropriate response to such lapses. One important aspect is that all responses should be rapid and appropriate. Protocols—including reporting and disclosure rules and channels—should be established well in advance of their needed use. It is essential to have thoroughly prepared and planned for everyone's role in responding to these events.

Recover

The recovery plan will naturally depend on the severity of the disaster. In some cases, recovery will entail only a minor response or a revision of the ethics program. On the other hand, once the dust of a scandal has begun to settle, the aftermath of these disasters can leave your company in disarray. Operations may have been disrupted to a significant degree. Legal and criminal investigations may drag on for years. Executives and mid-level managers may be away from their desks dealing with investigations, or worse, serving prison sentences, leaving a potential void in expertise that further impacts continuity. Employee motivation and morale may be reduced, which may make it more difficult to retain experienced employees and recruit new ones. Productivity may be down. Stock value and prices may have plummeted during the scandal, and investors may avoid your company's stock altogether. Consumers may have abandoned your products and services. Government regulators, court ordered oversight, mandated programs, and increased scrutiny may be a burden for years to come. The word "disaster" barely covers the range of possible devastation that may lie in the wake of a significant EMD. No matter how daunting the task may appear, it is essential to have a plan(s) in place and a roadmap for recovering from these scandals and getting back to business.

The road back to business as usual requires diligent, strategic and deliberate efforts aimed at recovery. A comprehensive coordinated communication plan to repair your image is an essential part of the post-disaster recovery operation. It is essential to have in place and to follow a detailed plan to stabilize the situation, and to resume the work of your business as quickly as feasible. Repairing the underlying ethical and compliance issues is only part of the tasks that face a company trying to recovery from these types of scandals.

Chapter

2

The Personal Disasters Behind the Headlines

Ethical misconduct disasters (EMDs) can disrupt routine operations, stifle productivity, imperil long-held reputations, erode stakeholder confidence, and have the potential to result in untold legal and financial costs. Although the headlines of financial papers reporting these scandals trumpet corporate earnings restatements, fines and even executive prison sentences, they rarely look at the toll EMDs take on individuals. The reality is that every ethical scandal has casualties behind the headlines—lost jobs, vanished pensions, disrupted families and communities, poor health, stress and ultimately a growing mistrust of corporate America.

In this chapter, we'll explore the ethical misconduct scandal at Enron from an internal perspective to try to better understand the individual and organizational factors and pressures that resulted in such a devastating disaster. In this chapter, co-author Lynn Brewer, as an executive in four different divisions at Enron, provides a front-row seat of Enron's implosion. Now CEO and founding chairman of The Integrity Institute, Inc., Brewer has written about her experiences in *Confessions of an Enron Executive: A Whistleblower's Story.*

An Insider's View of the Enron Culture

In the aftermath of Enron, just as the 9/11 Commission investigated the events that lead to the terrorist attacks on the United States, experts scrutinized Enron from every angle—looking at everything from the lack of controls to manipulation of energy markets to poor governance to poor leadership to the fraud created from the greed. From the outside world, the EMD at Enron appears to have been a "perfect storm," a convergence of systems to which no one paid much attention because alone they were insufficient to create significant damage. When each of the systems failed at the same time, however, Enron was unable to sustain itself.

As a former Enron executive, watching the converging storms that led to its EMD, I have a different perspective. Although the focus has been on Enron the corporation and on the misdeeds of a few contemptible individuals like Ken Lay, Jeff Skilling and Andrew Fastow, much larger forces at work created the storm. Clearly these three men were a contributing factor, but none of them would have had the strength to cause the damage they did without massive support.

Many experts would be surprised to learn that, in all likelihood, two-thirds of Enron employees were at one time or another aware of unethical behavior, not at the hands of Lay, Skilling and Fastow, but rather by the mid-level executives and those reporting to them. In my opinion, if you'd asked the employees at Enron whether it was a highly ethical or highly unethical company, 90 percent would have said highly unethical, but if you'd asked those same employees, including perhaps even Jeff Skilling or Andy Fastow, whether they themselves were highly unethical individuals, they clearly would deny such a claim. The unconscious disconnect between the individual and the corporation was perhaps the greatest threat to the sustainability of the organization.

Cognitive dissonance is, of course, the driving force that compels humans to acquire or invent new thoughts or beliefs, or to modify existing ones, in order to minimize the amount of conflict between their actions and their values. For most at Enron, it eventually became easier and more beneficial to adopt the doctrine of plausible deniability. But with every EMD that has occurred since Enron, we must ask ourselves: Is there a little bit of Enron in all of us?

Facts would indicate the answer is, yes. In 2001, the year Enron imploded, the Securities and Exchange Commission received on average 6,400 reports of securities and financial fraud every month from whistleblowers. In 2004, three years after the EMD at Enron and two years after the passage of the SOX, those reports had mushroomed to an astounding 40,000 reports per month. With approximately 16,000 public companies traded on the U.S. stock exchanges, one could surmise that even if half the reports are false positives or frivolous reports filed by disgruntled employees, there are still more reports filed every month than there are publicly traded companies. This naturally draws us to the conclusion there is indeed a little bit of Enron in at least a majority of us.

We must first acknowledge that while fraud has sadly become a large part of the history of capitalism, it is not restricted to public companies, as it has also occurred in a large number of nonprofit organizations. Even having witnessed and arguably participated in unethical behavior at Enron, I still believe that a majority of us are inherently good, which creates an inherent disconnect between those who believe they are doing the right thing and those who can be persuaded to behave in a certain manner that can, absent appropriate controls, ultimately put the company and the individual at risk. Of course, what most people fail to realize is that fraud often simply starts as good people coming together to create business solutions to satisfy some demand set by external forces. As the pressure increases, so too does the creativity or innovation of the solutions. Solutions that are unsustainable can ultimately lead to the sort of fraud seen at Enron.

Although most have focused on the accounting fraud at Enron, the schemes were simply a means to an end. The objective was best described by Tim Belden, the director of Enron's western power trading. When asked why he manipulated the California power market, he replied, "I wanted to make money for the company." Of course, no one would argue that making money for the company is not a good thing, but too few focused on how that money was being made. As a growing number of mid-level executives witnessed the rewards being offered to those who were creative, the innovation eventually spread. Make no mistake though, Enron's implosion was caused by two equally destructive forces: (1) contribution to the corruption and (2) complacency towards the corruption. Arguably in both instances, employees believed they were doing the "right thing."

While Tim Belden and I worked together briefly trading power in the California markets, he is going to jail and I am not. Tim Belden represents the Enron executives who contributed to the corruption, while I represent the Enron executives who grew complacent towards the corruption. Both of us represent everything that precipitated Enron's massive EMD, and we are equally guilty of contributing to Enron's downfall. Of course the difference is that Tim Belden was perpetrating crimes, falsely driving Enron's revenue from the sale of wholesale electricity from $50 million in 1999 to $800 million in

2001, while I was blowing the whistle to senior management and eventually to the United States government. But I am no less guilty of contributing to the EMD.

Although our methods may have been different, I'm certain our motivation was the same—financial gain. In less than three years, I would make nearly $250,000 in stock options in addition to my salary and bonus, while Tim Belden would receive an annual bonus of nearly $5 million plus salary and stock options, likely to be in the millions as well. For myself, the price eventually became too high, as I recognized I had become someone I no longer respected. For my sake, this awareness came sooner for me than it did for Tim Belden— had it not, perhaps I too would be going to prison.

I have learned a clear lesson from Enron in hindsight. Absent evidence to the contrary, I witnessed good people doing horrendous things—not because they lacked a conscience or because they intended to commit crimes—but because they were trying to solve business problems facing the corporation. Before you judge from the outside, allow me to take you inside my world as a mid-level executive.

The Road to Enron

I think it may be useful to give you a brief history of my personal background that led me to Enron. I grew up as a competitive figure skater, which set the tone for my "stop-at-nothing" attitude. By the time I was 10, I would wake myself every morning at 4:30 a.m. to be on the ice by 6:00 a.m. After two hours of practice, I would go to school for six hours and then return to practice from 2:30 p.m. to 6:30 p.m. every day. At age 16, my dreams were shattered when a drunk driver hit me.

Suffice it to say from that point forward, my life seemed to fall short. No matter where I turned, I always longed for something that would challenge me while nurturing my desire and drive to be competitive. Enron provided all of that and more, having just been named *Fortune* magazine's Most Innovative Company for the third year in a row. Enron was to the energy industry what the Chicago Bulls were to basketball.

Since I spent most of my early years away from home as a competitive ice skater, I rarely saw my own family, and after my father passed away when I was 23, I found myself desperate to reclaim my affiliation with someone or something. Approaching 40, having been unsuccessful at relationships or having a family of my own, I began to focus on a career—believing, perhaps, that Enron would be my family and a place I could call home. However, just as my relationships had quickly proven to be an illusion, failing to provide me with a sense of being, so too would Enron.

The Cult

I joined Enron in March 1998 after being recruited to head up a risk management group that would, among other things, brief the "off-the-balance sheet partnerships" of Andrew Fastow for senior management and Enron's board of directors. Of course, the morning of my first day was spent in new-hire training where, after completing employment and medical insurance forms, the head of each of Enron's business units paraded before us to highlight our potential growth opportunities within the organization. I felt a bit like a child on Christmas morning. One package after another had been opened—each with a better present than the last.

Heading from one smorgasbord of sorts to another, from endless possibilities to lunch, I was certain that I had finally made the right choice. Where I had failed in relationships, I had succeeded in finding a home at Enron. Of course, that was until the main course arrived and my boss leaned over and explained to me the real reason I had been hired—I was to fire two people on my team that she had been unable to get rid of during the last round of performance reviews. I quickly scanned my memory bank as to the illuminated banners ten feet in length hanging from the ceiling in the Enron lobby—the ones proclaiming Enron's Vision and Values. Was this a test to see whether I would adhere to those values or to a different set of rules? I sat quietly and listened, never proclaiming one way or the other what I was willing to do or not do.

The shock and awe of my first lunch dampened my spirits only a bit. Each day I was more amazed at the brain trust Enron had built. Every person I met seemed to raise the bar and IQ level to new highs. Clearly on my honeymoon, each meeting was exhilarating, each deal seemed to pump yet another dose of adrenaline into my system. If it wasn't the deals, it was the energy of the traders on the trading floor. Enron was the envy of every company in Houston, and my friends outside the company were envious of my new-found success. Of course, as with any new relationship, there were warning signs, but I remained hopeful—at least until I could deny it no longer. The messages I would receive would be subtle at first, but would grow eventually to the level that many would consider death threats.

At my first all-employee meeting in April 1998, it became clear that Enron was not all it represented itself to be. With all the fervor of a rock concert, Enron had launched its brand new "Vision and Values" program. If the banners boldly displayed in the lobby were saying one thing, the leadership was clearly saying something else. The Vision—to become "The World's Greatest Energy Company"— identified the direction we were heading, while the values—respect, integrity, communication and excellence—established the boundaries in which the company would operate, or so I thought.

As a promotional video ran defining Enron's purpose, Jeff Skilling, then COO, could be heard saying in a voiceover, "There may be a temptation to cut corners but we can't have that at Enron." As the film ended, Skilling emerged on stage and revealed his disconnect between what Enron was telling the outside world and what we were seeing inside. Surprisingly, he made no effort to hide the real purpose for us having any stated values. Like Tim Belden, it was all about making money. "We have found companies that have a written vision and values statement have a greater return on investment than those that don't," he would say as he introduced the film. The tone was definitely defined at the top—it's okay to cut corners if we provide a greater return on investment.

In November 1998, I discovered what appeared to be bank fraud when I learned that the natural gas in an underground storage facility used as collateral for a December 31, 1997 bank loan in the amount of $232 million did not exist. To complicate matters, Enron camouflaged the loan as a marketing agreement whereby the company could book the revenue from selling the gas rather than as a loan that would require the reporting of debt. Unfortunately, even if the gas that Enron pledged had existed, it was in a form that could never be extracted. "Cushion gas," as it is called, is required to create sufficient pressure to maintain the structural integrity of the underground aquifer where the natural gas is stored. Without the cushion gas, the storage field would collapse. If Enron had defaulted on the loan and the banks needed to seize the asset, they would have been unable to do so.

Upon learning of the dubious deal, I immediately went to my supervisor to alert her of the problem, where I was instructed to "leave that out of the brief." This would be the first of many directives I would receive that provided a consistent message across the organization. A culture of silence is the foundation for corruption. At the same time as my boss was telling me to remain quiet, I was receiving preprinted Post-It Notes proclaiming Enron's values. The "Communication" Post-It was green and had a quote from Dr. Martin

Luther King, Jr.: "Our lives begin to end the day we become silent about things that matter." Perhaps Dr. King was right. As I began to lay the foundation for a culture of complacency, I allowed those who would do so to seize upon the opportunity to commit the crimes, and my life as I knew it was beginning to end.

In the summer of 1998, I learned that Enron began the first of many efforts to manipulate the power markets, starting in the Midwest and then in California. In mid-June, my boss entered a meeting by saying, "Apparently today we're printing money." We were printing money all right and lots of it. During the week of June 22–26, 1998, wholesale prices of electricity rose from $25 per megawatt hour to $7,500 per megawatt hour at the hands of Enron's traders. The basis between Enron's purchase and sale of the power went from $35 per megawatt hour to $10,000 overnight.

Making money is one thing, making a killing is quite a different story. Because power cannot be stored, the market must buy at whatever the real-time market is selling it for unless individual parties have entered into long-term stable contracts. Even with a contract securing power prices, if the parties contracted to deliver power are unable to do so because everyone is buying power in a frenzy, a local utility may be forced to suddenly go to the real-time market and pay current market prices. Alternatively, it can cut off power to the customer, which is exactly what happened. As a result of Enron's manipulation of power prices, I watched as elderly people died that summer when no air conditioning was available due to Enron-induced power outages.

Of course, it didn't occur to me at the time that I was part of the culture and as such was in someway responsible for those deaths by remaining silent about what was causing the power outages. My mind could not afford to consider that. Any personal responsibility I should have felt was overtaken by the adrenaline I felt every day as I watched the monitors throughout every floor in the Enron building—watching Enron's stock tick upwards minute by minute. Like watching my horse at the racetrack lead around the corners, I could feel my heart racing. Of course, I was not alone in my anticipation that Enron's stock would soon be splitting—giving me twice as many shares, which hopefully would appreciate back to the pre-split level, doubling my money. However, I also began to realize that I was not sleeping through the night and my hands were going numb. The migraine headaches were also starting to escalate. Enron's culture was beginning to feel more like a cult—one I know I should leave but couldn't.

By summer of 1999, I was increasingly sickened by what I saw as Enron's unscrupulous business practices when I realized that Enron was violating its own contracts by allowing the traders to do deals that potentially put the structural integrity of Enron's natural gas pipelines at risk. Natural gas naturally contains carbon dioxide, and there are acceptable levels of the corrosive gas. When gas fields age and the quality of gas diminishes, however, the toxic gases can become elevated, and the price a producer can demand for the gas drops significantly. Enron's contracts generally allowed for CO_2 levels to be somewhere between 8 percent to 12 percent. This level is considered acceptable and will not jeopardize the structure of the walls of a pipeline. Higher levels can corrode the lining of the pipeline, which in essence diminishes the long-term value of Enron's asset. While prices for good gas were consistently trading between $1.75 and $2 per MMBtu, I suddenly realized there was a whole group of traders who were suddenly buying "sour" gas for $.02 per MMBtu containing CO_2 rates between 20 percent to 28 percent, commingling it with good gas, and then selling it at a profit of $1.98 per MMBtu, which drove Enron's profits through the roof while at the same time potentially setting Enron up for a natural disaster if the pipeline were to rupture.

The leaders at Enron were nothing if not consistent. They created one message that would be heard throughout the community while operating with a very different message behind close doors. To the outside world, Enron was committed to the community, but behind closed doors, it was all about money and it was willing to jeopardize the safety of the community to raise its earnings. None of this would have been possible without the rank and file employees carrying out the orders. We would be hard pressed to find a record of senior leaders getting their hands dirty. All of it was covered up with images and dollars—all of which were nothing more than an illusion.

By now, I was keenly aware of the commercial value of the traders to Enron's bottom line. In fact, Jeff Skilling once noted that the traders contributed $1 million per day to Enron's profit. Because he recognized the value of the traders, he clearly must have recognized the risk of rogue traders. I decided to raise the issue at a management meeting because I had been plainly informed to leave the traders alone. Even being in the legal department, I lacked the authority to pull any of the deals done by the traders. To my surprise, Skilling dismissed the notion that there was any problem with the practices and informed me that if it were a problem he would be told so. Of course, I also wondered what he thought I was doing by telling him about the problem—blowing into the wind?!

Complacency: The Glue That Held Enron Together

My public interaction with Skilling was my first real indication that senior managers weren't interested in knowing the dirty little secrets about how the company was making money—but only that they were making money. I had learned through Enron's performance review system—fondly known as "Rank and Yank"—that being voted "most likely to succeed" required one of two things: (1) contribution to the corruption or (2) complacency towards the corruption. Falling into one of those two categories allowed you to stay employed. Failing to do so meant you would be voted out the door, as you would be ranked against your class of executives. Every year 20 percent of Enron's work force was asked to leave, as they were arbitrarily ranked as "Needs Improvement" or "Issues."

The insatiable appetite for earnings increased as Wall Street began to ask questions about Enron's cash flow and the pressure to perform increased. We could feel it throughout the organization, but never more so than at review time. Twice a year, Enron employees underwent what amounted to running the gauntlet. If you survived, you were safe for another six months. The process involved providing a list of six external or internal customers who could provide feedback as to your performance for the previous six months. After this feedback was supplied, the managers would head to a conference room at a local hotel to begin a cockfight. One employee was pitted against another with the employees of the strongest managers ending up on top. Those who could fight to defend the honor of their employees would rise to the top, while the rest remain battered and bruised or, worse yet, left in ashes. The top 20 percent would be given the two highest rankings—"superior" and "excellent"—and thereby receive the largest portion of the bonus pool and significant raises. The middle or so 60 percent of employees would ride the bell curve, receiving moderate raises and bonuses, while the bottom 20 percent were moved out of the way with a needs improvement or issues. Needs improvement amounted to a forewarning you had better find another job within six months or else you too would be out of the door at the next review. This process further reminded employees that in order to rise to the top, you had better remain quiet if you weren't making money for the company—otherwise, the company would silence you.

As you can imagine, there were those who remained silent—at least until the review process was over. Figure 1 shows the whistle blowing reports to Enron's Office of the Chairman month by month.

Just prior to the review process in April and May, both in 2000 and 2001, reports dropped off significantly, and then began to rise again dramatically in June right after reviews had been completed. This would suggest that, at least for a time, employees were silenced out of fear—until they realized what an injustice had occurred. Eventually, the more employees were rewarded for the unethical behavior, the more the behavior became acceptable.

Figure 1

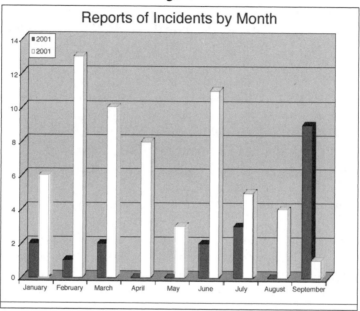

Of course, this chart can be used for another purpose—to understand the impact of Enron's stock price on the number of whistle blowing reports. As long as Enron's stock continued to rise, the employees enriched themselves from the stock options and remained silent—until the stock began to drop. There is a direct correlation between the increase in the number of whistle blowing reports and the drop in Enron's stock price. In the end, tolerance for the misconduct eventually deteriorated just as rapidly as the stock.

For a number of years, though, we all benefited. The complacency allowed the corruption to continue, which allowed the stock to keep rising. As the corruption persisted, even those who were complacent were being rewarded handsomely for their silence. Every day that Enron's stock went up $1, I was making $2,000 profit. Some days, as Enron's stock rose $10, I was making $20,000. While Enron paid all of its executives very well, nothing could compare to the gains we made from stock options.

Everyone inside Enron at one time or another benefited from this mutually beneficially arrangement. In fact, I doubt you could find any Enron employee who will tell you that he or she didn't enjoy the benefits of the stock options, even if it meant turning a blind eye from time to time or, worse yet, contributing to the corruption. The stunning reality came to me when Enron International's vice chairman told me he was "glad it came to an end because [he] didn't have the guts to leave because of the stock options"! Of course, put into perspective, he was making tens of millions of dollars every day that Enron stock went up $1—but it was the first time I realized I was not alone in my addiction.

Like the junkie and the crack dealer, the complacent employees were dependent upon the corrupt employees. I was just as dependent upon Andy Fastow's financial fraud as he was reliant upon my continuing to remain quiet. I needed him as much as he needed me. However, in order to continue to keep the silent workers quiet and the corrupt workers happy, Enron's stock had to keep going up, which required a form of accounting that Enron would quickly find as its own drug of choice. Enron had become addicted to something called "mark to market" accounting. This method of accounting allowed Enron to book the entire revenue expected over the term of a contract at the time the contract was "booked" or entered into the system. Even though the revenue would be received slowly over the long term of the contract, the company was able to appear to be making money when there was nothing coming in the door.

To achieve its revenue objectives, I watched Enron's contract management group move 10,000 of its gas contracts through assignment from one of Enron's subsidiaries to another, only to move those same contracts again to yet another subsidiary at the end of the next quarter—all to generate a false sense of revenue for Enron's balance sheet. It was then that I realized this company was nothing more than smoke and mirrors. But for me, leaving was a complex issue. Since joining Enron, likely from the stress, I had been diagnosed with pre-cancer and medical insurance would be virtually impossible to get anywhere else. I wasn't from Houston, so I had little support there. Blowing the whistle on the company would mean I would have to leave the city, and looking for another job in another city was impractical given the demands of my work schedule.

Personal and Corporate Desperation at Enron

I was becoming dependent on my stock options for my survival, and while they were rapidly becoming worth a small fortune, by the summer of 1999, I would receive what many would consider a death threat. Out of desperation, I decided to move to Enron's water subsidiary, Azurix, believing perhaps that I was better suited for a more traditionally asset-based business operation, where reality could be defined in the value of tangible property. Azurix was Enron's vice chairman Rebecca Mark's effort to make her own mark by transitioning from the predominantly testosterone driven world of Enron to pursue a more altruistic venture to privatize water and waste water treatment throughout the world—or so I thought.

Although originally hired to be responsible for deal structuring, I was quickly moved to the e-commerce group when Enron restructured Azurix's focus from an "asset-heavy" strategy to an "asset-light" e-commerce one focused on trading water and water rights. In the summer of 1999, Rebecca Mark encouraged the e-commerce group, of which I was a part, to form a joint venture with her then fiancé, now husband, Joachim Michael Jusbasche, to market water chemicals through a web portal. When it was obvious the deal was not going to come together, I witnessed the first of many efforts by Jusbasche to claim rights to trade secrets that clearly were not his.

In January 2000, now pursuing a commodities-based water trading platform, I would discover that Jusbasche, by this time married to Rebecca Mark, was actually helping himself to intellectual property and trade secrets and then selling them back to the company. Recognizing that Jusbasche had no connection to Azurix except for being married to its CEO, I realized there were only two ways he had learned of the trade secrets—from his wife or from her computer.

Rebecca Mark-Jusbasche was now *Fortune* Magazine's 14th "Most Powerful Woman" on its list of 50. From all indications, she was either a crook or married to one. Either way, given that Azurix's stock had gone from an IPO price of $19 per share to $4 per share in less than six months, I believed if the media were to become aware of the information, it would trigger an EMD. Although I found it hard to believe that the CEO of one of Enron's subsidiaries was involved in assisting her husband in espionage, I felt someone at Enron needed to know, so I carefully gathered the supporting documentation.

Initially driven by loyalty, believing the company was in a far better position to correct the problems if it was to recognize them first rather than have them played out in the media, I was also of the belief that senior management should be held to a higher standard. In this case, it appeared as though the CEO knew about the "problem," so I decided to offer my letter of resignation. Much to my surprise, rather than accepting my letter of resignation, my boss and I agreed he should discuss the matter with Mark-Jusbasche before I made any final decisions—which he agreed to do over the weekend.

On Monday morning, I was called into a meeting where I expected I would be fired, but instead I received what amounted to a promotion—to trade power with Enron's western power trading operations in Portland, Oregon. Realizing that such a move would permit me to remain at Enron while my stock options vested as well as to receive a significant bonus and a company-sponsored move to the Pacific Northwest where I was raised, I accepted the opportunity.

Corruption: The Force That Destroyed Enron

It took me all of one week to realize I had made a terrible mistake. The honeymoon with Enron was clearly over. Up close and personal, I would discover not only that Enron was manipulating wholesale power prices, but also how it was doing it. Weighing heavily on my mind was the realization that if I went outside the company with the details I knew, I could potentially collapse an entire commodity market and destabilize anything that ran off electricity because every trading contract was hedged with another contract, creating a house of cards. The overwhelming sense of responsibility was beginning to take its toll on me. I could no longer get my head around the separation between right and wrong—no longer did "doing the right thing" seem to be an easy decision. Sadly, this opportunity to reflect also brought me the greatest personal reflection on the impact of Enron's misdeeds that occurred right under the nose of employees like me without any ability to intervene.

This is where I would meet Jeff Richter, a young man in his 30s who had grown up in the Midwest. Straight from Wisconsin, he had had nearly as many problems with relationships as I had, so we related to each other in a sick sort of way. After graduating from college with a teaching degree, he decided to teach math, but failed to see the long-term financial opportunities in helping children within the confines of the educational system. I'm not certain how Jeff Richter ended up at Enron, but he did come under the counsel of my boss at Enron, who had agreed to hire him as a Lotus Notes programmer. Once inside Enron, Jeff realized, like most, the real money to be made was in trading energy. Jeff decided the best use of his quantitative skills was to buy "real estate" on Wall Street by becoming a power broker, becoming one of Enron's premiere traders in the California power markets. Little did Jeff know that the risk in playing any game of Monopoly is that you can "Go Directly to Jail." Like myself, he too had become a product of his environment. Playing by the rules meant being a team player, which meant that Jeff's life, like mine, had been irrevocably changed forever.

When I met Jeff Richter for the first time in 2000, he had transferred from Houston to Portland, Oregon, where he was responsible for trading power in the state of California. Sean Crandall traded at the California-Oregon Border (COB), and Jeff traded in the mid-section of the state between north and south. This is where the greatest crunch for power occurred because of the high demand for power in Silicon Valley and the weak infrastructure that failed to allow for sufficient power to be delivered between Northern California and Southern California. Quite literally, there was a disconnect in the ability to get power to where it was needed when it was needed most.

When I arrived in February 2000 to decide whether to accept a position as Jeff Richter's backup in trading power, I quickly realized the weaknesses in the system would be no match for these very smart men. Without going into great detail as to the specific schemes used to defraud customers, suffice it to say that at the direction of Tim Belden (director of Enron's western power trading), a group of whiz kids would look for ways to buy low and sell high, requiring them to drive the price of power up. They did everything from buying up all of the power to scheduling more power than the physical transmission line had the capacity to transmit, to causing the state of California to pay Enron rebates to relieve the falsely created demand.

Trading power suddenly brought everything into focus for me. At the hands of one leader, who claimed to have the keys to the Ark, a group of individuals blindly followed. Two by two they walked behind Tim Belden, seduced by the money, believing they would somehow be left off the boat when it set sail were they not willing to follow. By the time they awakened to the reality of the situation and the potential penalties for breaking the law, the cover-up naturally followed, which is what caused the EMD for Enron in the California power markets. Of course, a lot of really good people would be hurt by the actions of a few.

The radar screen for me in the three years at Enron never seemed to focus in on the damage I was potentially causing by my failure to stand up sooner. It never occurred to me that people would die or that teachers would not be able to retire simply because I sat on the sidelines and watched. I just knew I wasn't breaking the law so somehow I was justified. Of course, today I realize that is like saying you know your friends are robbing a bank but, as long as you are outside the bank, you have no responsibility for what is going on inside, even as you hear gunfire. Knowing that people have died because of my unwillingness to stand up against the bad guys makes me one of the bad guys. Perhaps I realized that our actions, no matter how big or small, have a large ripple effect when I learned from the general counsel of a small public utilities department in Snohomish, Washington that a customer had told him, "I can't even buy a prom dress for my daughter's senior prom because of my power rates."

I also learned in that week, and I remain committed to this today, that absent working for Enron, Jeff Richter was not a criminal outside his life at Enron. To assume otherwise means that in any situation Jeff would be drawn into a desire to commit crimes. He was not raised that way, but rather he committed crimes because he could. He, like most of us, never thought much about the consequences of his actions. Most believed they could get away with it, until it was obvious they couldn't. White male professionals don't go to jail, they must have thought from time to time, and certainly not ones who work for a company that had such close relationships with the politicians. Clearly they were wrong in their thinking. However, I could squarely look Mr. and Mrs. Richter in the eyes and say, "Your son became someone inside Enron he was not raised to be—but so did I."

Enron's world for me now was clearly defined. Staying in Portland trading power would require that I move from a place of complacency to corruption—something I was unwilling to do. The boundaries were blurred, but not gone. I decided accepting such a position would be the proverbial jump from the fire into the frying pan, so I returned to what I believed was the lesser of two evils—back to Houston to focus on the e-commerce initiatives at Azurix. In part, my responsibility was to write public relations content for the Internet and its intranet so as to promote the company. In doing so, I would happen upon public information that chairman and CEO Rebecca Mark's husband, Michael Jusbasche, had not only been stealing trade secrets from us, he had actually been indicted in 1980 for stealing exploration maps from Shell and pled "no contest." Recognizing the potential public relations disaster this could cause if the media were to begin to investigate the company and, more specifically, Rebecca Mark, I went to my boss, who was the managing director of public relations for Azurix and who had overseen Rebecca's career while serving as the chairman of Enron International and vice chairman of Enron.

Initially she appeared shocked. Although I believed it was in response to learning that espionage was being committed against one of Enron's subsidiaries at the hands of the CEO's husband, perhaps even at the direction of the CEO, in retrospect her shock was associated with someone discovering the details that would clearly implicate the CEO, whose reputation she had been charged to protect. She agreed to speak with Rebecca and get back to me. Nearly 15 minutes passed before my phone finally rang with instructions for me to remove every reference to Jusbasche within the context of Rebecca Mark on both the Azurix web site, as well as its intranet. Rebecca Mark-Jusbasche would once again be known simply as Rebecca Mark, so if the media were to investigate the poor performance of the company, they would not tie the two together.

I had gone from being asked to leave it out to remove it, which amounted in my mind to a cover-up. Legally, the line was clear, but ethically, the line was so fine it was growing increasingly fuzzy. But I knew it was wrong. The rationale in my mind remained that the people I had grown to respect immensely seemed to be fine with asking me to cover up the executive's misdeeds. Perhaps it is no different than agreeing to sign a confidentiality agreement to settle a sexual harassment case—the victim is paid for silence, leaving the perpetrator unidentified and allowed to strike again. It was the culmination of evidence that was beginning to weigh on me. This was no longer about a single perpetrator; this was about an entire culture of permissive behavior that had become a runaway freight train. The line between wrong and right was no longer black and white, but gray.

My days at work were beginning to feel a bit surreal. Loyalty to the brand was beginning to cost me a sense of health and well-being. The more I thought about what my father might think of my behavior, the more I began to justify my increasing complacency by simply moving the lines of right and wrong. As much as I was growing tired of "complaining" about the actions of those around me, including those who worked for me, I believe I was beginning to be seen as the "problem" rather than the solution.

Enron's world was becoming more vicious. Having received my own death threat and then seeing at least one person who had complained come to work severely beaten, claiming to have "fallen," I realized the time had come for me to leave the company no matter what the cost. I had two options: leave the company or transfer to another subsidiary. There was just one problem to the latter. As Azurix began taking on water and sinking fast, a mass exodus began, so Enron placed a moratorium on employee transfers, which left me with no alternative but to leave the company.

Out of desperation, I pleaded for a life raft. I clearly had enemies, but I also had friends inside the company. Enron had always been a place where rules were made to be broken, and sure enough, at the one time I needed to apply this rule in my case, it worked, and the company transferred me to Portland, Oregon to work for its broadband subsidiary. Although I never had to play that card, I do suppose that it helped that senior management knew that I knew what was really going on. I had gone from working indirectly for Andy Fastow, who was committing bank fraud, to working indirectly for Tim Belden, who was stealing from the state of California, to working for Rebecca Mark, who, at the very least, knew her husband was committing espionage.

Now heading up the competitive intelligence efforts in Portland, Oregon for Enron Broadband Services, I realized the media and analysts were being misled at the direction of Jeff Skilling as to the market potential for trading broadband. While Skilling was claiming that Enron's stock, trading at $80 per share, should be worth $40 more per share simply because Enron was creating new markets, I was telling him that there was no potential for trading broadband. In fact, our only two competitors were going out of business. Without competitors to trade, there is no liquidity in the market. Without liquidity in the market, there is no demand. Jeff continued his blatant lies right to the very end when he would say "the broadband market caught him by surprise."

But something else would catch him by surprise, as well as most of us in attendance at the all-employee meeting in Portland, Oregon. When Jeff presented Enron's financial statement, the numbers did not add up. In the spirit of inquiry, risking everything, the head of accounts payable asked him in the public forum, "Jeff, where are you getting your numbers?" He responded, "These are the numbers I was given." The final straw came for me when I heard her response, "No you weren't, because I give you those numbers!" Silence fell across the room and, for the first time, I realized the most senior man at Enron, actively engaged in Enron's operations, had his own way of ensuring Enron would once again be named the "Most Innovative Company."

As Enron tried desperately to justify its entry into the broadband market and Enron Broadband Services was financially hemorrhaging due to the capital expenditures required to build the switches necessary to trade broadband, pressure was coming from all angles to find the revenue. As the primary purchaser of market data, I knew that we had the potential to reduce our costs while developing a potential stream of revenue. Enron was telling the world it had an "Intelligent Network" that was to be hailed as the next generation Internet, which would allow content to be streamed across the globe. Given that Enron was spending nearly $10 million in market research data, I suggested that we offer the research data providers a free ride on the information superhighway in exchange for the data. Imagine the excitement when anyone presents an opportunity to leverage assets that can wipe out $10 million in expenses overnight.

My boss's first response to my idea was a bit shocking. "Who did you get this idea from?" When I explained to him it was my idea alone, he looked at me as though it was some covert operation. "Don't tell anyone of this idea. It is fabulous." What would happen next drove me to the place of reckoning within myself. As the pressure mounted for Enron Broadband Services, the pressure my boss placed on me increased immensely. Of course, I had seen the unscrupulous deals, but I had never assumed Enron was virtually bankrupt. As the pressure built to get the deal done, I began playing the "Enron card," suggesting that if the market data companies wouldn't play by Enron's rules, no division within Enron would be playing with them. Suddenly it dawned on me, as I heard myself aggressively going after the deals—never mind Enron's values, what had happened to my own?! Just as I had lost myself in a few too many relationships, I had lost myself within this company. I was no longer certain where Enron the company started and my own identity ended. If I was willing to practice what amounted to extortion, what else was I capable of? I knew if I didn't get out of the company, I would have a very long time to think about it from prison.

In early November 2000, I had a doctor's appointment with the head of surgical oncology at Oregon Health Sciences University Hospital. Having been diagnosed with pre-cancerous cells, discovered during a surgical procedure I had undergone while at Enron in Houston, it was a routine visit to establish a relationship with a local surgeon after my relocation. "You have an 86 percent chance of full-blown breast cancer in the next five years." The words stunned me, but the surgeon also gave me hope. "You can reduce your odds, but you have to remove all of the stress in your life." There was only one conclusion I could draw—I was not going to die for Enron.

On the way back to the office that afternoon, I realized I had nowhere to turn. The company was crooked. The more I stood up against the injustice, the more I was hammered by those above me who also felt helpless to go up the chain of command. But someone certainly needed to know what was going on, and if those inside the company were not going to listen, I was going to go outside the company. Using my company-issued cell phone, I pulled out my Enron health insurance card and dialed the employee assistance number listed on the bottom. The woman answering the phone took down my pertinent information and suggested she could perhaps help me. That was until I laid out the details of my experiences at Enron, to which she responded, "Ma'am, I'm sorry, inasmuch as our fees are paid by Enron, I can't take your call. You'll have to hire a private lawyer."

I didn't need a private lawyer, I needed help. Forcing the company to sever our relationship was the best thing I could hope for. Under Enron's severance package, I would be entitled to approximately six months worth of pay, plus my stock options. Of course, I could offer something the company needed—my silence. Agreeing to the terms of the severance agreement, I finally resigned from Enron in November of 2000.

Now bound by a confidentiality agreement, I was forced to remain silent until I could do so no more. I realized that Jeff Skilling had once again overstated Enron's financial position in his letter to the shareholders in early 2001 when he said, "Enron hit a record $1.3 billion in net income in 2000." The problem existed in the audited financials—Enron had hit only $978 million according to its auditor Arthur Andersen. And, perhaps more importantly, but more obscure, was footnote 16, which said that a member of Enron's senior management had an interest in an outside partnership. Of course, everyone inside the company knew who that member was—none other than Andy Fastow. We also knew that the board of directors had waived its code of conduct to allow the conflict of interest. But the media had no idea and did very little to investigate much further.

In the summer of 2001, we once again saw power rates in California and now the Pacific Northwest that were obviously being manipulated. No one had the details of how Enron was achieving what amounted to "gaming" of the system. But I did, and by now I realized I needed to alert the media, so quite innocently I sent an e-mail to one of Seattle's most respected radio show hosts for CBS that said "if you want the details of how Enron is manipulating the power prices, let me know." Of course, minutes later I got the call from his producer and was interviewed on air to describe the details of Enron's dirty tricks. It was liberating, but frightening at the same time. I don't know what I had been thinking. When you send an explosive e-mail, clearly you should expect to get a call. I realized I could no longer hide behind "I didn't know." I did know what went on at Enron and I had no reason to hide behind the veil of secrecy anymore. My loyalty wasn't to Enron anymore, I thought, but like an abused child I still expected to be beaten.

Shortly thereafter, at the urging of my new-found friend in the media, I went to the U.S. House of Representatives Energy and Commerce Committee and called Senator Byron Dorgan who heads the committee. Enron's stock was now virtually worthless, having lost $90 billion in 24 days because of the massive sell-off of its stock in what appeared to be an old-fashioned run on the bank. I explained to the young man from Dorgan's office that I had evidence of bank fraud and espionage on the part of Enron. He said, "Send us an e-mail," which I did within minutes. The reference line said, "I have evidence of bank fraud and espionage on the part of Enron." You didn't even need to open the e-mail to realize the content could be explosive. Yet today, despite this effort, no one from Dorgan's office has ever called me.

A Systemic Cover-Up: Complacency Compounded the Corruption

Enron was clearly a two-part story: 1) those who refused to tell the truth and 2) those who refused to listen. While those of us inside Enron were clearly complacent, so were the media and the analysts, and so was Enron's board of directors. The board members, like me, became complacent in their efforts to stand up against those who refused to tell the truth. If we look at the presentation made to Enron's board of directors by its internal auditors in September 2001 (see Figure 2), we can see there was a 300 percent increase in whistleblowing reports between 2000 and 2001.

Figure 2

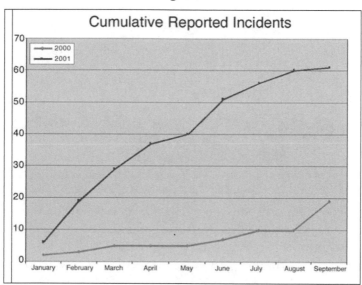

Among the 2001 incident reports received, 31 percent were reports of alleged criminal activity, of which 74 percent were cases of fraud (Figures 3 and 4). While one could certainly argue that Andrew Fastow had simply become more active in committing fraud, the truth was the lack of integrity throughout the culture had spread like cancer.

Figure 3

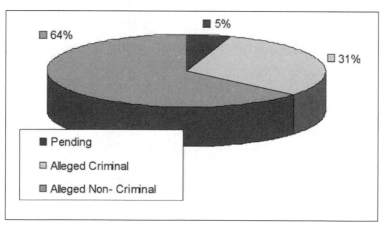

Figure 4

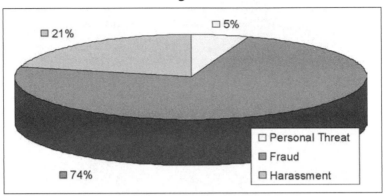

I'm sure most who are going to jail as a result of their actions and decisions inside Enron are doing, realize the value of an ethical disaster is about self-reflection as to our personal responsibility for our actions and perhaps forgiveness, both of ourselves and of others. I may never know the impact the good I do in this world may have, but I certainly know that whether for good or bad, my actions do have consequences. The awakening came for me in 2003 when I opened *The Wall Street Journal* on my birthday and read on the front page that Jeff Richter had pleaded guilty and was going to prison. "There but for the grace of God go I." Perhaps it was the irony of reading it on my birthday that I realized I was born to do something in this world and, for better or for worse, I am the one that holds the key to that car, and I alone decide what road I take—no one else chooses for me unless I give them the keys to the car.

Beyond Enron: Transcending Complacency to a Cause

The effects of my time at Enron have affected my life deeply. On an emotional level, I am reminded every day that people died because of my complacency. I am reminded that elderly people had to go back to work because their fixed incomes were insufficient to sustain them with the downturn in the market. I am reminded that millions of people lost millions of dollars of their retirement savings. I am reminded that at least one person could not buy a prom dress because of the rising power rates, and I am reminded our entire capital market system hung in the balance because of the corporate corruption that was brought to light with the Enron case. And I am reminded that I played a personal role in this destruction, and must accept personal responsibility for this.

On a physical level, while I have not seen any signs of cancer, I do suffer from symptoms commonly associated with post-traumatic stress disorder due to the elevated levels of adrenaline I endured over a prolonged period of time while at Enron. Apparently, people who live in danger produce high levels of natural opiates, which temporarily mask pain. However, when removed from the traumatic situation, the body has become addicted to what amounts to a drug. The prolonged exposure to adrenaline causes my body to crave what was once environmentally-induced adrenaline. Of course, if left untreated, the receptors apparently break down, causing a deficient immune system—hence the oncologist's suggestion that I remove all the stress in my life. Unfortunately, I was just a little too late! Rather than focus on the consequences of my experiences, I have decided to channel my energies towards positive change.

The Integrity Institute

If left undetected, an unethical environment will eventually metastasize like cancer and kill the body as it did at Enron. Personally, I have an obligation to make certain I apply the lessons I learned there for the greater good; otherwise that EMD will have served no purpose. I believe Enron was predictable, as were many of the other EMDs discussed in this book.

Yet, despite the wave of regulatory and legislative changes brought about in large part because of Enron, WorldCom and others, the corruption and EMDs have continued. While these changes have resulted in an expanded focus on governance, risk and compliance, this too has proven unsuccessful in curing the problem. Some would argue this disease has become an epidemic for which we have no cure. Often we don't know that an EMD is upon us until it is too late. Having been inside Enron and having watched the perfect storm build, I know there must be a better way, which is why I founded The Integrity Institute.

Similar to mapping the human genome, The Integrity Institute has mounted an effort to integrate ten validated models that will create a diagnostic tool to help organizations recognize the structural weaknesses early on in order to avoid or address problems appropriately rather than to respond to and recover from a crisis, which often proves too late. Rather than myopically focusing on silos of independent assessments, for the first time we will be able to understand how leadership influences organizational culture; how governance affects compensation; how compensation affects earnings; how earnings affect corporate citizenship; how corporate citizenship affects stakeholder perceptions; how stakeholder perceptions affect risk; how risk affects compliance and ethics efforts; how compliance and ethics affect communication; how communication affects culture; and how the interconnectivity of these "organisms" strengthens or weakens the dynamic organization.

Using non-financial information that discovers and assesses the soundness, wholeness and incorruptibility of corporate citizenship, communication, compensation, compliance and ethics, culture, earnings, governance, leadership, risk and stakeholder perceptions, we will be able to pinpoint more accurately where weaknesses may exist that influence the financial health and welfare of a company and its sustainability. By measuring these components we believe we will be able to measure an organization's ability to withstand market forces (e.g. EMDs) that may influence the company and destroy shareholder value.

The Integrity Institute is neither a watchdog organization nor a rating agency; rather, it operates similar to the Underwriter's Laboratory or Good Housekeeping Seal of Approval. It has four objectives:

1. Help companies sustain the momentum built as a result of Sarbanes-Oxley and the Federal Sentencing Guidelines for Organizations.

2. Reduce the fees associated with compliance with Sarbanes-Oxley and other mandated attempts to legalize business ethics.

3. Provide transparency as proposed by recent legislation and regulatory activities to increase shareholder value.

4. End the need for mandated regulatory bureaucracy such as Sarbanes-Oxley, designed to make companies act responsibly.

Health, of course, is the absence of disease. The Integrity Institute exists for the purposes of assessing and certifying the health of companies using nonfinancial performance indicators. It seeks not only to assess an organization's ethical health, but also ultimately to certify the results with an Integria seal when an organization meets the standards established by The Integrity Institute. More information about The Integrity Insitute's standards can be found in Appendix B.

We believe this seal of approval provides corporations with the opportunity to increase shareholder value. Beyond that, we believe that there are companies that desire to go beyond being simply disease free to reach a place which most would consider robust health to provide long-term growth, superior results, healthy companies, and happy employees, around which the culture is defined and without which they will not survive the pressures common to all organizations. Appendix B provides more detail on my approach to standardize and assess corporate integrity.

Moving Beyond Complacency

Lynn Brewer's experiences indicate that the collateral damage an ethical disaster creates can be devastating to those behind the headlines. Every person who experiences shock, humiliation, and fear, as well as career-threatening results from the disaster, will have their lives changed forever. In some cases, children and spouses have watched their loved ones go to jail. Communities have lost not only economic resources, but also the vitality and energy of citizens who wanted to contribute to a high quality of life but instead went to jail for their misconduct. If the stories behind the headlines were acknowledged, perhaps more corporate leaders would understand the ramifications of unethical conduct and recognize that pushing everything to the bottom line could result in human losses as well as financial ones. The goal of this book is to provide a blueprint to prevent these types of disasters.

The founding of The Integrity Institute was intended to create a proactive response from corporate America to recognize, avoid, discover, answer to, and if necessary, recover from ethical lapses that have the potential to grow into EMDs. Just as an athlete must recognize and develop the physical conditioning required to give a successful performance, a corporation must spend adequate time and resources to recognize and discover its ethical condition in order to develop programs to address any risks that are identified. There are no shortcuts to developing a corporate culture that can absorb ethical lapses, repair ethical damage and prevent major ethical disasters. All of the legislative attempts to create ethical cultures will fail if corporate leaders do not understand their role in developing, implementing, and modeling an ethical culture on a day-to-day basis. Indeed, as we saw at Enron, corporate leaders can even send messages that effectively counter an ethical culture. From Lynn Brewer's perspective at Enron, a highly unethical corporate culture resulted in subcultures that quickly recognized that corruption or complacency was the key to performance—and ever-increasing stock options.

As we shall see in the next chapter, leadership that creates an ethical culture understands both the formal and informal nature of communicating, assessing, and enhancing values and principles that can prevent an EMD. An ethical culture sets the tone for employees and other stakeholders and fosters accountability and transparency. An ethical culture is not created through codes of ethics, employment conduct manuals, and values statements that are not a part of how things operate on a daily basis. This was the case at Enron, and it should be an example to other companies that ethics is not simply a check-the-box or create-a-document activity. Everyone in the organization, through communications and actions, must become ethical role models for the people they interact with on a daily basis. Leaders must discuss the importance of ethics, model ethical behavior, and reinforce this with training on ethics.

3

The Role of Leadership in Recognizing and Avoiding Organizational Misconduct

---

To avoid an Ethical Misconduct Disaster (EMD), business people must recognize ethical issues and make ethical decisions. An ethical issue is a problem, situation or opportunity that requires an individual, group or organization to choose among several actions that must be evaluated as right or wrong, ethical or unethical.[1] Some obvious ethical issues involve clear-cut attempts to deceive or take advantage of a situation. For example, two former senior executives with Ogilvy & Mather advertising were sentenced to more than a year in prison for conspiring to overbill the government for an ad campaign warning children about the dangers of drugs. The executives were also required to perform 400 hours of community service, pay a fine and draft a proposed code of ethics for the advertising industry.[2] The requirement to draft a code of ethics implies that the court viewed the executives' wrongdoing as a lapse of ethical leadership in the advertising industry. Obviously, misrepresenting billing on accounts is a serious ethical issue that can evolve into misconduct with severe repercussions.

The 2002 SOX and the 2004 amendments to the Federal Sentencing Guidelines for Organizations (FSGO) emphasize the necessity of establishing an ethical organizational culture. This approach is to be realized through ethics and compliance programs. The Department of Justice's Thompson Memorandum sets forth nine factors for U.S. Attorneys to consider in determining whether to investigate, charge or negotiate a plea with an organization. An ethics and compliance program is key to avoiding prosecution. However, business ethics in organizations also require values-based leadership from top management, purposeful actions that include planning and implementation of standards of appropriate conduct, as well as openness and continuous effort to improve the organization's ethical performance. Although we often think of CEOs and other top managers as the most important leaders in an organization, a firm's board of directors is also an important required leadership and oversight component. Leadership and effective corporate governance are necessary to sustain an ethical organizational culture that prevents misconduct and supports appropriate conduct.

Understanding Ethical Decision Making[3]

Values-driven ethical leadership and compliance-driven ethics training, monitoring, and reporting systems help to create an ethical corporate culture that can recognize and respond appropriately to ethical issues before they escalate and become major, damaging events. However, according to David Gabler, president of a business ethics consulting firm, "It is not enough to merely ask whether controls are in place or if everyone has attended a class or signed a code. The organization has to understand what the drivers of behavior are, and how those align with integrity goals."[4] Thus, it is vital to understand *how* people make business ethics decisions. Figure 1 illustrates a model of ethical decision-making in an organizational environment. Although it is impossible to describe precisely how or why an individual or a work group may reach a particular decision, we can generalize about typical behavior patterns within organizations. It is important to understand that this framework does not explain how *to make a decision,* but rather describes how *decisions are made.* In other words, this framework facilitates understanding the factors that influence decision-making within an organizational culture. For an executive to make a specific ethical decision requires subject-matter knowledge, an assessment of risk, and the experience to understand the consequences of the decision on all stakeholders. While personal character and values are important, decisions are made in an organizational context.

Figure 1

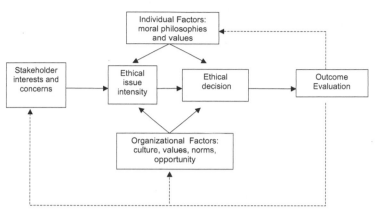

Source: O.C. Ferrell, 2006

The first step in Figure 1 is recognizing stakeholder interests and concerns. Stakeholders, obviously, are individuals, groups, and even communities that can directly or indirectly affect a firm's activities. Although most corporations have emphasized shareholders as the most important stakeholder group, the failure to consider all significant stakeholders can lead to ethical lapses. Some executives believe that if their companies adopt a market-orientation and focus only on customers and shareholders, everything else will be adequate. Unfortunately, failure to recognize the needs and potential impact of employees, suppliers, regulators, special-interest groups, communities and the media can lead to unfortunate consequences.

Thus, organizations need to identify and prioritize stakeholders and their respective concerns about organizational activities, and gather information to respond to significant individuals, groups, and communities. These groups apply their own values and standards to their perception of many diverse issues. They supply resources—e.g. capital, labor, expertise, infrastructure, sales, etc.—that are more or less critical to a firm's long-term survival, and their ability to withdraw—or threaten to withdraw—these resources gives them power.[5]

One approach is to deal proactively with stakeholders' concerns and ethical issues and stimulate a sense of bonding with the firm. When a company listens to their concerns and tries to resolve issues, the result is tangible benefits that can translate into customer loyalty, employee commitment, supplier partnerships and improved corporate reputation. This requires going beyond basic regulatory requirements and making a difference by genuinely listening to stakeholders and addressing their concerns. Such a stakeholder orientation secures continued support and stakeholder identification that promotes the success of the firm.

The purpose of understanding stakeholder concerns and risks is to pinpoint issues that could trigger the ethical decision-making process. If ethical issues are perceived as being related to the importance of stakeholders' interaction with the firm, a sound framework will exist for assessing the importance or relevance of a perceived issue—the intensity of the issue[6]—and the next step in Figure 1. The intensity of a particular issue is likely to vary over time and among individuals and is influenced by the organization's culture, the specific characteristics of the situation, and any personal pressures weighing on the decision. Different people perceive issues with varying intensity due to their own personal moral development and philosophies and because of the influence of organizational culture and coworkers.[7]

Understanding individuals' moral philosophies and reasoning processes is one approach that is often cited for recognizing and resolving ethical issues. However, the role of individuals and their values is one of the most difficult challenges in understanding organizational ethical decision-making. Although most of us would like to place the primary responsibility for decisions on individuals, years of research suggest that organizational factors have greater dominance in determining ethical decisions at work.[8] Nonetheless, individual factors are clearly important in evaluating and resolving ethical issues, and familiarity with theoretical frameworks from the field of moral philosophy is helpful in understanding ethical decision-making in business.[9] Two significant factors in business ethics are an individual's personal moral philosophy and stage of personal moral development. Through socialization, individuals develop their own ethical principles or rules to decide what is right or wrong, and with knowledge and experience, they advance in their level of moral development. This socialization occurs from family, friends, formal education, religion and other philosophical frameworks that an individual may embrace.

Although individuals must make ethical choices, they often do so in committees, group meetings, and through discussion with colleagues. Ethical decisions in the workplace are guided by the organization's culture and the influence of co-workers, superiors and subordinates. A significant element of organizational culture is a firm's ethical climate—its character or conscience. Whereas a firm's overall culture establishes ideals that guide a wide range of behaviors for members of the organization, its ethical climate focuses specifically on issues of right and wrong. Codes of conduct and ethics policies, top management's actions on ethical issues, the values and moral development and philosophies of coworkers, and the opportunity for misconduct all contribute to an organization's ethical climate. In fact, the ethical climate actually determines whether certain dilemmas are perceived as having a level of ethical intensity that requires a decision.

Together, organizational culture and the influence of coworkers may create conditions that limit or permit misconduct. If these conditions act to provide rewards for unethical conduct—such as financial gain, recognition, promotion or simply the good feeling from a job well done—the opportunity for further unethical conduct may exist. For example, a company policy that does not provide for punishment of employees who violate a rule (e.g. not to accept large gifts from clients) effectively provides an opportunity for that behavior to continue because it allows individuals to break the rule without fear of consequences. Thus, organizational policies, processes and other factors may contribute to the opportunity to act unethically.

Such opportunities often relate to employees' immediate job context—where they work, with whom they work, and the nature of the work. The specific work situation includes the motivational carrots and sticks that managers can use to influence employee behavior. Pay raises, bonuses, and public recognition are carrots, or positive reinforcement, whereas reprimands, pay penalties, demotions, and even firings act as sticks, the negative reinforcement. For example, a salesperson that is publicly recognized and given a large bonus for making a valuable sale that he obtained through unethical tactics will probably be motivated to use unethical sales tactics in the future, even if such behavior goes against his personal value system.

Business Ethics Does Not Equal Personal Ethics

According to ethics consultant David Gebler, "Most unethical behavior is not done for personal gain, it's done to meet performance goals."[10] Unfortunately, failure to understand this basic fact is a major barrier to educating corporations as to how to avoid an ethical disaster. Many executives believe that the moral values learned within the family and through religion and education are the major drivers of ethical decision-making in business. Indeed, some companies and many business schools focus on personal character or moral philosophy development in their training programs to prevent unethical business decisions. Although a personal moral compass is certainly important, it is not sufficient to prevent ethical misconduct in the complex world of business. The rewards for meeting performance goals and the corporate culture, especially for coworkers and managers, have been found to be the most important drivers of ethical decision-making.[11] Although there are many factors that influence the final decisions of individuals—including the workplace, family, religion, legal system, community, and profession—the level of these "spheres of influence" varies depending on how important the decision-maker perceives the issue to be.[12]

In evaluating the key influences of ethical decision-making, it is important to remember that ethical decisions are often made in groups or committees, and groupthink combined with peer pressure often becomes more important than the influence of the individual. Usually, a strong leader evolves who assures others that a particular action is legal and acceptable, and if the other individuals do not feel good about the decision, they are reminded that it is just a business decision that is necessary to stay competitive. For example, Betty Vinson, an accountant at WorldCom, objected when her superiors asked her to make improper accounting entries in order to conceal the telecom's deteriorating financial condition. She gave in only after being told that it was the only way to save the beleaguered company. She, along with several other WorldCom accountants, eventually pleaded guilty to conspiracy and fraud charges related to WorldCom's bankruptcy after the accounting improprieties came to light. She was sentenced to five months in prison and five months house arrest.[13]

This situation is made more dynamic because individuals are culturally diverse, have different values, and have different personal attributes, such as personality, age and gender, which may influence how they will react in an organizational decision-making situation. In fact, academic studies have shown that in any workplace, at least 10 percent of employees will take advantage of situations if the opportunity exists and the risk of being caught is low. About 40 percent of workers will go along with the work group on most matters; these employees are most concerned about the social implications of their actions and want to fit into the organization. Another 40 percent of a company's employees will always try to follow company rules and policies, including codes of ethics, ethics training and other communications about appropriate conduct. The final 10 percent of employees try to maintain formal ethical standards that focus on rights, duties and rules.[14] For a corporation like Wal-Mart, with 1.6 million employees, this suggests that 160,000 employees are likely to engage in misconduct if given the opportunity.

Ethical Leadership

To move from just being an ethical person in everyday life experiences to being an ethical leader in a corporation requires an understanding of the ethical decision-making process described earlier. Leadership also requires an understanding of the firm's vision and values, as well as the challenges of responsibility and the risk in achieving organizational objectives.

Lapses in ethical leadership do occur even in people who possess strong ethical character, especially if they view the organization's ethical culture as being outside of the realm of decision-making that exists in the home, family, and community. This phenomenon has been observed in countless cases of so-called good community citizens engaging in ethical misconduct that sometimes lead to corporate ethical disasters. An ethical individual can be a cautious and conforming participant in a corporate culture that tolerates unethical conduct. Consider that many executives facing ethical disasters were viewed as outstanding community leaders in their personal lives, yet became embroiled in scandals at their companies. For example, Robin Szeliga, CFO of Qwest, who pleaded guilty for insider trading, was an excellent community leader, even serving on a college-of-business advisory board.[15]

In the long run, if a company's leader fails to satisfy stakeholders, he or she will not retain a leadership position. A leader must not only have the respect of stakeholders, but must also provide a standard of ethical conduct for them. Sunbeam, for example, fired CEO Al Dunlap after the Securities and Exchange Commission launched an investigation into whether the firm had fraudulently manipulated its financial reports. "Chainsaw Al" Dunlap had previously written a book entitled *Mean Business*, in which he took a somewhat questionable approach to achieving organizational profitability.[16] He ultimately paid $500,000 to settle the SEC's charges that he defrauded investors by inflating the small-appliance maker's sales. He also paid $15 million to shareholders, who filed a class-action suit on similar charges.[17]

Leadership Styles[18]

Employees often look to their organizational leaders to determine how to resolve ethical issues. Leadership styles influence many aspects of organizational behavior, including employees' acceptance of and adherence to organizational ethical standards. Styles that focus on building strong organizational values among employees contribute to shared standards of conduct. In short, the leadership style of an organization influences how its employees act. Studying a firm's leadership styles and attitudes can also help pinpoint where future ethical issues may arise.

Psychologist Daniel Goleman identified six leadership styles based on "emotional intelligence"—that contribute to the ability to manage ourselves and our relationships effectively.

1. The coercive leader demands instant compliance and focuses on achievement, initiative and self-control. This approach can be quite effective during a crisis turnaround, but it otherwise fosters a negative climate for organizational performance.

2. The authoritative leader—often regarded as one of the most effective styles—motivates employees to follow a vision, promotes change, and builds a positive climate for corporate performance.

3. The affiliative leader respects people, their emotions, and their needs and relies on friendship and trust to encourage flexibility, innovation, and risk-taking.

4. The democratic leader fosters participation and teamwork to reach collaborative decisions. This approach focuses on communication and creates a positive climate for achieving results.

5. The pacesetting leader can create a negative climate because of the high standards he or she sets. This approach works best for achieving rapid results from highly motivated people who value achievement and take the initiative.

6. The coaching leader establishes a positive climate by cultivating skills to foster long-lasting success, delegating responsibility and issuing challenging assignments.

The most successful leaders do not rely on one style but adapt their techniques based on the situation at hand. Different styles can be effective in developing an ethical climate depending on the leader's judgment of risks and desire to achieve a positive climate for organizational performance.[19]

Another way to study leadership styles is to classify them as transactional or transformational. Transactional leaders strive to satisfy employees through negotiating or bartering for desired behaviors or performance, whereas transformational leaders attempt to boost employees' level of commitment and to inspire trust and motivation.[20] Both types of leaders can positively influence the organizational culture.

Transformational leaders communicate a sense of purpose, inspire new ways of thinking, and foster new learning experiences. They think about employee needs and desires as well as organizational needs. These leaders also instill commitment and respect for values that provide guidance on how to deal with ethical issues. Thus, transformational leaders strive to promote activities and behavior through a shared vision and common learning experience. Consequently, they may have a greater influence on employee support in building an ethical culture and in making ethical decisions than do transactional leaders. A transformational approach is best suited for companies that have higher levels of ethical commitment among employees as well as strong stakeholder support for an ethical climate. A number of industry trade associations, including the American Institute of Certified Public Accountants, Defense Industry Initiative on Business Ethics and Conduct, Ethics and Compliance, Ethics Officer Association and Mortgage Bankers Association of America are helping companies provide transformational leadership.[21]

Transactional leaders, in contrast, concentrate on ensuring that required conduct and procedures are employed. Their negotiations to realize desired outcomes result in dynamic interactions with subordinates in which reactions, conflict, and crisis affect the relationship more than ethical concerns. Transactional leadership yields employees who work to attain a negotiated level of performance, including compliance with ethical and legal standards. As long as both employees and managers find this approach mutually satisfying, the relationship is likely to be successful. Nevertheless, transactional leadership is best suited for rapidly changing situations, including those caused by ethical problems or issues. When Michael Capellas took over as CEO and president of WorldCom (now called MCI) after an accounting scandal forced the company into bankruptcy proceedings, he employed transactional leadership to change the firm's culture and ethical conduct. Capellas sought to restore WorldCom's reputation by bringing in a new board of directors, establishing a corporate ethics office, enhancing the code of ethics, and initiating new employee financial-reporting and ethics-training initiatives.[22]

Habits of Strong Ethical Leaders

Archie Carroll, University of Georgia business professor, crafted "7 Habits of Highly Moral Leaders" based on the idea of the Stephen Covey's *The 7 Habits of Highly Effective People.*[23] We have adapted Carroll's "7 Habits of Highly Moral Leaders"[24] to create our own "7 Habits of Strong Ethical Leaders" (Table 1). In particular, we believe that ethical leadership is based on holistic thinking that embraces the complex and challenging issues companies face on a daily basis. Ethical leaders need both knowledge and experience to make the right decision. Strong ethical leaders have both the courage and the most complete information to make decisions that will be the best in the long run. Strong ethical leaders must stick to their principles and, if necessary, be ready to leave the organization if its corporate governance system is so flawed that it is impossible to make the right choice.

Table 1 Habits of Strong Ethical Leaders	
1.	Ethical leaders have strong personal character.
2.	Ethical leaders have a passion to do right.
3.	Ethical leaders are proactive.
4.	Ethical leaders consider stakeholders' interests.
5.	Ethical leaders are role models for the organization's values.
6.	Ethical leaders are transparent and actively involved in organizational decision-making.
7.	Ethical leaders are competent managers who take a holistic view of the firm's ethical culture.

Founders of corporations such as Sam Walton, Bill Gates, Milton Hershey, Martha Stewart, Michael Dell and Steve Jobs, as well as

Ben Cohen and Jerry Greenfield, left their ethical stamp on their companies. Their conduct set the tone, making them role models for desired conduct in the early growth of their respective corporations. In the case of Milton Hershey, his legacy endures, and Hershey Foods continues to be a role model for ethical corporate culture. In the case of Sam Walton, Wal-Mart embarked on a course of rapid growth after his death and became involved in numerous conflicts with various stakeholder groups, especially employees, regulators, competitors and communities. Despite the ethical foundation left by Sam Walton, Wal-Mart, as well as most large corporations, deals with hundreds of reported ethical lapses every month.[25]

Ethical Leaders Have Strong Personal Character

There is general agreement that ethical leadership is highly unlikely without a strong personal character. The question is how to teach or develop a moral person in a corporate environment. Thomas I. White, a leading authority on character development, believes the focus should be on "ethical reasoning" rather than on being a "moral person." According to White, the ability to resolve the complex ethical dilemmas encountered in a corporate culture requires intellectual skills.[26] For example, when Lawrence S. Benjamin took over as president of U.S. Food Service after a major ethical disaster, he initiated an ethics and compliance program to promote transparency and to teach employees how to make difficult ethical choices.

A fundamental problem in traditional character development is that specific values and virtues are used to teach a belief or philosophy. This approach may be inappropriate for a business environment where cultural diversity and privacy must be respected. On the other hand, teaching individuals who want to do the right thing corporate values and ethical codes, and equipping them with the intellectual skills to address the complexities of ethical issues, is the correct approach.

Ethical Leaders Have a Passion to Do Right

Archie Carroll describes the passion to do right as "the glue that holds ethical concepts together." Some leaders develop this trait early in life, while others develop it over time through experience, reason, or spiritual growth. They often cite familiar arguments for doing right; to keep society from disintegrating; to alleviate human suffering; to advance human prosperity; to resolve conflicts of interest fairly and logically; to praise the good and punish the guilty; or just because something "is the right thing to do."[27] Having a passion to do right indicates a personal characteristic of not only recognizing the importance of ethical behavior, but also of the willingness to face challenges and make tough choices. Consider the crisis faced by Harry Kraemer, the CEO of Baxter International, after 53 dialysis patients died during treatment. The dialysis filters used in each of the cases came from a single lot manufactured by Althin Medical AB, a firm that Baxter had acquired the year before. After investigating, Kraemer chose to take responsibility, apologize, recall all of Althin's dialysis filters, and ultimately close down Althin's operations— actions that would eventually cost Baxter $189 million. Afterward, Kraemer asked Baxter's board of directors to reduce his bonus because of the deaths. He could have made different choices, but he put the situation in a larger context: "We have this situation. The financial people will assess the potential financial impact. The legal people will do the same. But at the end of the day, if we think it's a problem that a Baxter product was involved in the deaths of 53 people, then those other issues become pretty easy. If we don't do the right thing, then we won't be around to address those other issues."[28]

Ethical Leaders Are Proactive

Ethical leaders do not hang around waiting for ethical problems to arise. They anticipate, plan and act proactively to avoid potential ethical crises.[29] One way to be proactive is to take a leadership role in developing effective programs that provide employees with guidance and support for making more ethical choices even in the face of considerable pressure to do otherwise. Ethical leaders who are proactive understand social needs and apply or even develop "the best practices" of ethical leadership that exist in their industry. PepsiCo has made diversity a high priority not only to make its work force better reflect its customer demographics, but also to channel those diverse perspectives into innovative marketing and products, like Mountain Dew Code Red. To enforce the importance of that goal, CEO Steve Reinemund made eight members of his senior-management team executive sponsors, each for a specific group of employees: African-Americans, Latinos, women, women of color, white males, the disabled, gays, lesbians and the transgendered. Reinemund expects each of the executives to understand his or her group members' unique needs, discover new talent and personally mentor at least three people from within the group. Reinemund's directive exemplifies the proactive approach PepsiCo has adopted toward diversity in recent years and illustrates why the company was recently named the best workplace for Latinos and African-Americans.[30]

Ethical Leaders Consider Stakeholders' Interests

Ethical leaders consider the interests of and implications for all stakeholders, not just those that have an economic impact on the firm. This requires acknowledging and monitoring the concerns of all legitimate stakeholders, actively communicating and cooperating with them, employing processes that are respectful of them, recognizing interdependencies among them, avoiding activities that would harm their human rights, and recognizing the potential conflicts between leaders' "own role as corporate stakeholders and their legal and moral responsibilities for the interests of other stakeholders."[31]

Ethical leaders have the responsibility to balance stakeholder interests to ensure that the organization maximizes its role as a responsible corporate citizen. Wal-Mart, for example, opened a 206,000-square foot "green" store in McKinney, Texas that features a 120-foot tall wind turbine to generate electricity, a rain-water harvesting pond that provides 95 percent of the water needed for irrigation, and many other environmentally friendly and energy-saving features. One such effort is reclaiming used motor oil from the auto center to help heat the building. Long criticized by environmentalists, consumer activists and neighborhood groups, Wal-Mart says the new store is evidence that the retail giant is listening to stakeholders' desires for it to support sustainability, be more economical, and be more environmentally responsible. Although the store is a prototype, the store manager says many of its features may one day be standard in all new Wal-Mart stores.[32]

Ethical Leaders Are Role Models for the Organization's Values

If leaders do not actively serve as role models for the organization's core values, then those values become nothing more than lip service. According to behavioral scientist Brent Smith, as role models, leaders are the primary influence on individual ethical behavior. Leaders whose decisions and actions are contrary to the firm's values send a signal that the firm's values are trivial or irrelevant.[33] Firms such as Enron and WorldCom articulated core values that were only used as window dressing. On the other hand, when leaders model the firm's core values at every turn, the results can be powerful.

Consider New Belgium Brewing Company, the third-largest craft brewer in the U.S. Early in the firm's history, founders Jeff Lebesch and Kim Jordan wrestled with defining New Belgium's core purpose above and beyond profitability. The values they developed (see Table 2) have changed little over the years despite mostly double-digit growth. Indeed, those values dictated a more controlled pace of growth to ensure quality, even when so-called experts believed the firm could have grown much faster. Those values were also behind the company's state-of-the-art, wind-powered brew house with numerous award-winning environmentally friendly and waste-minimizing features. They are also behind the firm's generous donations to many charitable causes and event sponsorships. New Belgium also gives employees a piece of the company (and a fat-tire bicycle) after one year's tenure. The owners believe that employee ownership and open-book management policy translate into a community of trust and mutual responsibility. This proactive approach and devotion to core values have helped New Belgium gain a cult-like customer base, devoted employee-owners, and numerous awards for environmental stewardship, ethics, entrepreneurship and beer making.[34]

Table 2 New Belgium Brewing Company's Core Values
• **Producing world-class beers**
• **Promoting beer culture and the responsible enjoyment of beer**
• **Continuous, innovative quality and efficiency improvements**
• **Transcending customers' expectations**
• **Environmental stewardship: minimizing resource consumption, maximizing energy efficiency, and recycling**
• **Kindling social, environmental, and cultural change as a business role model**
• **Cultivating potential through learning, participative management, and the pursuit of opportunities**
• **Balancing the myriad needs of the company, staff and their families**
• **Committing ourselves to authentic relationships, communications and promises**
• **Having fun**

Ethical Leaders Are Transparent and Actively Involved in Organizational Decision-Making

Being transparent fosters openness, freedom to express ideas and the ability to question conduct, and it encourages stakeholders to learn about and comment on what a firm is doing. Transparent leaders will not be effective unless they are personally involved in the key decisions that have ethical ramifications. Transformational leaders are collaborative, which opens the door for transparency through interpersonal exchange. Earlier we said that transformational leaders instill commitment and respect for values that provide guidance on how to deal with ethical issues. Herb Baum, former CEO of the Dial Corporation, says, "In today's business environment, if you're a leader—or want to be—and you aren't contributing to a values-based business culture that encourages your entire organization to operate with integrity, your company is as vulnerable as a baby chick in a pit of rattlesnakes." Baum's three remarkably simple principles of transparency are 1) tell the whole truth; 2) build a values-based culture; and 3) hire "people people."[35]

Ethical Leaders Are Competent Managers Who Take a Holistic View of the Firm's Ethical Culture

Ethical leaders can see a holistic view of their organization and therefore view ethics as a strategic component of decision-making, much like marketing, information systems, production and so on. When Charles O. Prince took over as chairman of Citigroup, Inc., he sought not only to placate regulators and other stakeholders, but also to reshape the troubled company from the inside out. He viewed Citigroup not just as a profit-seeking business, but also as a "quasi-public institution." Prince instituted numerous internal controls, slashed costs, and slowed the huge company's pace of expansion, but he spent a major portion of his time addressing issues related to the company's culture and values. Although his inward focus and management style resulted in the exodus of a number of executives and the first earnings drop in years, Prince says, "You can never sacrifice your long-term growth, your long-term reputation, to the short term."[36]

Discovering and Responding to Organizational Ethics

Our model of ethical decision-making illustrates that the individual is only one element in the complex web of influences that determine how ethical decisions are made in business. Business school deans and professors often tell their students and future business leaders just to stand up to challenges by doing the right thing, and simply making correct ethical decisions. If this is all the help they get on the topic of business ethics, then they are doomed from the start when entering an ethically-challenged organizational culture. Business students and new employees who want to be ethical leaders need a holistic understanding of how ethical decisions are made in an organizational environment and the required organizational infrastructure of checks and balances, including formal and informal cultural structures that support ethical conduct.

Understanding organizational ethical decision-making means that strategic continuity planning is necessary to anticipate, discover and respond to the potential for an ethical disaster. With an understanding of the corporate ethical decision-making environment, the failure to establish ethical corporate values, an effective ethics program, a corporate culture that has zero tolerance for misconduct, and compliance mechanisms such as anonymous reporting, would constitute failure to follow due diligence.

Successful ethics initiatives depend on effective leadership and corporate governance. If leaders at the top are immoral and driven by selfish desires for individual and organizational gains at the expense of others, ethics programs will be nothing more than window dressing and decisions will be only marginally legalistic. In general, more managers are amoral—intentionally or unintentionally—than immoral. Intentionally amoral managers tend to push ethics out of the business decision-making process because they view business as outside the realm of moral judgments. These managers tend to feel that if something is legal, or if they can make a defense that the action does not violate a law, then it is okay to do it.[37] An intentionally amoral approach to an ethical dilemma would be to tell subordinates not to communicate information that could help someone else uncover wrongdoing. Scott Sullivan's actions as chief financial officer of WorldCom suggest that he may have been intentionally amoral in that he attempted to push the envelope to the point of collapse. On the other hand, unintentionally amoral leaders are ethically careless, ignorant and generally heedless as to how ethical decisions affect the organization's stakeholders. These managers simply lack a moral compass and do not think about how their actions damage others. As a result, the letter of the law rather than the true spirit of the law guides them.[38]

With lawyers and courts debating the proper interpretation of law, the amoral leader is a ticking time bomb on the road to ethical disaster. This leader is like a horse wearing blinders that sees only the course in front of it, and cannot consider collateral damage that might occur to stakeholders in decision-making. The largest ethical disasters have occurred in environments where lawyers and accountants certified that the letter of the law was being followed. Viewing ethics as a cost rather than an investment in future success, the amoral leader does not warrant the expenditure necessary. It is interesting that most business schools preparing future business leaders have downplayed ethics in degree programs as common sense or as an attribute that is developed through character education or studying moral philosophies. The key reason that both amoral leaders and business schools avoid ethics is because business schools tend to use neoclassical economics that holds the practice of business to be value-free.[39]

Business ethics consulting companies are reacting to the mushrooming attention many firms are paying to business ethics, but most of this is driven by SOX.[40] Very little of this new interest in business ethics is related to the emergence of ethical leadership at the top. There is more of a scared rabbit syndrome among top executives looking to dodge, hide and protect themselves from the wolves—otherwise known as the SEC. Our model of ethical decision-making would suggest that without a change of corporate culture, consulting companies will install ethics programs and nothing more, which might be equated to a minimalist burglar alarm system that organizational members learn to set when needed. Only through committed strong leadership that is implemented into strategic planning and effective corporate governance can effective ethical leadership be a driving force in creating an ethical organizational culture.

Chapter
4

Discovering and Assessing a Corporation's Ethical Risk

Once there is a commitment to recognize the potential for and avoid a corporate ethical disaster, the next step is to discover and assess the firm's ethical climate and condition. To execute these activities effectively, top executives and the board of directors need to develop both formal and informal feedback systems. Formal feedback systems consist of mechanisms in the ethics program such as monitoring, anonymous reporting and management oversight. Informal systems include things like walking around, listening to discussions, tuning in to the grapevine, encouraging questions and creating an open and transparent culture. For example, a member of the board of directors and chair of the audit committee of a leading information technology company gave his personal cell phone number to hundreds of managers at an ethics training meeting. He encouraged any manager to call it with a question or to report an ethical lapse. Such efforts help to identify risks and shortfalls in developing compliance with codes, policies, and regulatory requirements.

The formal feedback mechanisms should provide systematic, consistent and accurate discovery and assessment. The informal feedback systems should provide checks on the gaps in the formal reporting system and a robust understanding of all emerging developments that could lead to a potential ethical disaster.

In this chapter, we explore the concepts of discovering and assessing a firm's ethical condition as a means of implementing and monitoring an effective ethics program. We begin by defining the terms "discovery" and "assessment" and examining their benefits and limitations, especially with regard to avoiding a management crisis. Next, we take a more detailed look at the discovery process. We then detail our framework for the steps of an ethics assessment. Finally, we consider the strategic importance of ethical discovery and assessment.

The Importance of Discovery and Assessment

The 2004 amendments to the FSGO make it clear that a corporation's governing authority must be well-informed about its ethics program with respect to implementation and effectiveness. This places the responsibility squarely on the shoulders of the firm's leadership, usually the board of directors. The board must ensure that there is a high-ranking officer accountable for the day-to-day operational responsibility of the ethics program. The board must also provide for adequate authority, resources and access to the board or an appropriate subcommittee of the board. The guidelines further call for confidential mechanisms whereby the organization's employees and agents may report or seek guidance about potential or actual misconduct without fear of retaliation. Finally, the board is required to oversee the discovery of risks and to design, implement and modify approaches to deal with those risks. Thus, the board of directors is clearly accountable for discovering risks associated with a firm's specific industry and assessing the firm's ethics program to ensure that it is capable of uncovering ethical misconduct before it turns into a disaster.

The process of discovery uncovers the existence of activities or events that relate to ethical issues. Through discovery it is possible to identify facts and perceptions of conduct that could lead to an ethical disaster. The term discovery is also used in legal investigations, where it involves a process of compulsory disclosure of relevant facts or documents to the opposing party. We are using the term differently to describe a process of ethical discovery as both a formal and informal feedback mechanism to get people to communicate about issues before they become an EMD. Although we are not using discovery as a legal term, we recognize that when events or actions that have legal ramifications have been detected, it is important to follow established legal requirements to secure and protect evidence. Obstruction of justice is a serious breach of the law. Companies must embrace the idea that it is better to know what is happening and deal with it as soon as possible, rather than attempting to cover up and ignore misconduct.

The process of assessment involves evaluating and measuring the effectiveness of the formal and informal ethical systems and programs embedded in the corporate culture. The purpose of an assessment is to gauge the opportunity for addressing issues and improvements to existing programs, as required by the FSGO. Assessment has often been associated with an ethics audit, which can be viewed as a systematic evaluation of an organization's ethics program and performance to determine its effectiveness. The ethics audit includes "regular, complete and documented measurements of compliance with the company's published policies and procedures."[1] As such, the audit provides an opportunity to measure conformity to the firm's desired ethical standards. An audit can even be a precursor to setting up an ethics program to identify the firm's current ethical standards, policies and risk areas so that an ethics program can effectively address problem areas. Although few companies have conducted ethics audits, recent legislation will encourage greater ethics auditing and assessments as companies attempt to demonstrate to various stakeholders that they are abiding by the law and have established programs to improve ethical decision making.

Regardless of its formality, assessment is a tool that companies can employ to display and measure their ethical commitment to stakeholders—including employees and investors—who are increasingly demanding that companies be ethical and accountable for their conduct. In response, businesses are working to incorporate accountability into actions ranging from long-term planning to everyday decision-making, including rethinking processes.

Discovery has both formal and informal dimensions important for accountability. First, the formal aspects require that the right questions be asked related to the existence of codes, policies, monitoring methods and response mechanisms. The state of ethical decision-making must be observed and documented. Comprehending ethical leaders' strengths and distinguishing weaknesses in ethical decision making is important in understanding the ethical climate. The more informal aspects include developing cultural and structural systems that allow employees and other stakeholders to ask questions, identify issues and make suggestions.

Assessment is an objective approach for a company to demonstrate its commitment to improving strategic planning, including compliance with legal and ethical standards and social responsibility. The assessment process is important to business because it can improve organizational performance and effectiveness, increase attractiveness to investors, improve relationships with stakeholders, identify potential risks, and decrease the risk of misconduct and adverse publicity that could harm reputation.[2]

It is important to understand financial auditing and ethics assessments or audits. Whereas financial auditing focuses on all systems related to money flow and financial assessments of value for tax purposes and managerial accountability, discovery and assessment deal with the internal and broad external impact of the ethical performance of an organization. Another significant difference is that managing ethics is a self-governing process, whereas financial audits are required of public companies. Because of the voluntary approach that we are describing, there are few standards that a company can apply with regard to reporting frequency, disclosure requirements,and remedial actions that a company should take in response to assessment results. This may change as more companies build voluntary ethics programs and ethical leadership in an environment where there are requirements for board of directors' oversight over all ethics programs. For boards to track the effectiveness of ethics programs, more formal assessments such as an ethics audit will be required.

Benefits of Discovery and Assessments

The processes of discovery and assessments can provide benefits for both organizations and their stakeholders. They can help companies identify priorities and assess the effectiveness of programs and policies, often improving operating efficiencies and reducing costs. Of course, the processes of ethics assessments and auditing can also help a company identify potential risks and liabilities and improve its compliance with the law. Furthermore, an audit report may help to document the firm's compliance with mandatory requirements as well as to demonstrate its progress in areas of previous noncompliance, including the systems implemented to reduce the likelihood of a recurrence of misconduct.[3]

One of the most significant benefits of ethics assessments is that they may help prevent public relations crises associated with ethical or legal misconduct, which can potentially be more devastating than traditional natural disasters or technological disruptions. Measuring a firm's ethical condition could help more executives identify potential risks and liabilities in order to implement plans to eliminate or reduce them before they reach crisis dimensions. An ethics assessment may even discover rogue employees who are violating the firm's ethical standards and policies or laws and regulations. Thus, the ethics assessment provides the key link to preventing ethical disasters.

The Risks of Not Discovering Risks

Most corporate leaders' greatest fear is discovering serious misconduct or illegal activity somewhere in their organization. The fear is that a public discovery can immediately be used by critics in the mass media, competitors and skeptical stakeholders to undermine a firm's reputation. Corporate leaders worry that something will be uncovered outside their control that will jeopardize their careers and their organizations. Fear is a paralyzing emotion. Of course there are executives such as Bernard Ebbers, Dennis Kozlowski and John Rigas who may have experienced fear because they knew about and perhaps even participated in serious misconduct that debilitated their companies and hurt many groups of stakeholders. These leaders were the captains of their respective ships, and they made a conscious decision to steer their firms into treacherous waters with a high probability of striking an iceberg. For many corporate leaders, concern for ethics is limited to the notion that if misconduct is not discovered, then nothing will go wrong. One of the authors of this book witnessed a sales manager tell a salesperson to stop talking when he brought up the need to pay a bribe to secure a key account. The manager told the sales rep, "You're job is to get the business any way you can. ... I don't want to know the details." This conversation can be replayed many times throughout Corporate America.

Corporate leaders do fear the possibility of reputation harm, financial loss or a regulatory event that could potentially end their careers and even threaten their personal lives through fines or prison sentences. Indeed, the whole concept of risk management involves recognizing the possibility of a possible misfortune that could jeopardize or even destroy the corporation. For example, there was always a risk that a Category 5 hurricane could strike New Orleans, flooding the city and destroying most business operations. This risk became a reality in 2005 with Hurricane Katrina.

Yet dispite all of the risk analysis that predicted the devastation that such a storm would cause, precautions were not taken that would prevail against such a torm. Crises management became the focus because the risks had not been appropriately managed.

Risk managers use insurance, hedging, derivatives and other financial instruments to plan for risk. They also use information technology backup systems, geographic dispersion of manufacturing, diversified customer bases, alternative suppliers and competitive intelligence. Yet only a few risk managers are managing the potential risks associated with a Category 5 ethical hurricane.

Unfortunately, for most executives, ethical misconduct risks have the lowest priority. These risks are not a major area of concern because they are submerged like 90 percent of the volume of an iceberg. Top managers tend to deal with more visible and dramatic risks associated with hurricanes, fires, electrical blackouts, and more. However, the risks of an ethical disaster have the potential for even more damage than most natural disasters. It is believed that even our corporate governance systems have operated only in theory, and directors have ignored risks associated with ethics because of their social relationships with each other and their ability to use the system mainly for their own advantage. Typically, directors serve on a number of boards and the impact of interlocking boards of directors has not created an environment of discovery and assessment.

The risks associated with corporate governance shortfalls are tied directly to the ethical climate and ethical risk of an organization. Too often ethical risks are viewed as something to be delegated to lawyers or risk managers whose concerns and responsibilities relate to traditional financial and natural disaster risks. Ignoring the possibility of an ethical disaster occurs because of being too preoccupied with the next quarterly earnings report. However, focusing only on the bottom line and avoiding an ethical risks management initiative is the fastest track to creating an ethical disaster.

The Discovery Process

As mentioned earlier, the FSGO requires that high-level personnel with substantial authority must be well-versed about the content and operation of a business' ethics program. The board of directors must also ensure that there is a high-ranking officer accountable for the day-to-day operational responsibility of the ethics program. For simplicity's sake, we'll refer to this person as the ethics officer (EO), as this term is increasingly being used, although other terms are also used. In today's post-Enron climate, it is not unusual for ethics officers to receive salaries in the range of $750,000 because of the complexities of their responsibilities.[4] These officers are required to report information on the program's implementation and effectiveness to the board of directors or an appropriate subgroup of the board. This means that informal mechanisms for the discovery of risk and conduct are essentially a requirement of the amended guidelines. Indeed, the discovery process that we present is based on the philosophy of the FSGO (Table 1). The questions that follow provide a systematic formal method of discovery. The alignment of formal approaches with informal cultural methods of listening and discovering, however, is just as important.

| Table 1 |
| Important Elements of the Discovery Process[5] |
| • Emphasize the importance of organizational culture that encourages a commitment to compliance and ethics. |
| • Specify the responsibilities of the organization's governing authority and leadership. |
| • Include training and dissemination of training materials and other information as needed. |
| • Establish periodic assessment of the effectiveness of the ethics program. |
| • Conduct risk assessments as a part of the implementation of an effective program. |

Does the Company Have a Written Code of Business Ethics or Code of Conduct?

Of course, the answer to this question is increasingly "yes", especially for corporations required to do so by the FSGO and SOX, section 406. Codes of ethics/conduct are formal statements that describe what an organization expects of its employees. To address this query, the ethics officer should indicate whether the firm's code reflects the standards that are common to its industry. He or she should describe the process through which the code was developed (how, when, why, where and who participated in the development). The response should indicate whether the code includes statements of management philosophy—formal pronouncements about the firm's way of doing business—and corporate credos—broad statements of corporate commitment to stakeholders, values, corporate citizenship and objectives. The response to the question also should indicate how often the code is communicated to employees and describe the types/kinds of employees who receive these communications. The officer should describe whether the code addresses social concerns associated with the use of the firm's products. Finally, this response should examine whether the elements of the code are enforceable and are, in fact, enforced. Tyco, for example, established a Guide to Ethical Conduct in the wake of a major accounting scandal. The new code was part of a major corporate overhaul that involved forcing out nearly 300 managers, dramatically changing reporting relationships, and making many more initiatives to ensure that Tyco developed an ethical corporate culture.[6]

Have specific individuals within high-level positions in the organization been assigned overall responsibility to oversee compliance with standards and procedures?

The corporation must be able to identify at least one individual who is officially in charge of directing the legal compliance and ethics programs and describe that person's job title and overall responsibilities. At Tyco, for example, Eric Pillmore took up the daunting task of recovering from a major scandal as senior vice-president of corporate governance. He reports directly to the nominating and governance committee.[7] Many other firms have created ethics officer positions recently, including the New York Stock Exchange, Marsh & McLennan, Nortel Networks and Computer Associates International.[8] Individuals with operational responsibility should report periodically to the ethics officer and to the board of directors.

What are the procedures, processes, methods, forums or other means by which ethical considerations are integrated into any and all manufacturing, marketing, distribution, advertising, sales, electronic commerce, and general corporate strategy decisions?

To respond to this question, the ethics officer should indicate whether ethical considerations related to various business functions are ever put in writing and, if so, by whom, when and where. The response should also examine whether ethics and corporate citizenship are addressed in strategic plans. If the company has a code-of-conduct provision or associated policy addressing marketing and/or product development strategy, this section should describe that in detail. HCA, for example, developed a comprehensive ethics and compliance program in response to ethical and legal crises in the past. Its code of conduct addresses ethical and legal considerations related to patient information, coding and billing, accreditation and many other issues related to its role as a health-care provider. The company also has additional policies and procedures that provide specific guidance in these areas.[9]

Is there a review process whereby ethical, legal, and business practice considerations are presented, reviewed, or otherwise considered by the board of directors?

The revised FSGO guidelines require directors to be knowledgeable about their firm's ethics program and to exercise reasonable oversight with respect to the implementation and effectiveness of the program. Thus, this response must describe the procedures that link the review process to operations and the board of directors. If the firm does not have a periodic review process, then the ethics officer should attempt to explain why and remedy the situation. He or she should also address whether the high-level ethical review has been considered and rejected by high-ranking corporate officers and whether an information system has been developed to gather data useful in assessing ethical risks. The board should be aware of industry best practices for ethical conduct, as well as all applicable state and regulatory requirements.

In addition, the board should help set the tone for the informal culture dimensions of the firm's ethical climate that includes appropriate rewards for ethical conduct and punishment for misconduct. There should even be informal walkarounds by board members to capture the informal aspects of a firm's culture. For example, board members of Lowe's, the home-improvement chain, visit a number of stores every year to get a personal feel for each store's environment, including any ethical issues. This is a key discovery element that is essential to prevent an EMD. Failure to discover risks and exercise reasonable oversight could result in a less-than-effective program, which could lead to allegations that the firm failed to demonstrate due diligence to prevent and detect misconduct.

What steps has the company taken to communicate its standards, procedures, and policies to all employees and other agents through training programs or publications that explain what is required in a practical manner? Detail the ethical compliance training program in which all employees are required to participate, complete, take, or otherwise experience.

In this response, the ethics officer should outline the steps the company has taken to communicate its standards, policies and procedures to all appropriate stakeholders through training programs or publications. It is important that these materials be communicated at an appropriate level (i.e. if most employees read at a 6th grade level, the communications should be written at a 6th grade level). For most firms, this response will include media such as written codes of ethics/conduct (which typically must be signed by employees on a regular basis), wall posters, web sites, newsletters, speeches and classroom training. The EO should also describe these training efforts and specify the types of employees (and additional stakeholders) required to attend ethical training. Lockheed Martin, for example, maintains an ethics department at each of its operational locations to provide training and a face-to-face presence with employees.

Ideally, all ethics training should contribute to a culture of openness and a commitment where only ethical conduct is acceptable. At a minimum, training programs typically strive to instruct employees about the firm's policies and expectations, as well as pertinent laws, regulations and social standards. Training can also inform employees of available resources, support systems, and designated personnel who can help them with ethical and legal advice. HCA, for example, requires two hours of orientation training on the company's code of conduct for each employee within 30 days of employment, as well as an annual code-of-conduct refresher course for every employee. Employees involved in specific areas of the company—e.g. billing— are required to undergo additional annual compliance training in their areas of operation.[10]

Has the organization taken reasonable steps to achieve compliance with its standards by utilizing, monitoring, and auditing systems reasonably designed to detect misconduct and by providing a reporting system whereby employees and other agents can report events, outcomes, or activities within the organization without fear of retribution?

The ethics officer should describe all resources and systems employed to monitor and enforce ethical conduct and measure the ethics program's effectiveness. A company's failure to provide resources to support these systems could render them ineffective in the case of a major legal event. This response should detail any regular monitoring and auditing efforts and delineate to whom such audits are reported. This step should also include descriptions of the role of the board of directors, ombudsman, corporate compliance efforts, ethics officer, hotline, or other available vehicles through which employees may question various conduct of the organization and its employees without fear of retribution from the corporation or their own supervisors. At Tyco, employees with concerns can now turn to an ombudsman, who reports any wrongdoing directly to the audit committee.[11]

In addition to ethics officers to whom employees can direct questions, corporations increasingly are setting up internal or external hotlines for employees and other stakeholders to ask questions or report misconduct they have observed, even anonymously if that is their preference. Sears, for example, has two hotlines through which its 330,000 employees can ask questions about how to interpret company policy as well as specific work-related issues. Most of these calls are directed to a human resources manager and five associates who are trained in negotiation, conflict resolution and investigation.[12] Additionally, companies can turn to independent ethics consulting firms that provide some of these services or solutions to implement them. For example, they can employ incident management reporting software, which allows for analytical assessment to effectively manage and resolve issues before they become potential disasters. Some software packages permit and track anonymous reporting of a wide range of issues, such as internal theft, harassment, discrimination, accounting fraud and environmental violations.

Is adherence to, and implementation of, the code of ethics one of the standards by which the corporate culture can be linked directly to performance measures?

While the revised FSGO require compliance, the focus is on creating an ethical culture with values acting as a buffer to unethical and illegal activities. A statement of values should make it clear to all stakeholders that core principles guide all decisions. For values to be effective, leaders must explain, reinforce, and provide examples through their actions about how the values are implemented. Tyco, for example, has tied its performance management system to the four core values named in its code of conduct: integrity, accountability, teamwork, and excellence. Managers are evaluated on nine behaviors that relate to the core values, such as "managerial courage," and their bonuses are at least partially tied to these evaluations.[13] Ethical leadership is needed to implement a code of ethics and ethics program. Executives and directors must be role models for their own programs as well as meeting the standards and best practices of similar organizations.

Has the organization used due care not to delegate substantial discretionary authority to individuals whom the organization knew, or should have known through the exercise of due diligence, did not have the capacity to implement organizational wide risk-reduction processes?

This response should detail any efforts the firm has taken to ensure that all individuals with significant discretionary authority have a background of appropriate ethical conduct, are well-versed in all relevant laws and regulations as well as company values and standards, and have the capacity to implement these processes. It is difficult to discover details about an individual's background and to forecast future behavior. There are legal protections for individual privacy, and organizations must also respect diversity and the rights of individuals to express themselves. On the other hand, many business leaders and educators believe that a person's general character is the primary influence of ethical decisions made in an organizational context. Jeffrey E. Garten, former dean of the Yale school of management, has suggested that "Andrew Fastow [Enron's former chief financial officer] would have turned out to be a bad apple no matter what he was taught in graduate school." Garten further believes that "When soliciting references, business schools should specifically request input on a candidate's character."[14] If Garten is right, then business schools cannot teach future business managers how to be ethical leaders.

There seems to be a general belief that business ethics is just character attributes that exist in the individual from some source other than education and organizational training. This perspective does not explain why many individuals with excellent personal character, such as WorldCom's Betty Vinson, discussed in Chapter 3, caved in to organizational pressure after many repeated attempts to reject requests to make false accounting entries.[15] Apparently, the developers of the FSGO believe that ethical leadership can be developed with values, training, compliance, monitoring, and an effective ethics program linked to effective corporate governance.

The backbone of organizational ethics is an understanding that ethical decisions are made in groups and through social interaction, and individual character is only one of a number of variables that influence outcomes. Of course, the background of the individual in a responsible position should be known, and previous legal violations or unethical patterns in decision-making should be identified. At its current state of development, there is no guarantee that personal character or ethics tests will identify rogue employees who may be good at covering up their true ethical intent. Finally, academic research supports the creation of an organizational ethical culture as having more influence on decision-making than a person's character references at home and in the community.

Have the standards been consistently enforced through appropriate mechanisms, including, as appropriate, discipline of individuals responsible for violating compliance and ethics requirements? Describe any appropriate mechanisms in place in the organization to follow up on reports of suspected threats to employees, resellers or consumers to determine what occurred, who was responsible, and recommend corrective actions.

The ethics officer's response to this question should specify all disciplinary mechanisms available for sanctioning individuals who violate the company's code, policies or the law. It should also describe how these mechanisms have been communicated to all affected employees to ensure that employees recognize that there are clear consequences for violations. At HCA, for example, the code of conduct specifies that a violation may result in an oral warning, written warning, written reprimand, suspension, termination and/ or restitution, depending on the nature, severity and frequency of the violation.[16] The ethics officer should also describe all mechanisms available to follow up on any reports of suspected harm to employees, consumers, resellers or other stakeholders in order to determine what happened, who was responsible and appropriate corrective actions. This step should delineate all steps the company should take after a negative outcome, such as a consumer injury, to respond appropriately and quickly to the event and to prevent further injuries. In short, this response should briefly summarize the organization's crisis management plan.

The discovery stage is vital to establishing and documenting the current state of an organization's ethical culture as demonstrated through its activities, mechanisms and systems. The ethical decision-making of people within the organization should be the main focus of the discovery process because misconduct develops from not only purposeful actions, but also through unconscious lapses and the failure to recognize and understand what to do when confronted with a dilemma. The most important risk is an individual choosing to go along with the group or caving in to pressure to make a decision to improve performance in a questionable manner.

In today's business climate, the pressures for corporate governance mandate that senior executives and the board of directors implement intelligent solutions that promote immediate transparency and early resolution of all problematic risks and compliance and ethics issues. As mentioned earlier, a number of ethics consulting companies are springing up to provide services that help address these concerns. Intercede and EthicsPoint, for example, have developed monitoring software solutions that provide companies with instantaneous visibility of critical operational risk issues, as well as a business process that enhances company-wide management of corporate ethics. This type of software permits anonymous reporting that promotes the early resolution of issues through accurate and informative incident reports and can even be integrated into performance review systems to ensure personnel who may be the source of unethical practices are not unsuspectingly promoted. Regardless of the system or technology used to track episodes of developing concern, the discovery process must be managed effectively. The more thorough or complete the feedback method developed, the less likely there will be an ethical disaster.

The Assessment Process[17]

After the establishment of a systematic approach to discovery, there should be assessment to measure, evaluate, correct or revise and take managerial actions to prevent misconduct. In our view, discovery and assessment overlap and work together to establish a framework for ethical leadership and an ethical organizational culture. Assessment is unique because it focuses on taking a snapshot of the current situation for use by top executives and the board of directors for continuous improvement.

There are many questions to be addressed in conducting an assessment, such as how formal it should be, how broad it should be, what standards of performance should be applied, how often it should be conducted, and what actions should be taken in response. It is our belief that an assessment should be unique to each company based on its size, industry, corporate culture and identified risks, as well as the regulatory environment in which it operates. Thus, an assessment for a banking firm will differ from one for an automobile manufacturer or a food processor. Each has different regulatory concerns and unique risks related to the nature of its business. Thus, corporate approaches to assessment are as varied as approaches to discovery. For this reason, we have mapped out a framework that is somewhat generic and can therefore be readily expanded upon by most companies. The steps of this framework are presented in Table 2. As with any new initiative, companies may choose to begin with a smaller, less formal approach and then work up to a more comprehensive assessment. For example, a firm may choose to focus on employees in its initial assessment and then expand to additional stakeholder groups in subsequent assessments.

Table 2
Framework for an Ethics Assessment
• **Secure commitment of top executives and board of directors.**
• **Establish a committee to oversee the assessment.**
• **Define the scope of the assessment process, including all relevant subject matter areas.**
• **Review the organization's mission, values, and compliance relative to ethical priorities.**
• **Collect and analyze relevant information in each designated subject matter area.**
• **Report the findings to top executives and board of directors as appropriate.**

Our framework encompasses a wide range of business responsibilities and relationships. The assessment entails an individualized process and outcomes for a particular firm, as it requires the careful consideration of the unique issues that face a particular organization. It is important to recognize that our focus at this stage is not a formal audit, but rather an internal evaluation that can capture both formal and informal aspects of the organization that support leadership and an ethical climate. Formal financial audits conducted by the Big Four accounting firms do not necessarily prevent financial misconduct by top executives who want to cheat.

Secure Commitment of Top Executives and Board of Directors

The first step in conducting any assessment or audit is securing the commitment of the firm's top management and, if it is a corporation, its board of directors. Indeed, the push for an assessment may come directly from the board of directors in response to specific stakeholder concerns or corporate governance reforms related to the SOX, which suggests that boards of directors should provide oversight for *all* assessment activities. In addition, the FSGO holds board members responsible for the ethical and legal compliance programs of the firms they oversee. Rules and regulations associated with SOX require that board members be informed and qualified to oversee accounting and other types of financial matters to ensure that these reports are accurate and include all material information. While a board's financial audit committee will examine ethical standards throughout the organization as they relate to financial matters, it also must implement a code of ethics for top financial officers, according to section 406 of SOX. This requirement is an attempt to bring ethics into financial oversight and to act as a buffer to prevent misconduct that even the government cannot anticipate. An assessment can demonstrate that a firm has taken steps to prevent misconduct, which can be useful in cases where civil lawsuits blame the firm and its directors for the actions of a rogue employee. Thus, many corporate directors are quite motivated to push for ethics assessments.

Pressure for an assessment can also come from top executives looking for ways to track and improve ethical performance and perhaps to give their firm an advantage over competitors facing questions about their ethical conduct. Regardless of where the impetus for an assessment comes from, its success hinges on the full support of top management, particularly the CEO and the board of directors. Without this support, an assessment will not be effective in improving the ethics program and corporate culture. For example, after a negative publicity documentary, "Wal-Mart: The High Cost of Low Price," was released, the company asked economists to assess its effect on the economy. A conference, "An In-Depth Look at Wal-Mart and Society," was part of a campaign to address criticism of wages, health care benefits, workplace policies and economic impact on communities. Wal-Mart attempted to develop an objective and balanced assessment to respond to a very one-sided documentary. [18]

Establish a Committee to Oversee the Assessment

The next step in our framework is the establishment of a committee or team to administer the assessment process. While the board of directors' financial audit committee oversees the financial audit, it may not have the capacity to oversee an ethics assessment. As we mentioned earlier, many executives view ethics from a personal character perspective and do not recognize the organizational dimensions of an effective approach to ethics in the context of a business. In most firms, assessments are conducted by ethics officers who, unfortunately, do not always report to the board of directors. In any case, the assessment committee should include members who are conversant in the nature and role of ethics and the various risks and issues the firm faces. The members should come from various functional areas within the firm and be able to articulate the concerns of various stakeholder interests. Ethics and compliance areas often exist in silos, with communication and even turf wars over responsibility for issues and assessment. Bringing areas such as human resources, legal compliance, as well as ethics together for an integrated assessment can build bridges for cooperation.

Define the Scope of the Assessment

The assessment committee should determine the scope of the assessment and supervise its progress to keep it on track. The scope of an assessment depends on the type of business, the risks faced by the firm and the available opportunities to manage ethics. This step also entails defining key subject matter or risk areas that should be addressed in the assessment (e.g. environment, discrimination, product liability, employee rights, privacy, fraud, financial reporting, legal compliance) as well as the bases on which they should be assessed. Some firms use third party organizations to determine the scope of their assessment in established criteria for determining risk areas in the assessment process.

Review the Organization's Mission, Values, and Compliance Practices Relative to Ethical Priorities

Because assessments generally involve a comparison of organizational performance to the firm's goals, values, and policies, the assessment process should include a review of the current mission statement and existing strategies. The company's overall mission statement may spell out ethics objectives, but these may also be found in other documents, including those that focus specifically on ethics and social responsibility. Niagara Mohawk, for example, specifies five core values in its ethics program: management by fact, respect for people, focus on the customer, continuous improvement and ethical behavior.[19] This step should examine all formal documents that make explicit commitments with regard to ethical and legal issues, as well as less-formal documents, including marketing materials, workplace policies, and ethics policies and standards for suppliers or vendors. This review may reveal a need to create additional statements to fill identified gaps or to craft a new comprehensive mission statement or ethical policy that addresses discovered deficiencies.[20]

It is also important to examine all of the firm's policies and practices for the specific areas covered by the assessment. For example, in an assessment that includes discrimination issues in its scope, this step would consider the company's goals and objectives regarding discrimination, the company's policies on discrimination, the means for communicating these policies, and the effectiveness of this communication. This assessment should also look at whether and how managers are rewarded for meeting their goals and the systems available for employees to give and receive feedback. An effective assessment should review all these systems and assess their strengths and weaknesses.[21]

During this step, the firm should articulate its ethical priorities. Determining a company's ethical priorities is a balancing act, as it can be difficult to identify the needs and assess the priorities of each stakeholder. Because there may be no legal requirements for ethical priorities, it is up to management's strategic planning processes to determine appropriate standards, principles, duties, and required action to deal with ethics issues. It is very important in this stage to describe these priorities and values as a set of parameters or performance indicators that can be objectively and quantitatively assessed.

At some point, the firm must demonstrate action-oriented responsiveness to its top priority ethics issues. For example, HCA's ethics program requires not only articulating standards of compliance and ethical conduct, but also a system for auditing performance in areas of compliance risk to ensure that established policies and procedures are being followed and are effective.[22]

Collect and Analyze Relevant Information

The next step in our framework is identifying all tools and methods that can be employed to measure the firm's current ethical situation and its progress in improving ethical decisions and conduct. Then the firm should collect all relevant information for each designated subject matter area. To understand employee issues, for example, the committee would work with the firm's human resources department in gathering employee survey information and other statistics and feedback. A thorough assessment should include a review of all relevant documents, including those sent to government agencies and others. Table 3 lists a number of sources where this information can be obtained.

Table 3
Sources of Information for Assessment Analysis

- The extent of standards and procedures designed to reduce the prospect of injury to consumers, which may be reflected by the existence of internal memoranda or methods used in data collection or analysis;

- The extent to which high-level personnel are involved in activities to improve the safety of products, as reflected by time records, diaries, minutes of meetings, internal memoranda or documents evidencing formal delegation of responsibility;

- Efforts made by the organization to identify employees responsible for maintaining records and data on consumer complaints, such as standard job application forms, supervisor questionnaires and consumer questionnaires;

- Material used in connection with compensation and promotion decisions, and the existence of lines of communication for supervisors to communicate such information;

- The extent of efforts to communicate effectively the organization's standards and procedures designed to reduce the risks to consumers or the general public, which may be reflected by the existence of internal memoranda and publications (such as corporate newsletters) or materials used in, or relating to, the employee orientation and training process;

- The level of monitoring and auditing systems to obtain information about the product concerns of resellers, consumers and the general public, as reflected by the number of employees involved in such activities, the amount of time spent on such systems, the amount of money spent on the systems and the amount of monitoring and auditing efforts;

- Documents relating to systems that encourage employees to log concerns, complaints, and information about the negative social consequences of the firm's manufacturing, marketing and consumer information programs;

- Disciplinary actions taken against wrongdoers, in particular the frequency and severity of such discipline, the efforts to publicize it within the organization, and the extent to which supervisory personnel were subject to the discipline; and

- Whether any changes in the organization's ethical compliance program have been made in response to detected internal violations, consumer concerns, or negative consequences to society—any document critical of the compliance program, including those comparing the program to industry standards in the company's records.

The information collected in this step will help determine baseline levels of ethics and compliance, as well as the internal and external stakeholders' expectations of the company. This step can identify where the company has, or has not, met its commitments, including those prescribed by its mission statement and other policy documents. The documents reviewed in this process will vary from company to company, depending on the firm's size, the nature of its business and the scope of the process.[23] For example, Ford Motor Company launched a formal inquiry into whether former president and CEO Nick Scheele violated company purchasing policies after he ordered that all of Ford's advertising and marketing business be directed toward WPP Group PLC, a London-based advertising firm that already handles much of the automaker's advertising and for which Scheele's son works. Ford has a specific purchasing policy governing single-source contracts.[24] This inquiry should reveal relevant information related to the subject matter area of conflicts of interest and purchasing policies.

Some techniques of evidence collection might involve examination of both internal and external documents, observation of the data collection process (such as stakeholder consultation) and confirmation of information in the organization's accounting records. Ratio analysis of relevant indicators may also be used to identify any inconsistencies or unexpected patterns. The importance of objective measurement is the key consideration of the committee.[25]

Because stakeholder integration is so crucial to the assessment, a company's stakeholders may need to be defined and interviewed during the data-collection stage. For most companies, stakeholders include employees, customers, investors, suppliers, community groups, regulators, nongovernmental organizations and the media. For example, the Chris Hani Baragwanath Hospital (CHBH) in Johannesburg, South Africa conducted an ethics audit that included focus groups with hospital management, doctors, nurses, related health professionals, support staff and patients. Based on the trends uncovered in these focus groups, CHBH then developed a questionnaire for an ethics survey, which it administered to a larger group of individual stakeholders.[26] The greater the number of stakeholders included in this stage, the more time and resources will be required to carry out the assessment; however, a larger sample of stakeholders may yield a more useful variety of opinions about the company.

Because employees carry out a business's operations, including its ethics initiatives, understanding employee issues is vital. Among the useful indicators for assessing employee issues are staff turnover and employee satisfaction rates. Clearly, high turnover rates may indicate poor working conditions, inadequate compensation, general employee dissatisfaction or an unethical climate. Additionally, employees may be surveyed as to their ethical perceptions of the company, their superiors, their coworkers, and even themselves, as well as their ratings of ethical or unethical practices within the firm and industry. For example, the Chris Hani Baragwanath Hospital ethics survey asked employees about many issues, including organizational culture and values, their physical workplace, human resources issues, misconduct, standards of patient care and problems and sources of stress.[27] The results of these surveys can serve as benchmarks in an ongoing assessment of ethical performance. Then, if unethical behavior is perceived to increase, management will have a better understanding of what types of unethical practices may be occurring and why.

Customers are another primary stakeholder group. Providing meaningful feedback through a number of mechanisms is critical to creating and maintaining customer satisfaction. Through surveys and customer-initiated communication systems, such as response cards, e-mail and toll-free telephone systems, a company can monitor and respond to customer issues. Sears, for example, surveyed more than two million customers to investigate their attitudes toward products, advertising, and the company's social and ethical performance.

Investors are another important stakeholder group, and they seem to be more aware of the financial benefits desired from ethical management systems—as well as the negative consequences of a lack of ethics. They are also increasingly taking legal action for financial losses resulting from ethical misconduct. For example, after the Securities and Exchange Commission filed civil fraud charges against HealthSouth Corporation for overstating its earnings by $1.4 billion over a three-and-a-half year period, the company's stock price plummeted 44 percent. The suit, which also accused the company of overstating assets by $800 million and its chief executive officer, Richard Scrushy, of instructing staff to inflate earnings to meet estimates, sparked additional lawsuits against the company by shareholders (although Scrushy himself was later acquitted).[28] Even the hint of wrongdoing can harm a company's relations with shareholders if the value of their portfolio declines. It is, therefore, critical for companies to understand the issues that this very important group of stakeholders have and what they expect from corporations financially, ethically and socially.

Feedback from stakeholders may be obtained through surveys, interviews, and focus groups. Companies can even invite specific groups together for beneficial exchanges. Such meetings also may include an office or facility tour or a field trip by company representatives to visit sites in the community. Regardless of how information about stakeholder views is collected, the primary objective is to generate a variety of opinions about how the company is perceived and whether it is fulfilling stakeholders' expectations.[29]

Once this data has been collected, the firm should then compare its internal perceptions to those discovered during the stakeholder assessment stage and summarize these findings. During this phase, the committee should draw some conclusions about the information obtained in the previous stages. These conclusions may involve descriptive assessments of the findings, including the costs and benefits of the company's ethics program, the strengths and weaknesses in the firm's policies and practices, and feedback from stakeholders, as well as issues that should be addressed in future assessments. In some cases, it may be appropriate to weigh the findings against standards identified earlier, both quantitatively and qualitatively.[30]

Data analysis can also include an exploration of how other organizations in the industry are performing in the designated subject matter areas. The committee can investigate the successes of peer companies that are considered the best in a particular area and compare its company's performance to the benchmarks established by those firms. Some common examples of benchmark information available from most corporate ethics audits include employee or customer satisfaction, the perception of the company by community groups, and the impact of the company's philanthropy. For example, the Ethics and Compliance Officer Association (ECOA) conducts research on legal and ethical issues in the workplace. The studies allow members of the ECOA to compare their responses to the aggregate results obtained through the study.[31] Such comparisons can help the committee identify best practices for a particular industry or establish a baseline of minimum requirements for ethics. It is important to note that a wide variety of standards are emerging that apply to ethics accountability. The aim of these standards is to create a tool for benchmarking and a framework for businesses to follow.[32]

Report the Findings and Act upon Them

The final step in our framework is reporting the findings of the assessment to relevant internal parties—namely the board of directors and top executives. At this point, the assessment committee needs to make the purpose methodology assumptions and limitations clear. The assessment is more meaningful if integrated with other organizational information available, such as financial reports, employee surveys, regulatory filings, and customer feedback. The use of information such as the Open Compliance and Ethics Group Benchmarking Study that is provided in Appendix A evaluates key elements of corporate and ethics programs could help assess best-practices across industry.[33]

The organization may prefer not to publicly release the assessment to various stakeholders, although some companies, such as Shell, Johnson & Johnson and the Body Shop, are posting all or part of their assessment reports on their website to promote their transparency. All organizations have areas that can be improved and openly addressing their concerns can be helpful. On the other hand, it is necessary to protect information that a competitor or the mass media could exploit. An action plan to address weak links in the firm's programs, culture, and performance should be the end result of the assessment. Finally, it is important to note that SOX Section 301 requires companies treat the problem, making it mandatory to act upon issues raised as a result of the assessment.

The Value of Discovery and Assessments

Corporate governance is at the heart of an effective ethics program. Chief executives and corporate directors must have the knowledge needed to provide oversight and take responsibility for the ethics of their organizations. The time when board members could just attend meetings, play golf, socialize and collect their checks is over. The view that ethics is a personal or character issue that just bubbles up in daily decisions fails to recognize the complexity of business ethics and the influence that organizations have over their members. There should be an embedded ethical culture that rejects the idea that it is okay to move to the edge of the line that divides acceptable conduct from misconduct. Lawyers and accountants have a poor record in the first part of the 21st century in telling companies that they have moved beyond that line and into ethical crises.

A central message that both the amended FSGO and SOX send to businesses is that the corporate governance system must take responsibility for creating an ethical culture that prevents misconduct. The alignment of formal compliance systems with more informal discovery and assessment processes can help in quickly resolving ethical issues that could escalate into an EMD. In fact, discovery and assessment should be conducted regularly rather than in response to problems or questions about a firm's priorities and conduct. In other words, these tools are not designed for a crisis management situation, although they can be used to pinpoint potential problem areas and generate solutions in a crisis situation.

Although the concepts of discovery and assessments imply a formal examination of ethical performance, many organizations assess their performance in this area informally. Indeed, many smaller firms probably take a highly informal approach. Because these steps are not legally required, effective informal methods are certainly acceptable. Regardless of formality, any attempt to measure outcomes and compare them against standards can be useful in improving ethics programs. The important thing is to establish an organizational commitment to transparency and to identify risks and address problems before it's too late.

Discovery and assessment are avoided by many corporations and executives or are treated superficially as check-off-the-box approaches because of the fear of discovery. Findings related to risk, existing conditions and organizational misconduct can be extremely disruptive. Many corporate leaders are paralyzed by the fear of discovery. They hope that questionable conduct will stay invisible to those both inside and outside the organization. Most ethical disasters occur because of poor leadership in the early stages of misconduct where a dilemma was either ignored or covered up.

Discovery and assessment can generate many benefits, as we have seen throughout this chapter. The assessment of a company's overall ethical performance as compared to its core values, internal operating practices, management systems, and most importantly, the expectations of key stakeholders is the best approach to prevent an ethical disaster. As such, discovery and assessments are useful organizational tools to help companies identify and define their impact, facilitate improvements in vital areas, reallocate resources and activities and focus on new opportunities.

Most managers view profitability and ethics and social responsibility as a trade-off, which prevents them from moving from an either/or mind-set to a more proactive both/and approach.[34] However, the cost of an ethical disaster can not only destroy profitability, but also the existence of the firm. Ask former employees and Arthur Andersen, WorldCom, Global Crossing and Enron about the costs of not discovering and preventing an EMD.

Chapter
5

Planning to Prevent and Survive Corporate Ethical Disasters

Most organizations have long acknowledged that business continuity planning is an essential priority in order to effectively anticipate, prevent, mitigate and survive natural disasters, data loss, accidents and deliberate malevolent acts. What many are only now discovering is that ethics continuity planning is likewise a due diligence policy and business priority. Earlier, we defined ethics continuity planning as the strategies, systems and procedures that help ensure that a firm's ethics programs are in place and operating (with all necessary redundancies, back-up checks and balances, safeguards, monitoring, etc.). Ethical issues must be on the strategic agenda. Such planning must go beyond compliance issues and reactive disciplinary policies to actually managing ethics and compliance. Managing ethics and integrity should be a priority because it is legally required and because it is the right thing to do.[1]

In ethics continuity planning, it is very important to synchronize formal ethics codes and policies, ethics programs and organizational culture with all decision-making within the company. There must be regular discovery, assessment, and other checks and balances to keep the firm on an ethical course. The planning component stresses the need to establish goals and objectives and to carefully document required approaches for implementing an ethics and compliance program.

In this chapter, we consider how to initiate planning for ethical continuity, especially through decision making; design and develop measures for ethics continuity; implement actions and programs for ethics continuity; test and strengthen continuity programs; and revise and update ethics continuity plans. Each organization should undergo a thorough review and examination of the various ethical and regulatory contingencies to prepare for the possibility of ethical misconduct. Making a commitment to ethical conduct will help send a strong message to all employees that only ethical conduct is acceptable. Such a commitment is demonstrated through both thorough planning and effective programs.

Preventing Ethical Corporate Disasters through Planning and Compliance Programs

Ignoring the risks of ethical misconduct disasters (EMDs) is the absolute least effective strategy for surviving ethics scandals. Despite the stories of corporate scandals, the news media headlines of ethical disasters, the growing regulatory and legal scrutiny of management responsibility to ensure ethical compliance, and most significantly the increased accountability and responsibility for executives to demonstrate a pro-active program for ensuring ethical conduct in their corporations, far too many managers continue to bury their heads in the sand and pretend that the risks of scandals and EMDs are not threats to their company. Senior management, particularly at the chief executive level, commonly ignores ethics continuity considerations. Research has found that 60 percent of chief executives and boards of directors fail to discuss ethics planning or to include such considerations in their strategic planning. Furthermore, 57 percent of companies have never incorporated ethics or compliance training at the strategic executive or board level.[2] More than half of all businesses fail to assess ethical misconduct risks and plans to ensure ethics continuity.[3] For example, less than half of companies include measurements of ethics in their employee performance appraisal criteria.[4] Over one-half of companies have never conducted an ethics assessment or audit, and about one-quarter have never engaged senior management in ethics/compliance training efforts.[5]

As we have emphasized, EMDs are serious, costly risks to the continuity of your business. News headlines seem to provide nearly daily evidence that breakdowns of ethics collectively cost businesses billions of dollars in litigation, fraudulent financial acts, increased costs, fines, reputation and image damage, customer/client trust, lost sales and recovery costs. Although many executives fail to grasp it, organizational ethics is the first line and fundamental strategic planning area to address the risks of major misconduct scandals.

There is no universal approach for establishing structures, processes and cultures that foster ethical conduct and ensure full compliance with all rules, norms, laws and regulations. However, the strategic development of a comprehensive organizational program appears to be a cornerstone of achieving ethical conduct. Such programs must go far beyond an emphasis on legal compliance and provide incentives for ethical behavior, facilitating ethical decision-making, sustaining an ethical organizational culture, and developing and enforcing specific disciplinary policies that explicitly and immediately sanction employee misconduct.

Ethicial behavior does not just happen within an organization. Consistent patterns of ethical conduct require a commitment and prominent place on the strategic agenda and proactive ongoing management and effective ethics and compliance programs. The company must have a clear-cut code of acceptable conduct and standards of compliance. It must designate responsibility for the management of these programs. There must be ongoing efforts to discover, assess, evaluate and enforce standards of ethical compliance. These programs depend on effective communication, training and modeling of ethical expectations. Finally, there must be efforts for continuous improvement of these compliance programs.

This proactive management can be implemented on many levels and through a wide variety of efforts aimed at ensuring compliance and ethical conduct, but it requires thorough and detailed planning. Such planning is interdependent with compliance and training programs. In addition, planning must go beyond all of the combined efforts to prevent ethical disasters. Ethics continuity planning can reduce a company's exposure to the risks of these disasters; increase confidence in its ability to prevent, mitigate, respond to, and recover from ethical lapses; and offer stakeholders some reassurance for stability in operations.

No company is immune from the threat of disruptive ethical breakdowns and their associated costs. Consider that even such a well-admired company as Berkshire Hathaway was under scrutiny for dealings its subsidiary General Re had with American International Group (AIG), which has admitted that it may have improperly recorded some transactions to improve the appearance of its bottom line. While neither General Re nor Berkshire Hathaway have been accused of legal violations, the investigation cast a dark shadow over a well-respected firm and its founder, Warren Buffet.[6]

Prudent businesses must plan to manage ethics by discovering their vulnerability to ethical disasters, taking proactive measures, assessing the effects of those measures, and preparing their organizations to mitigate and survive when such scandals break. Achieving consistent ethics is much more than simply ensuring legal and regulatory compliance. It requires that a company have a fundamental strategic commitment to ethics, be aware of intrinsic risks, and build an ethical culture that ensures that company employees are likely to make ethical decisions and behave ethically. Managing ethics depends on creating an ethical context in which employee decisions and behaviors are consistent with the mission-critical goals of professional, ethical and strategic processes. Managing ethics (as in managing people) involves managing employees' perceptions of situations. It also requires a commitment to a comprehensive training strategy to ensure that employees understand how they should act, behave and make choices in the performance of their work.

The basic model for ethics continuity planning can serve as a guide for getting started and following through on efforts to ensure ethical continuity. As with most strategic planning processes, ethics continuity planning must be initiated by a demonstrated commitment to such an on-going effort. This is subsequently followed by the steps of assessment, decision-making, designing and developing measures, implementing actions and programs, and testing and revising such programs. These final steps are on-going and frequently repeated to maintain relevance and functionality. Table 1 provides a sample checklist for an Ethics Continuity Planning Model.

Table 1
Ethics Continuity Planning Model
1. Initiate planning for ethics continuity.
2. Make decisions for ethics continuity.
3. Design and develop measures for ethics continuity.
4. Implement actions and programs for ethics continuity.
5. Test and strengthen ethics continuity programs.
6. Revise and update ethics continuity plans.

Initiate Planning for Ethics Continuity

The process of ethics continuity planning begins with consensus on and thorough identification of potential threats (of EMDs) to the ongoing success of the organization's business operations, mission and return on investment. This requires discussions about the company's strategic goals and prudent consideration of the potential impact of such negative episodes. This planning also calls for a strategic-level revision of corporate ethics statements and codes of conduct to address these risks. The strategic mission statement for every company must articulate specific statements that address the goals for ethical behavior and standards for conduct in all circumstances.

It is appropriate at this stage of planning to determine the scope, structure, resources and costs of efforts to sustain ethical performance, if it has not already been accomplished in the discovery phase (Chapter 4). It is useful to gather diverse perspectives on the challenges of sustaining ethical conduct, including legal, human resources, ethics officers, personnel, training, finance, information technology, public relations, systems and training. The challenge of sustaining ethics can be best met from an integrated and comprehensive perspective of the nature of the problems and the potential resources available that can be brought to bear on the problems.

If you have not already done so, the initiation of planning for ethics continuity is an opportune time to designate or select an ethics officer (also called a compliance officer, as well as many other titles). The ethics officer should sit on the overall crisis management team (CMT). Indeed, EMDs should be regarded as serious threats to continuity as are natural disasters, malevolent acts, and accidents and, as such, should be on the agenda for your overall business continuity preparations.

Make Decisions for Ethics Continuity

The next task is to make the decisions that will better ensure ethical conduct. This requires a comprehensive investigation of all threat risks and potential ethics vulnerabilities. As discussed in the last chapter, you should conduct a comprehensive risk analysis for specific contexts where unethical conduct could mushroom into an ethical disaster as part of the discovery and assessment processes. Consider management decision-making, financial accounting, sales reporting, personnel decisions and contexts where ethical lapses might originate. The types of decision-making, value norms, reward systems and monitoring policies should be reviewed.

The most important decisions involve developing a detailed plan for what actions should be taken and by whom in the event that misconduct is discovered. The plan should include detailed and specific steps and designate responsibilities to everyone involved in the management of these issues. It is important to make these decisions for creating the plan long before disaster strikes. Never try to make it up as you go along.

The plan should include response procedures for all types of misconduct that are possible in your company. In fact, it is useful to draft a plan that addresses different variations of potential misconduct. Of course, no list can be considered universally exhaustive, but there are general categories of ethical misconduct that can serve as a starting place for the creation of these plans. These include workplace harassment or discrimination, criminal or illegal activities, financial improprieties, customer deception, bribery or improper influence, regulatory violations, corruption and undisclosed conflict of interest. In addition, different industries may have specific legal or regulatory requirements that should be addressed (e.g., some companies might add a category related to the requirements of the Health Insurance Portability and Accountability Act of 1996).

One aspect of planning is to review the potential threats identified during the discovery process and calculate the risk probabilities for the occurrence of certain types of ethical lapses. Further, one might also calculate the risk probabilities of what types of ethical lapses are more likely to become major scandals or ethical disasters. This process of threat forecasting can also provide analysis of the damage potential and seriousness of each type of disaster and identify those that pose the greatest likelihood of occurrence, the greatest cost and the greatest potential to annihilate the organization.

For example, a plan may have a section that addresses charges of sexual harassment. In that case, the plan should reference the ethics programs or training programs devoted to educating the workforce about harassment. The plan might include assessment data to demonstrate the overall effectiveness of the harassment training programs. The plan should define each type of harassment and its potential impact (legal, economic and reputation). The plan should also provide a detailed set of actions and procedures that should be followed in the event that sexual harassment is detected. This should include investigatory, disciplinary, notification and delegated responsibilities for managing the misconduct.

The plan should be created with input and review from all

perspectives (ethics and compliance officers, legal, human resources, public relations, etc.), and it should detail all of the appropriate responses. Some plans may even offer several different decision-tree options based on the specifics of any given incident. The plans should be written so as to be fully consistent and integrated with codes of ethics and disciplinary policies.

The plan should also contain response steps for all possible escalation paths of misconduct. It should include directions and planned messages to address stakeholders, the media and the general public when the situation warrants. A complete communication plan should be prepared well in advance of a misconduct occurrence. Additionally, the threshold for such notification should be included in the plan. That is, the plan should specifically define under what circumstances or at what stage of investigation or disciplinary proceedings (if at all) that disclosure to law enforcement or the public will be made. The plan should incorporate all of the relevant policies and procedures and should, at each stage of discovered misconduct, explicitly answer the question "what should we do now?"

A plan should provide specific steps to be followed at the discovery of misconduct. As much as possible, factors should be anticipated so that no major decision is made hastily and without time for reflection on strategies. However, no amount of brainstorming and advance work can realistically anticipate every possible permutation of events in these types of crises. Therefore, in addition to having a detailed playbook to follow, the team must continue to revaluate and reassess the circumstances, facts of the case, as well as factors that may have been impossible to anticipate. Taking these real-time factors into account to make decisions and reevaluate the existing plan procedures is what decision-making research calls "double-loop decision-making."

Double-loop decision-making describes the process where a premeditated and detailed plan is followed to guide actions and procedures to ensure consistency and validity of responses. The decision-makers should not just blindly follow the plan, no matter how well conceived and comprehensive, without simultaneously reevaluating and reassessing the relevancy, appropriateness and consequences of following that plan given the many changing and unpredictable variables that arise. The analogy to navigating a sailboat may be helpful. Charting a detailed course, including calculations of course, speed and drift is an essential and necessary plan for every skipper. Nonetheless, merely following the charted course without monitoring (and making required adjustments to) the wind, currents or debris clinging to the hull would inevitably lead the sailor off course and, consequently, result in failure to reach the desired destination. Of course, simply tossing the detailed navigational plan overboard and making course corrections on the fly without regard to the detailed plan is equally a poor navigational strategy that does little to assure the sailor of ever reaching the desired destination. Likewise, developing a detailed plan for responding to EMDs is a necessary but insufficient step in successfully navigating the treacherous shoals of ethical disasters. The plan should be followed, but must simultaneously be monitored and necessary adjustments made to steps taken and policies enacted.

The value in having a precise plan written in a calm time well in advance of the pressures of a crisis is that it serves as a guidebook that is not unduly influenced by the pressures of the moment. On the other hand, mechanically following a plan that inherently cannot take into account factors that may be unique to a given situation is not likely to produce the best results. The solution is to have a plan that has been prepared well in advance that provides clear-cut steps and procedures to serve as a roadmap for responding to these events. At the same time, knowledgeable and well-trained managers should proactively and dynamically assess and evaluate the recommendations of the plan in the context of the given situation. The best practice is not either/or but rather both forms of decision-making. Managers can be trained in this double-loop decision-making skill so they are capable of consistently following the plan that has been prepared while simultaneously making decisions in real time that assure that the roadmap is appropriate for the circumstances of the given situation.

As part of the decision-making and planning process, it is also important to conduct a thorough business impact analysis for ethics lapses. This analysis should include creative consideration of worst-case scenarios. Using a hypothetical case-study approach, each scenario should be analyzed for possible actions that might prevent or discourage such an ethical lapse; how monitoring, disciplinary and mitigation processes might be best designed to minimize the impact of such lapses; how such lapses might affect business operations and the company's reputation; and, finally, what types of strategies and responses would be most effective at restoring or repairing the harm caused by such lapses. It is important to fully understand the harmful impact of a major ethical lapse as part of the planning process. A diverse team of planners should conduct a periodic Ethics Continuity Business Impact Analysis as part of the planning process.

It is important to assess a company's vulnerability to various contingencies. You should conduct a thorough and systematic review of all of the impacts that an EMD would hold for your company and your management. It is helpful for planners and trainers to meet with legal counsel to identify specific areas of regulatory compliance that can be assessed and checked. Ethics disasters may violate statutes and could leave your company executives facing indictment, trial and even prison time. It is helpful for planners and trainers to meet with public relations and branding professionals to identify specific areas of planning that can be assessed and checked. A major EMD can impact your company's brand and corporate reputation, specifically in terms of lost sales, diminished capitalization, degradation of credit worthiness ratings and loss of public goodwill. The primary point is that you should bring in a diverse range of perspectives to best help you understand the risks as well as to take the preventative steps necessary to help your company prevent or survive the disastrous effects of ethics scandals. It is imperative that companies carefully assess the ethics risks that are unique to their business, organizational culture and performance reward systems, codes of ethics, compliance training, and employee development programs. Table 2 provides basic questions that can assist in analyzing a company's ethics, strengths, weaknesses, opportunities and threats.

Table 2
Ethics Continuity Business Impact Analysis
• On what criteria do you base confidence in your company's ethics continuity?
• Do all company personnel know how to act or behave ethically and appropriately in all situations and contexts?
• Do employees know the rules for each situation that may arise?
• How does the company know the employees have this information?
• Do you have reliable and valid data to predict how employees act in various situations?
• Do you have an accurate measure of the state of ethics in your company?
• How would you learn of an ethical violation in your company?
• Do you have functional monitoring, whistleblower and feedback channels?
• What procedures and policies are in place to response to ethical misconduct?
• What would be the financial, legal and reputational impact on your company of a major ethical misconduct scandal?

Formal codes of ethical conduct alone are insufficient to prevent scandals or ensure ethical conduct. Ethical concerns must be regarded similarly to other business disruption concerns, and active efforts are key in ensuring continuity. In most cases, ethical disasters involve employees who have failed to follow corporate codes and policies. Rarely, if ever, does a scandal arise from a single individual who has acted independently from the larger culture, processes and reinforcement systems, all of which tend to facilitate, encourage or reward the unethical behavior.

These risks can be minimized by assessing employee conduct and the integrity of the organizational culture (including measuring employees' knowledge and familiarity with polices, rules and protocol); conducting effective, active ethical conduct training; and evaluating the effectiveness of ethical codes of conduct and training efforts. One approach that has been used effectively to assess a company's strengths, weaknesses, opportunities and threats is the Ethical Conduct Audit.[7] Such an assessment can provide insight into both legal compliance behaviors as well as into the ethical reasoning and decision-making that is often difficult to see with unfocused or by casual observation.

Another critical set of decisions involves the steps and commitments made towards prevention planning. How best can these threats be minimized? What are the key things that can be done to reduce the likelihood of such ethical lapses? What policies can be implemented now to limit the escalation of ethical lapses into full-blown misconduct disasters or public scandals? This may involve employee training programs, the dissemination of ethical expectations, unique training in ethical decision-making, and changes in reward and disciplinary systems to discourage unethical behaviors.

Rapid response to unethical conduct in terms of discipline and disclosure is also an important dimension of planning preparedness. What types of policies and procedures, including reporting, disclosing, disciplinary and investigative steps, should be addressed? What types of arrangements would stop the escalation of unethical conduct into a full-blown scandal?

Another important planning aspect is to determine the steps and procedures of recovery and resumption of business operations after a major scandal has occurred. Planning should include consideration of specific policies and steps needed to get back to routine business as rapidly as possible. The disruptions to employee morale and investor and consumer confidence, as well as damage to image, reputation and brands all need to be addressed. A specific plan to repair image, restore morale and reestablish positive aspects of the corporate reputation is needed.

The final aspect of this stage of planning is budgeting and undertaking a cost analysis of ethics continuity. The return on investment for ethics continuity is sufficient to justify the devotion of resources, time, and personnel to this task. These are investment costs that must be budgeted and allocated. There should be oversight and active management of resources to most effectively utilize these resources so as to ensure ethics continuity.

Design and Develop Measures for Ethics Continuity

After making decisions and generating plans, it is time to design and develop specific measures to ensure ethics continuity. The crisis management team should prepare to respond to EMDs just as they prepare for other potential disruptions to business operations. Every company should have an executable playbook that details who gets called, what steps are taken, who is in charge, and what should happen next for every possible type of emerging or potentially escalating ethical misconduct scandal. The plan should be comprehensive and assign roles, tasks and other activities for every member of the response team and senior management during these types of events.

Each member of the crisis team should have specific roles and responsibilities during ethical misconduct events. An area that should not be overlooked is crisis communication planning. One unique challenge of EMDs is the nature of culpability and constituent attributions. Unlike natural disasters or accidents, ethical misconduct inherently invites assignment of blame and guilt. The importance of having an effective internal and public communication plan is critical in events of this nature.

Planning for the Worst Case

A prudently prepared organizational playbook has detailed plans to mitigate, respond and recover from ethical disasters. To survive scandals requires much more than simply flying-by-the-seat-of-your pants management. It requires vigilant decision-making, careful adherence to well-designed procedures, and the implementation of a response plan that allows for control of situations that could potentially escalate into disasters. Such plans should cover disciplinary issues, disclosure protocols, communication and procedures for working with legal and regulatory investigators.

Although the primary goal is to prevent ethical disasters or, at the very least, nip them in bud before they escalate into a damaging scandal, it is equally critical to have a well-developed plan for recovering from ethical disasters. This will help the company get back to routine operations, heal the damage to morale and motivation, achieve certification for ethical processes, repair or restore damaged reputation and brands, and rebuild the business. The plans to recover should also provide alternatives for contingencies where mid-level and senior managers may be serving prison time—taking with them knowledge, skills and experiences that will provide further challenges to resuming normal business operations.

Companies must establish standards and procedures to prevent and detect misconduct. They also need specific procedures to follow if they do detect instances of misconduct. The procedures should cover reporting guidelines, whistle-blower protection, specific disciplinary policies, responsibility for investigation, responsibility to disclose misconduct to law enforcement or regulatory authorities, and, in the cases where the potential for escalation into a misconduct disaster is present, a procedure to activate a crisis management team to oversee the crisis.

Once misconduct has been detected, the company is required to take reasonable steps to respond appropriately to the misconduct and to prevent further similar misconduct, including making any necessary modifications to the organization's compliance and ethics program. More importantly, companies should immediately respond with a number of important steps to quickly mitigate and manage incidents of misconduct to prevent them from escalating into full-blown EMDs. Furthermore, if misconduct does escalate into a disaster, following planned strategies may mitigate the harm and loss that such scenarios entail. Because every business and every situation is unique, each plan will be different. However, each plan should address the same basic need to have action steps planned out well in advance of the discovery of misconduct. It is important to be prepared to handle a wide variety of these types of events.

Plan Employee Response

Managing ethics requires creating formal and informal systems so employees will act in ways that ensure legal compliance as well as adherence to the corporate code of conduct in ways that are consistently professional, ethical and desirable. Managing ethics is intertwined with managing the larger corporate culture and informal reward/motivation processes that influence employee decisions and behaviors in ways that transcend policies printed in a written code of conduct. In many instances, major ethical scandals have occurred even in companies that have clear and explicit policies and codes of conduct. Consider that Tyco had an ethics program and was even a member of the Ethics Officer Association, yet its CEO, Dennis Kozlowski, was convicted of grand larceny, conspiracy, securities fraud and falsifying business records after raiding millions of dollars of company funds for his personal use.[8] There needs to be more than merely having policies in place to avoid, mitigate and survive these risks. Obviously, every business needs to strategically create structures and processes that fundamentally require all employees and managers to obey all legal requirements and regulations.

Implement Actions and Programs for Ethical Continuity

Integrated comprehensive compliance and training programs are an essential factor in preventing and mitigating the damage from ethical lapses. These programs are useful inasmuch as they disseminate rules, expectations, and polices. Such efforts should also provide clear modeling for recognizing ethical situations and making ethical decisions, and provide guidance for reporting misconduct. Ethics training programs are discussed in Chapter 6 in greater detail, but it is important to note that training is most effective when it includes instruction for ethical reasoning and decision-making. Such programs must also cover reporting channels, discipline and reward systems, assessment, and coordinated oversight of all compliance activities.

One integral aspect of compliance programs is the ongoing monitoring of compliance across the organization. This includes both formal and informal monitoring of employee behavior. This type of surveillance is an important part of the early detection system to identify and recognize ethical lapses quickly before they have time to escalate into ethical disasters. It is helpful to incorporate systematic observation to detect and analyze the warning signs of underlying potential ethical problems.

Another important key to effectively managing ethical lapses is swift and immediate response at the first indication of unethical behavior that has the potential to escalate into a full-blown misconduct disaster. Policies and training need to focus on the disciplinary policies of your organization. Such policies must be quickly and consistently enforced. Be wary of how these policies (and their implementation) will be used as implicit messages and frames in which other employees will interpret the real or underlying values that they believe you want them to enact. Senior managers too often fail to recognize that every decision or action (or inaction) is itself a message that subordinates will scrutinize. When these implicit messages contradict your written code of ethics or explicit policies, some employees will adhere, model and enact the implicit norms and rules that they perceive as set by example.

Another issue that must be addressed at this stage is procedures for notifying authorities and disclosing to relevant stakeholders any misconduct. Do not overlook the impact of your firm's grapevine. Rumors among your employees, while beyond your direct control, are predictable outcomes of incidents of misconduct. What you tell (or do not tell) your employees becomes part of the overall drama during scandals. How, when, and what you disclosure to the news media also becomes part of the scandal drama. Remember that the Federal Sentencing Guidelines for Organizations (FSGO) instruct the courts to provide a break to those companies who disclose misconduct and cooperate fully with the authorities. Once a scandal begins to escalate on the public stage, what you say (don't say), when you say it (or don't say it), and how you say it are all part of the fabric that will be woven together in the minds of your stakeholders into the overall integrated drama of the scandal.

It is also important at this stage to specify plans for identifying target audiences, developing your message, choosing channels to reach the key audiences, and specifying means of assessing the effectiveness of your communication. It is important to build relationships with stakeholders, particularly members of the news media on whom you can draw upon during these types of dramatic spectacles. It is crucial to designate a well-prepared, effective spokesperson for your company, who can stay on message in all of your communications with the news media and all stakeholders.

Test and Strengthen Ethics Continuity Programs

Having your plan in place is not enough. It is important to test your plan, to practice and rehearse. The role of exercises, simulations and practice runs is very important. These may take the form of tabletop exercises, specific simulations or even complete mock drills. Just as government agencies conduct mock drills to test their readiness for natural disasters or terrorist attacks, so too can companies conduct exercises to assess their readiness for ethical misconduct incidents. These exercises can reveal deficiencies in plans or highlight areas where employees need additional training to be able to execute the plan during times of crisis. External review of the plan may also be an essential means to evaluate your readiness.

Training programs for employees on what to anticipate or their role during a scandal is an important aspect of strengthening response readiness. It is important to get an idea of ethical behavior in the workplace. You need to anticipate and monitor for warning signs of potential EMDs. You should also have ongoing employee awareness programs to reinforce your commitment and to create a context in which your response to these types of events is consistent and expected.

There are a number of steps that you can make towards building a culture of ethics. Do not underestimate the importance that simply making ethics a featured aspect on your strategic agenda will have on the culture and focus of everyone in your organization. Declaring ethics continuity a strategic goal for your company itself will raise the salience of this issue in the minds of everyone connected with your business.

Revise and Update Ethics Continuity Plans

Continuity planning is not a one-shot affair. To be effective, it must be an ongoing process. It requires a continuous commitment to constant diligence and active management. Complacency is a threat to preparedness, and vigilance is always an intrinsic aspect to the planning process. It is essential to monitor and regularly revise your planning efforts and documents. Periodic updates are necessary to revise plans to keep pace with changes in the climate, culture, operations, personnel, regulations and legal requirements.

There are many strategic actions that can prevent or minimize the risks for ethical lapses and ethical disasters. However, it is essential that these efforts do not become outdated or out of touch with the realities of your business operations. Continuous review and consideration of a variety of programs, structural and cultural changes, procedural and policy changes, and plans that can limit or mitigate the damage caused by ethical lapses should be a routine feature of your strategic processes.

Remember, all of the best efforts cannot assure that there will be zero instances of ethical lapses. This is even more true in situations where there is a static and one-shot approach that does not build in continuous review and revision of the tactics selected to ensure ethical continuity. Furthermore, despite such superior, on-going efforts, there is always the risk of misconduct escalating into a scandal or disaster that threatens your firm's survival. Therefore, in addition to excellence in due diligence in preventing ethical breakdowns, prudent companies will develop, and have on hand, complete response and recovery plans in order to best manage and survive the threats of ethical disasters. This approach to surviving EMDs is the most prudent and most likely to succeed and protect your company, your assets, and the careers of your management.

Plan Assessment: Measuring Ethics

It is somewhat more abstract, but nevertheless important, to determine the current state of ethics in an organization. Part of initiating continuity planning is to establish on-going assessment and monitoring systems for ethical compliance and conduct in your organization. A strategic commitment to assess ethical practices as well as a multiple method approach to gaining information, insight, and evaluation of ethical decisions and conduct should be part of the continuity planning package.

An ideal ethics or compliance continuity program (as well as perhaps the soundness of overall corporate governance) should stand up to the scrutiny and assessment of an independent expert authority. A valid and reliable evaluation of the cumulative efforts to promote ethical behavior and legal compliance provides an objective assessment of your plans and planning efforts. Such an evaluation can confirm the strengths of the program, as well as offer suggestions for ongoing improvements. An assessment model, such as The Integrity Institute's Integra™ model, is an example of a standardized measurement method that provides a consistent and valid measure of the state of integrity in an organization. With a means of evaluating ethics, a company can minimize the risks associated with ethical disasters.

The assessment of ethical behaviors should focus on the prescribed areas of compliance, the contexts of ethical decision-making, and the locations in your business setting that are subject to ethical problems. After you have formulated policies and procedures governing the ethical conduct of employees, you have to have a developed plan for implementation, testing, assessing and preparing for failures in these efforts. This planning should include the assessment of the state of ethical compliance, including the utilization of an Ethical Conduct Audit.

Planning Checklists

Each organization should undergo a thorough review and examination of the various ethical and regulatory contingencies. What should your company be doing to plan to manage these contingencies? The following ten-step checklist may be helpful as you consider your company's unique situation.

1. Develop, revise and review clear corporate goal statements of ideal ethical values and incorporate them centrally in the

overall strategic mission statement. It is important to define essential or priority values.

2. Articulate those ideal values in relevant objectives, credible policies, specific behaviors and decision-making criteria. Use narratives, case studies and typical situations to clearly describe ethical and unethical behaviors. Distinguish between value-based ethical (i.e. "the right thing to do") and regulatory required standards of conduct.

3. Review with counsel all applicable federal, state and local regulations that govern corporate and employee conduct, decisions, communications and behaviors.

4. Identify key situations, contexts, and behaviors that should be included in prevention strategies.

5. Designate a high-level ethics officer or team to oversee the development of all regulatory compliance programs, ethical training and ethical crisis preparedness. Integrate ethical considerations and contingency preparedness into the master crisis management plan.

6. Establish formal channels and systems to monitor and audit for ethical and/or regulatory misconduct and to monitor compliance with all regulatory requirements.

7. Create a supportive climate for reporting and eliminating misbehavior and/or criminal activity.

8. Communicate standards and proper procedures to employees and company agents through ongoing and thorough training efforts.

9. Build consensus and support for a corporate conscience for ethically valid and regulatory compliant behaviors. This is part persuasion, part mutual participation and part consciousness raising (i.e. getting employees to think about these issues).

10. Enforce ethical standards and employee codes of conduct consistently and fairly.

11. Respond immediately to reports of unethical behavior, employee misconduct or criminal activity to prevent such contingencies from escalating into a major crisis.

12. Frequently, consistently, and regularly assess or even audit company preparedness for ethical and compliance contingencies. Continuously improve ethical and regulatory contingency preparedness.

There are a number of key questions that must be asked and

answered to determine whether your company has adequately integrated ethical considerations into its crisis management plan.

In addition to identifying all of the various ethical dimensions of employee conduct and pertinent workplace regulation, planners must ask questions about worst-case misconduct from employees. A thorough consideration of various "what if" situations should be analyzed, tactics developed to prevent such occurrences, and, of course, remedial response plans for the occurrence of each potential contingency should be developed and implemented. Response plans ought to be integrated with company discipline policy, and tied to specific employee code of conduct and job expectation descriptions.

The following review questions might be helpful as you think about your own company:

1. Does your ethical misconduct management plan explicitly include a list of all potential ethical and regulatory compliance contingencies and areas of general vulnerability?
2. Does your ethical misconduct management plan explicitly include specific situations and contexts of potential contingencies and vulnerabilities?
3. Does your ethical misconduct management plan explicitly include a review by legal counsel of policies, training, avenues of redress and codes of conduct?
4. Does your ethical misconduct management plan explicitly state and reflect corporate ethical values as a consideration in each and every contingency?
5. Does your ethical misconduct management plan explicitly include planning for ethical and regulatory compliance crises?
6. Does your ethical misconduct management plan explicitly include a provision for training for ethical and regulatory compliance considerations in employees' task roles, decision-making and communication acts?
7. Does your ethical misconduct management plan explicitly include periodic assessment and evaluation of planning and training for ethical and regulatory contingencies?
8. Does your ethical misconduct management plan explicitly include both ethical values and legal requirements?
9. Does your ethical misconduct management plan explicitly include an analysis of other policies, rules, expectations, traditions, assignments and responsibilities for their consistency with the corporate values and ethical expectations?
10. Does your ethical misconduct management plan explicitly include revisions and updates since the changes in corporate

vicarious liability for employee actions have been expanded by statue and court decisions?

Commitment to Ethics Continuity

To survive crises of ethics, a company must maintain a fundamental commitment to the strategic goals of proactively managing ethics. Corporations should expect, reward and encourage ethical behavior of their employees. Post-crisis analysis of many of the major ethical scandals has revealed that employees were frequently motivated by formal and informal reward systems and explicit and implicit expectations of management, or that they believed themselves to be acting consistently with the behavior of other employees in the organization. Far too many corporate scandals have occurred because the organization (culture, policies or reward system) was an enabler of the employee's unethical behavior.

Specifically, employees should not be required to bend the rules to perform their job tasks successfully. The consistent message (not mere words, but also reflected in reward structures) needs to be that employees can and should act in ethical ways to complete their work. Managers should never, even inadvertently, reward an employee whose performance was achieved at the expense of integrity or ethical behaviors. Ethical decisions and behavior should be facilitated by culture, attitudes and actions of the other employees and managers. Ethics is a process and way of working. Employees can be trained to make ethics a work habit. Ethical conduct is a dividend-paying, long-term investment, not an expense. Ethical misconduct is a fundamental breach of obligation to stakeholders.

On-going commitment to ethics continuity can aid in preventing, mitigating and recovering from ethical corporate disasters. Through continuous planning and compliance programs it is possible for your company to manage and survive the risks of EMDs. However, even the best planning does not guarantee that you won't experience a significant ethical breakdown in your company. At every level your company should prepare for the eventuality of an ethical breakdown. You should assess and test your response plans. You should practice how you will respond to ethical breakdowns. You should carefully review and revise your plans. Most significantly, in the wake of major ethics scandals, it is important that you develop a comprehensive crisis communication plan. Such a plan should have multiple contingency scenarios and step-by-step response procedure for each scenario.

The Crisis Communication Plan

Crisis communication planning is the process of preparing what, when and how to communicate both information and your advocacy messages to key constituent audiences in the most effective means possible. Such crisis communication may occur before, during or after a scandal rocks your company. Effective communication planning is an aspect of successfully surviving the hit that a major scandal or EMD will have on your company.

Crisis communication plans need to have a strategy and tactics to reach both internal and external audiences (as well as spanners between those two groups). You should also consider the nature of your company's existing reputation and image, your credibility with key constituents, your message goals, the nature of your target audience(s), the timing and appropriateness of messages, and the method (channel) of getting your message and information to specific audiences.

The bottom line is that a well thought out and detailed communication plan is essential to managing both a crisis and the consequences of a crisis for your organization. The plan should have many of the materials and preparations already in place, including background and historical information on your business, established communication channels and strategies, pre-planned procedures and messages and other useful tools to help the spokesperson.

Start Communicating about Corporate Ethics Now

An EMD can shipwreck your company. Loss of investor and customer support can wreak economic havoc. Ensuring the continuity of your positive corporate image and reputation is one of the major goals of ethical continuity. You have to be prepared to communicate effectively with all of these audiences to ensure the continuity of your operations. All of these goals depend on effective and successful communication. Effective communication should not be left to happenstance. Successful crisis communication requires a strategic commitment and substantial efforts to prepare and implement. It also requires a focus on communicating (building) a positive image and reputation long before a hint of scandal is sweeping across public opinion.

These image building messages can be included in a variety of routine communication channels including company reports, newsletters, press releases, advertisements as well as public and media appearances by your senior management. You can also utilize some of the emerging direct to audience communication technologies that are discussed later in this chapter to target specific messages to specific audiences. This can enhance your efforts to shape how a particular audience might frame or interpret subsequent news of an ethical issue.

Reputation and relationship building communication must begin before a crisis happens. This is where you can go beyond merely having a published code of ethical conduct and focus your pre-scandal messages on your strategic commitment to achieve integrity continuity. An analysis of your audiences and the potential impact of news of a scandal should be conducted now. Messages should be developed that cultivate your credibility (reputation for honesty and self-assessment) as well as sharing the proactive steps that you are taking to ensure integrity continuity in the company. You should inform your constituents about training and compliance programs that are in place. Feature the efforts to provide support for those who consistently work with integrity. You can share your efforts for ethics assessment, including Ethical Conduct Audits© and external review of the state of integrity in your company. Publicize the reporting mechanisms and practices.

Efforts for ensuring ethical continuity are themselves a positive aspect of your corporate reputation and image. It is important to follow through on promises made to discover, report and respond to instances of ethical misconduct. Your subsequent actions should be consistent with the expectations that such communication generates in the minds of your audiences.

Planning to Communicate during a Scandal

Survival of a major ethics scandal requires you to get your message out to your key constituent audiences as well as the general public. Whether your business survives depends to a large degree on your communication during and after the scandal emerges. Effective communication, information coordination and message control during and after ethical disasters is achievable only to the extent that you have a sound and workable plan for communicating during the crisis.

Hopefully, you developed a communication plan as part of your overall ethics continuity planning efforts. In any case, a crisis communication plan should detail how your organization plans to communicate with employees, families, customers, the local community, emergency responders, government authorities, and the news media during and in the aftermath of the crisis, whether that be a natural disaster, technological disaster, or one prompted by an ethical lapse. Appropriate employees will need to be alerted that an ethical problem has occurred and notified of the disciplinary steps taken by management. Ethics managers will need immediate and reliable intelligence during critical events and will need to provide feedback to senior management, access and utilize all relevant information necessary for ensuring continuity of business operations, and communicate with customers, vendors, suppliers and other stakeholders. The public in general and the news media in particular, will certainly have specific informational needs during and after such crises. It is important to communicate with the public frequently through the news media. Communicating with the news media is a challenge for which it is essential to be prepared. Your customers, investors, employees and other stakeholders will have questions about the impact of any scandal to your ongoing operations.

Plan Best Practice Guidelines for Crisis Communication Thoroughly and Carefully

- Begin with clear, explicit objectives—such as providing information, establishing trust, encouraging appropriate actions, stimulating emergency response or involving stakeholders in dialogues, partnerships and joint problem solving.
- Identify important stakeholders and subgroups within the audience; respect their diversity and design communications for specific stakeholders.
- Recruit spokespersons with effective presentation and personal interaction skills.
- Train staff–including technical staff–in basic, intermediate, and advanced risk and crisis communication skills. Recognize and reward outstanding performance.
- Anticipate questions and issues.
- Prepare and pretest messages.
- Carefully evaluate risk communication efforts and learn from mistakes.
- Share what you have learned with others.

In addition to creating a crisis communication plan, an effective leader makes sure that every employee—from the board of directors to the custodial staff—knows key information about the business.

What does your business stand for? What is its purpose? What are the important values and goals held by its employees? These values and goals should help guide employees when making decisions in ambiguous situations.

Employees should also know how to respond in crisis situations. What is their role? Where can they turn for information during a crisis? Who is the company's spokesperson and how can employees refer the media to that person? Orientation is a great place to begin this training, but training messages should be reinforced throughout the year because most people forget orientation information after they begin working. Actually applying what they have learned and practicing drills allows employees to sharpen skills and keep this knowledge fresh in their minds.

Monthly reviews and meetings can also be helpful in developing open lines of communication about crisis situations while enhancing employees' skills. Some companies even give employees a Crisis-Communication Survival Card (C-CS), which includes emergency information such as the business's hotline number, web sites set up strictly for times of crisis, specific name and contact information of the business spokesperson, and do and don't reminders. Some companies have more elaborate versions of these cards that include four fold double sided editions with condensed information and details. This same information can be available in electronic data files, but there is a better sense of fail safe for your people to have old-fashioned paper copies readily at hand in the event of a sudden crisis.

Sample Front

C-CS Emergency Information

Spokesperson contact information for all public inquires/questions:
    Ms Susan Smith, Corporate Spokesperson
    24/7 on-call line (212) 555-6400
    E-mail: smith@companyname.com
Automated Communication System Activation (800) 555-2222
Press Center – Corporate East – 2700 Major Blvd. NW
               Washington 20001

Media Inquiries	800-555-1000
Company Information:	800-555-4000
Family Line:	800-555-3000
Webpage Updates at	www.companyname.com

Sample Reverse

Quick Business Facts

Employees Worldwide
Various Units
Locations
Industry Segment

Key Points

Corporate Mission
Company Mottos
Company Values
Key Messages

Employee Report Procedures

1. Who to contact after a major disruption.
2. Alternative work arrangement information.
3. Report your status request.

These C-CS cards can be customized for specific businesses and for specific employees in your company. You may want to provide information about evacuation routes, disaster assembly points, first aid, what to say/not say to the news media and other information employees would need to have on hand. For ethical concerns, you might want to include excerpts from your corporate ethics policies or even specific ethical do's and don'ts. You will need to adapt cards for different categories of employees. You might even want to have three or four color-coded cards for different categories of crises.

Obviously, for any type of crisis, a card for a senior executive might contain different information than a card for a clerical worker. For public relations concerns, you might want to include some basic reference information so employees can direct the news media to your company spokesperson. There is an infinite number of ways to use this type of basic resource; the challenge is to explore and exploit all of the different types of emergency information reminders that you might want your people to have at hand in a variety of different types of crises.

C-CS cards can be expanded to a tri-fold or quad-fold format that would contain even more information that can be readily available. For ethical concerns, you can list the contract information for your ethics compliance officer, ethical compliance programs, ethics training programs, the results of recent ethical assessments, a copy of your company code of ethical conduct and routine steps taken to ensure adherence to the code. It might even be possible to include brief prepared statements about the corporate commitment to integrity, as well as phrases that can be used to express both concern and a commitment to a prompt follow-though on resolving the issues. This same information can be stored as electronic files on portable electronic devices. Expanded editions of this information can be kept in both hard copy and electronic format at different locations (work, car, office, etc.) of your key senior management so that it can be quickly assessable if they are put on the spot in a fast-breaking scandal.

There are many challenges to effective communication during crisis events, including poor business performance, lack of business ethics, bad stakeholder experiences, lack of communication skills by management—internally and externally, lack of transparency and not being proactive during a crisis. Each of these challenges must be overcome to maintain positive image and reputation. The importance of communication cannot be undervalued. How your business manages, or fails to manage, the communication game may make or break your business. Make sure that your crisis communication team is prepared to perform effectively. Your business may have done nothing wrong, but failure to confront the matter with effective communication can cost you dearly.

Stakeholder Analysis

Successful crisis communication requires careful preparation. First, you must identify and consider the characteristics and needs of all key stakeholders. Some people like to classify stakeholders as internal—employees, managers, executives, boards of directors and functional departments—or external—customers, competitors, suppliers, advertising agencies, regulators and special-interest groups.[9] Others like to classify them as primary or secondary stakeholders.

Primary stakeholders are those whose continued participation is essential for the company's survival; they include employees, customers, investors, suppliers and shareholders who provide necessary infrastructure. Secondary stakeholders, who generally do not engage in transactions with the firm, are not essential to its survival; they include the media, trade associations and special-interest groups. Primary and secondary stakeholders exert different pressures and have different priorities associated with them.[10] It is also worth noting that some individuals may be members of more than one stakeholder group. An employee, for example, may also be a shareholder, neighborhood or community resident and member of a special-interest group. In any case, it is important to target your message to the needs, characteristics, and capabilities of all relevant stakeholder groups during an ethics crisis.

Three central aspects help assess stakeholder groups: the power, legitimacy and urgency of their issues.[11] Power generally refers to one's ability to influence the behavior and decisions of others. Legitimacy relates to socially accepted and expected structures that help define whose concerns or claims really count, while urgency relates to the time-sensitive nature of stakeholder interactions.[12] Power and legitimacy may be independent, but urgency sets the stage for a dynamic interaction focusing on addressing and resolving ethical issues. Companies may at times view highly visible secondary stakeholders, such as the media or an outspoken special-interest group, with greater concern or urgency than a primary group, such as employees or customers, when the former has the power to harm the business.[13]

Regardless of how they are classified, major stakeholder groups have different needs, issues and agendas, and a fine-grained approach may be necessary to ascertain those differences even within major groups such as customers, employees, suppliers and investors.[14] As shown in Figure 1, various stakeholder groups exert pressure on the company, as well as on each other, to promote their own ethical values, standards and agendas. Despite their differences, individual stakeholders often share similar ethical values and expectations.[15] Some even choose to join formal organizations dedicated to advocating these ethical values and expectations. In Figure 1, each business has its own values and customs, which prescribe desirable behaviors based on corporate culture. These organizational values often overlap with those of other stakeholder groups, especially primary stakeholders, who are in the best position to exercise influence over the organization.

Figure 1

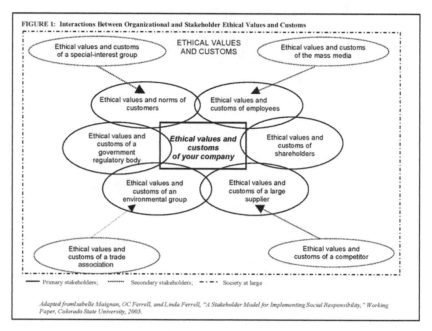

FIGURE 1: Interactions Between Organizational and Stakeholder Ethical Values and Customs

Adapted from Isabelle Maignan, OC Ferrell, and Linda Ferrell, "A Stakeholder Model for Implementing Social Responsibility," Working Paper, Colorado State University, 2005.

The second step in stakeholder analysis for crisis communication requires recognizing all communication media or channels available for reaching key stakeholders or target audiences. Then, you must decide which channels are most appropriate for each message and stakeholder audience. One way that companies can communicate with key stakeholders is through the use of third-party services, such as Global Compliance Service's stakeholder service, which permits stakeholders to interact with a corporation through the Internet or telephone. Although EMDs always entail numerous unique complications, it is still important to have various roadmaps that can help your firm manage its message during these events.

Analyzing Stakeholders' Communication Needs

Be aware that you have a multifaceted audience. It is important to tailor your message to address all of your audiences, to keep all stakeholders informed of your message. This will require planning before an ethical lapse occurs to lesson the burden when time is a scarce commodity. During a crisis, it is important to understand the expectations of all of the different stakeholder groups and audiences waiting for you to communicate. It is essential to anticipate their agendas and information needs. You must define your objectives when designing messages and selecting the best means of reaching key audiences with your message. You must have a consistent message and have your crisis communication team support the effort to stay on message.

The nature of crises demands communication to audiences (e.g. What happened? What is being done about it? Who is affected and how?). It is useful to remember that crises create anxiety and information voids. It is also a product of human nature that crises raise implicit questions of blame or responsibility and inquiring minds want to know the answers to such questions. Obviously, one of the biggest communication failures during a crisis is the failure to communicate altogether. You must engage in appropriate communication when ethics crises strike. You must be prepared to communicate appropriately before a scandal happens.

There are many steps you can take to preventing ethical corporate disasters through planning and compliance programs. These plans can be assessed and evaluated to better enhance their capability to prevent and mitigate scandals. It is also beneficial to measure the state of ethical conduct and compliance within your organization as part of the prevention and mitigation process. There are a number of items on the planning checklist that should help prepare your company to prevent, mitigate, and survive ethical disasters. However, true due diligence requires an on-going commitment to ethics continuity. In addition, you should begin your crisis communication planning before misconduct occurs and the threat of a major ethics scandal looms over your company.

Chapter

6

Disaster Prevention Answers: Culture, Programs, and Training

Managing ethics and avoiding misconduct disasters requires proactive efforts to develop and sustain an ethical organizational culture. The prevention and management of ethical misconduct situations requires dedicated planning and thorough preparedness to be able to respond quickly and to take measures to assure continuity of operations. The plan includes developing and implementing an effective ethics program and providing ethics training to sustain an ethical organizational culture. This process provides an integrated system that can discover potential ethical lapses before they occur and establish appropriate response mechanisms when lapses are detected. With such a system in place, a company's answer to any ethical issue should be rapid and appropriate. Without such a system, the possibility of an ethical misconduct disaster (EMD) is a giant cloud over the entire corporation.

In this chapter, we will examine a framework for developing and implementing an effective ethics and compliance program. In addition to those specific steps, we will examine the responsibilities for the ethics system and the role of training in helping employees recognize ethical issues, understand the decision-making process, be aware of the ethical resources available to them, and understand their role in fostering an ethical organizational culture. We will also explore the process that occurs when it is necessary to activate the ethics crisis management team.

Building an Effective Ethics Program[1]

Recent regulatory changes require senior executives and directors to be knowledgeable about the content and operation of the ethics program and to demonstrate active direct oversight regarding its implementation and effectiveness. Thus, senior managers should ensure that there is an effective ethics program in place and that this program has oversight from a corporate officer who has specific responsibly for the program. The reason for this high-level commitment is to ensure that there are sufficient resources, support, endorsement and direct access to the decision makers to ensure that such programs are central and vital to the organizational agenda. Table 1 describes a framework for creating an effective ethics program. This framework is compatible with the requirements for an effective compliance and ethics program under the 2004 amendments to the Federal Sentencing Guidelines for Organizations (FSGO). These requirements can be used as a template to determine if due diligence has occurred should there be legal action against the company.

Table 1
Framework for Creating an Effective Ethics Program
1. Establish the responsibilities of the governing authority (board of directors) for ethical leadership.
2. Assess risks to help in the establishment of codes of conduct and other components of the ethics program through the discovery process.
3. Implement operational oversight through an ethics officer or committee, compliance officer or human resource manager.
4. Develop a code of ethics and comprehensive standards of conduct.
5. Communicate values, standards, culture and expectations of employees.
6. Establish systems to monitor and report misconduct.
7. Enforce standards with rewards and punishment in support of organizational culture and standards.
8. Continuously improve and revise the program and monitor organizational culture and employee behavior.

Establish the Responsibilities for Ethical Leadership

Successful ethics programs depend on effective leadership and corporate governance. If leaders at the top are unethical or fail to set an ethical example, ethics programs will be nothing more than window dressing and the decisions made will be only marginally legalistic. Dwight "Ike" Reighard, "chief people officer" at HomeBanc Mortgage Corp., reminds us that, "A lot of the companies that flamed out so spectacularly had ethics policies as thick as phone books. But the leaders of those companies were not following their own policies, and many people within those organizations knew it. All the ethics training in the world won't help if your leaders don't live it."[2]

The 2004 amendments to the FSGO require that a business's governing authority be well informed about its ethics program with respect to content, implementation, and effectiveness. This places the responsibility squarely on the shoulders of the firm's leadership, usually the board of directors. The board must ensure that there is a high-ranking manager accountable for the day-to-day operational oversight of the ethics program. The board must provide for adequate authority, resources and access to the board or an appropriate subcommittee of the board. The board must ensure that there are confidential mechanisms available so that the organization's employees and agents may report or seek guidance about potential or actual misconduct without fear of retaliation. Finally, the board is required to oversee the discovery of risks and to design, implement and modify approaches to deal with those risks. If board members do not understand the nature, purpose and methods available to implement an ethics program, the firm is at risk of inadequate oversight in the event of ethical misconduct that escalates into a scandal.

Assess Risks through the Discovery Process

A firm's leadership is accountable for discovering risks associated with its specific industry and assessing the firm's ethics program to ensure that it is capable of uncovering ethical misconduct before it turns into a disaster. There are a number of categories of potential ethical misconduct risk. Such categorization is mostly useful in the brainstorming phase when it is important to generate a master list of types of risks that one might anticipate in the planning process. The discovery process discussed in Chapter 4 can help executives and planners identify risks, facts and perceptions of conduct that could lead to an ethical disaster. The categories of EMD risk include harassment and discrimination (e.g. ethnic, age, religion, sexual/gender), financial improprieties (e.g., fraud, falsifying records), consumer fraud, bribery and improper influence, environmental harm, failure to adhere to laws/regulations, communication improprieties (e.g., false advertising, deceptive selling practices, Internet fraud), violations of personal privacy, corruption, undisclosed conflicts of interest, and all other criminal, illegal or unethical activities.

Possibly one of the greatest risks that could trigger a potential disaster is a failure to have effective corporate governance with those in authority understanding and implementing effective programs to prevent misconduct. The ethical disasters at Adelphia and Tyco occurred because of corporate governance failures. Roy Disney, a former director of the Walt Disney Company, believes that poor corporate governance systems at Walt Disney permitted excessive executive compensation and other decisions that were not in the interests of shareholders.

Implement Operational Oversight

An effective ethics program requires a high-ranking manager or a committee to be responsible for its administration and oversight. This executive is typically called the ethics officer, compliance officer or compliance coordinator, but some firms have more distinctive or specific titles for this role. At Tyco, for example, Eric Pillmore took up the challenge of helping the firm recover from a major scandal as senior vice president of corporate governance.[3] That the role of this position is increasing in importance is highlighted by the dramatic growth of the Ethics and Compliance Officer Association, from 30 officers in 1991 to more than 1,200 members today, representing nearly every industry.[4] In large corporations, one or more senior managers are usually appointed to serve as ethics officers, but the entire senior management, including the board of directors, should be involved in creating, implementing, and supporting the ethics and compliance program. In the past, ethics officers have not always reported directly to the board of directors, but that is changing due to pressure from Sarbanes-Oxley Act (SOX) and the FSGO. At Tyco, for example, Eric Pillmore reports directly to the nominating and governance committee.[5]

Regardless of the title they go by and their reporting authority, ethics officers typically have the following duties:

- Coordinating the ethics program with top managers and the board of directors;
- Developing, revising, and disseminating a code of conduct;
- Developing effective communication and training devices;
- Establishing monitoring and control systems to determine the effectiveness of the system;
- Reviewing and modifying the ethics program to improve its effectiveness;
- Monitoring changes in the industry and environment that may affect organizational ethics and compliance; and
- Dealing with internal issues, including employee questions, concerns, and complaints

Without an effective officer in charge of the program, it will be impossible to implement effective training programs and prepare records that document the company's steps in managing the program.

Although it should be obvious, it is crucial that the manager who oversees the ethics program avoids delegating substantial discretionary authority to any individual known to have engaged in misconduct. Those in charge of ethical oversight within the organization have the obligation to prevent unethical people from holding positions of authority.

Develop a Code of Ethics and Comprehensive Standards of Conduct

The next step in creating an ethics or compliance program is to establish organizational standards of conduct. These standards often take the form of codes of conduct, which are formal statements of what a company expects in the way of ethical behavior. These codes and standards help employees understand what behaviors the company views as acceptable or improper, and they often spell out the ramifications of unethical or illegal behavior as well. At HCA, for example, the code of conduct specifies that any violation of the code may trigger an oral warning, written warning, written reprimand, suspension, termination and / or restitution, depending on the nature, severity and frequency of the violation.[6]

If your firm is developing a code of conduct from scratch, you may want to begin by looking at other companies' codes, especially those of firms within your industry. However, your code, and all other ethical policies and standards, should reflect your firm's needs, issues, practices, and history. Thus, other codes should serve only as guides. The table below presents some guidelines for drafting an effective code of conduct.

Table 2
Guidelines for Drafting a Code of Conduct or Ethics
1. **Provide leadership by upper-level management.**
2. **Identify the principle uses, purposes and stakeholders of the code.**
3. **Define essential values.**
4. **Differentiate between ethical and legal standards of conduct.**
5. **Make the ethics code relevant, credible and concise.**
6. **Include formal mechanisms for resolving ethical issues.**
7. **Have a small representative group write the draft.**
8. **Have upper management and a sample group of employees, suppliers/vendors and customers review the code.**
9. **Have all employees read and sign the code with periodic revisions**
Source: Debbie Thorne, O.C. Ferrell, and John P. Fraedrich, *Integrity Management: A Guide to Legal and Ethical Issues in the Workplace* (Tampa: University of Tampa Press, 1998), pp. 86-90.

Communicate Values, Standards, Culture, and Expectations to Employees

Communication by the firm's leadership helps keep the firm on its ethical course, and these executives must ensure that the ethical climate is consistent with the company's overall mission and objectives. Developing a values-based orientation fosters a system that provides a core of ideals such as respect, honesty, trust and responsibility. In a values-centered program, employees become more open, are willing to deliver necessary information to supervisors and generally begin to feel comfortable about how to make decisions in situations where there are no defined rules.

Managers cannot motivate employees or coordinate their efforts without effective communication about values, standards, and expectations. Communications is important in providing guidance for ethical standards and activities that provide integration between the functional areas of the business. No program can be implemented without complete understanding of its objectives and employee cooperation to make it work. While most managers and employees don't have ethics in their job title, everyone is ultimately accountable.

There are no formal guidelines for the correct way to communicate and establish shared values in an organizational context. It starts at the top with the CEO, board and other chief executives, and it involves formal communications, but it also takes place through informal stories, myths and water-cooler conversations. Additionally, executives must set the values in ways that are consistent with public proclamations about ethical expectations. Senior managers, in turn, model their expectations for ethical conduct. In so doing, they contribute to the collective culture. These are observable indicators of the values and ethical standards that are expected in a given organization. Organizational members will interpret instances of public accountability, acts of responsibility, openness and choices of integrity that are made in trade-offs with other outcomes as messages about expectations of ethical conduct. These symbolic actions are more powerful persuasive messages than are written codes of conduct that may not ever be read by every employee.

Organizations can communicate their ethical standards and other ethics-related messages through training, publishing the code of ethics, having employees sign the code of ethics and creating various reminders throughout the year. Many firms now elect to post their codes of conduct and basic ethics policies on their web sites so that suppliers, shareholders and prospective employees can easily view them. In addition, employees need guidance on where to go for assistance from managers or other designated personnel in resolving ethical problems. To communicate ethical values and implement an effective ethics program, training is crucial. Ethics training is discussed in detail later in this chapter.

Establish Systems to Monitor and Report Misconduct

Monitoring compliance is an ongoing activity that requires measuring organizational performance against the firm's stated ethical standards. Compliance can be appraised through the observation of employees and by adopting a proactive approach to dealing with ethical and legal issues. An effective ethics program uses investigatory reporting and case management systems. A hotline can assist with reporting more advanced case management systems, as well as assist with analysis, investigations, follow up, tracking and reporting. Sometimes external auditing of other organizations' programs can be helpful in developing benchmarks of compliance.

Questionnaires that survey employees' perceptions of the ethics of their superiors, colleague and themselves, as well as their ratings of ethical or unethical practices within the firm and industry, can serve as benchmarks in an ongoing assessment of ethical performance. Then, if unethical behavior is perceived to increase, managers will have a better grasp of what types of misconduct are occurring and why. A change in the ethics training within the company may be a necessary response.

A system for employees to report their observations of wrong doing or to ask questions is particularly valuable in monitoring and evaluating ethical performance. A growing number of corporations have established ethics hotlines and case management systems to offer support and to give employees an opportunity to register ethical concerns. Initially, these hotlines were operated internally, but the trend today is for companies to outsource their hotlines to firms with expertise in managing hotlines and providing other compliance services, such as EthicsPoint (Portland, Oregon) and Global Compliance Services (Charlotte, NC). Research suggests that employees are 50 percent more likely to make use of a hotline managed by an independent provider.[7] While there is always some concern that people may misreport a situation or misuse the hotline to retaliate against another employee, hotlines have become widespread and employees do utilize them. For example, more than half of the calls EthicsPoint receives relate to human resource issues such as workplace conditions or harassment, while just 10 percent relate to SOX concerns.[8]

Effective monitoring systems also require prompt investigation of any recognized or suspected misconduct. Once an investigation is complete, the ethics officer or other appropriate manager needs to make a recommendation to senior management on how to respond. In some cases, a company may be required to report substantial misconduct to a designated government or regulatory agent. As with hotlines, there is a growing number of experts and consulting firms providing services that businesses can rely on to manage incidents of misconduct, sometimes called case management. One such firm is Greenfire/Intercede (Charlotte, NC), which provides professional case management services and software. Intercede's software system enables companies to receive reports of employee concerns, complaints, or observations of misconduct anonymously and to track and manage these reports. The Intercede system helps in investigations, analysis, resolutions, and documentation of misconduct reports. Among the benefits of such systems is that the management of conflicts can help prevent the possibility of lawsuits and that shared management and prevention can help a company analyze and learn about ethical lapses.[9]

Finally, an ethics programs should be regularly assessed or audited to determine its effectiveness. In particular, it is useful to focus on the key factors that influence how ethical decisions are made, including organizational culture, peers, superiors and formal systems of reward and punishment. Understanding the ethical issues in an assessment can help in refining the codes of ethics and developing other programs to encourage ethical behavior in your organization.

Enforce Standards with Rewards and Punishment

Consistent enforcement and necessary disciplinary action are essential to an effective ethics program. When employees comply with organizational standards, their efforts should be acknowledged and rewarded, perhaps through public recognition, bonuses, raises or some other means. Conoco, for example, gives an annual President's Award for Business Ethics to individual employees and groups who provide extraordinary examples of Conoco's ethical values and demonstrate ethical leadership.[10] Conversely, when employees deviate from organizational standards, they should be reprimanded, transferred, docked, suspended or even fired.

Increasingly, corporations are firing employees who violate ethical standards. The ethics officer is usually responsible for implementing disciplinary actions for violations of a firm's ethical standards. Bank of America, for example, fired two senior investment bankers, not for violating the law or securities regulations, but for revealing confidential information to a competitor, an ethical breach.[11] Many companies are including ethical compliance in employee performance appraisals. During performance appraisals, employees may be asked to sign an acknowledgment that they have read the code of conduct or ethical guidelines.

To foster ethical and legal behavior, your firm's policies, rules and standards must be integrated into its compliance system. Reducing unethical behavior is a goal no different from reducing costs, increasing profits or improving quality. An ethics program that is aggressively enforced and integrated into the organizational culture can be effective in improving ethical and legal behavior within the organization.

Continuously Improve and Revise the Program and Monitor Organizational Culture and Employee Behavior

If the assessment process, or worse, a major ethical scandal, reveals that your ethics program has been less than effective at deterring misconduct, the program should be modified as necessary. If performance has not been satisfactory, the company may need to reorganize the ways certain kinds of decisions are made. Modification may also involve setting higher standards, improving reporting processes, toughening punishments, improving communication of standards, strengthening training programs, as well as participating in legal discussions with other organizations and their ethics officers. The Ethics and Compliance Officer Association, for example, provides a forum where ethics officers can share their best practices and ideas for improving ethics programs.

Although we can offer general advice for creating an effective ethics program, in the end, it is up to your firm's leaders and ethics officer to determine what is best and right for your company. There are a growing number of consulting firms, such as LRN, that specialize in the ethics and legal compliance area who can help companies create, monitor and improve their ethics programs. Ultimately, your company must make the commitment to evaluate its risks, organizational culture, employees and stakeholders and then go through the long process of building an ethical culture. With the need to continuously refine and improve an ethics program, this is usually a multiyear process.

Roles and Responsibilities for the Ethics Program

Every company should have a team that steps in to oversee compliance programs, respond to each discovery of misconduct, and manage ethical lapses so that they do not escalate into ethical disasters. An ethics officer or some other senior executive may lead this team. This may be the same team that manages all organizational crises (natural disasters, accidents, public relations crises, etc.). At the very least, your ethical misconduct crisis team should work closely with a general crisis management team to coordinate and organize response strategies, as well as to draw upon resources that can be shared without unnecessary duplication. The team that handles these events should be broad-based and be comprised of many different perspectives and voices, including legal, security, human resources/personnel, public relations, operations, and, of course, managers directly overseeing the day-to-day implementation of your ethics and compliance programs. You want to establish or, if you already have one, reevaluate your existing crisis management team.

Everyone on the team should have a clear understanding of his or her roles and responsibilities during these sessions. The team should oversee all of the internal preparations for what happens in the event of discovered misconduct. The team should ensure that all organizational members know their roles during these events. A systematic consideration of confidential reporting channels, whistle-blower protection, a means of disseminating appropriate information and correcting misinformation carried in rumors, and disciplinary policies are also some of the factors that the team should assess.

Importance and Benefits of Ethics Training

To prevent and alleviate the dangers of EMDs requires sustained commitment to a program of ongoing training and development. Such a program must have the support of top management. The training should educate the workforce on all of the expected codes of conduct and governing policies. This includes efforts to communicate with employees the expectations, reporting mechanisms, responsibilities, reward systems, disciplinary systems and the process for continuous development of the essential knowledge, skills, abilities and motivation for a culture of integrity. It is particularly important to help employees recognize ethical and legal issues and give them the resources to address and resolve such issues in ambiguous situations. A survey by the Ethics Resource Center suggests that 54 percent of organizations provide training in ethics.[12]

Training should provide adequate information to employees to make appropriate decisions, evaluate conduct and communicate appropriately in all circumstances. It should communicate to employees the acceptable norms for conduct, communication, behavior, and decision-making. Training should enable employees to anticipate negative effects of misconduct and failure to act in ethical and legal ways. It must make employees aware of company support resources, procedures and communication channels available to help them manage ethical and legal contingencies.

Ethics training appears to be most effective when it:

- is regular and ongoing;
- is tied to real workplace situations and decision-making scenarios;
- employs diverse participative training methods, such as

role-playing, case studies, and simulations;
- has a formal debriefing element;
- is consistent with company values, behavioral climate, other expectations, and is integrated into a shared corporate culture;
- is not directly or unwittingly contradicted by managers' messages or actions;
- distinguishes between individual ethics and the responsibilities and values of the corporate culture;
- is based on current, accurate regulatory and legal information;
- enhances employees' ethical reasoning skills to analyze situations where ethics or regulatory code is applicable;
- encourages employees to seek support and information when they are uncertain of the ethics or appropriateness of a given message, behavior, action, or decision;
- empowers employees to "speak up" about misconduct and fosters a climate of integrity in the workplace; and
- is regularly assessed and evaluated to measure its effectiveness.

Suggested Objectives for Ethics Training

A primary role of training is to communicate, coordinate and integrate employees' behaviors into a consistent system of corporate ethics. In addition, training should provide guidance, resources, and support for ethical conduct; assess the performance of ethical conduct; identify and resolve issues before they become problems; and oversee ethical compliance activities. The objective of training programs should be to promote decisions and behaviors that are consistent with and directly exemplify the corporate mission, values, and goals. Every employee should act in a manner consistent with the corporate ethical standards and policies, as well as regulatory requirements. Each deviation or misconduct sets up the potential for a costly contingency.

The central goal of ethics training is to create employees who have the knowledge, skills, abilities and motivation to act in ethical ways, make ethical choices, and comply with regulatory and legal requirements. Employees are more likely to conduct themselves in ethically appropriate ways when they have the knowledge, skills, habits and motivation of ethical and legal compliant conduct. To achieve this goal, the trainer must assess what specific knowledge, skills, abilities, and motivations employees already have and then identify what needs to be addressed in the training. Training efforts must be integrated with the overall corporate mission and woven together in a climate in which appropriate conduct is expected, modeled, rewarded, and supported.

Table 3 Training Supports an Ethical Culture
1. Generate personal sense of responsibility and accountability for ethical and legal conduct.
2. Create an appropriate climate of openness and support for ethical and legal conduct.
3. Make it normative and expected for each employee to act ethically and appropriately.
4. Give employees models and experiences for ethical functioning to remove incentives and motivations for misconduct.
5. Enable ethical and legal behavioral competence in wide variety of situations.

It is important to integrate training into an overall strategic plan to achieve ethics and compliance goals, as well as with other ongoing organizational development and transformation activities. You must have clear goals and objectives. An organization with a strong overall commitment to ethics is a more productive environment for ethical and legal compliance training.

Training Methods[13]

In general, training methods for ethics training differ little from those employed for other areas of business. However, the sensitive nature of ethics means that managers may have to modify their expectations and approach. In any case, employees need to recognize both the seriousness of training under the FSGO and the role they play in organizational culture. To accomplish these goals, most trainers will employ a combination of approaches listed below.

Lecture and Presentations

The lecture method has become the favored method for teaching many subjects. The lecture approach is efficient because it can reach a large number of people quickly and does not require the active participation of trainees in the process. In this context, however, employees are usually passive learners, and it is questionable as to whether their decision-making skills are truly enhanced by listening to lectures. As we've mentioned before, organizational decision-making is the result of both personal and work influences, neither of which can be adequately experienced through passive learning. Moreover, few lectures will be able to expose employees to the diverse viewpoints that can be taken on ethical issues. The use of short lectures and presentations is usually appropriate when a company introduces its code of conduct and ethics initiatives, as trainees need to understand the background and purpose of the program. This method can also be used to expedite compliance efforts and to set the stage for follow-up training sessions.

Cases and Scenarios

Cases and scenarios can be excellent tools for spawning discussion among class participants because they incorporate real-life problems and situations. Many organizations have found the case-analysis method beneficial for helping employees understand the various personal and organizational factors that interact to contribute to an ethical or legal dilemma. With the case method, employees can become active learners because they must read the case, analyze its issues and make recommendations based on case facts. After this process, trainers can link participants' recommendations to specific company values, standards and policies, as well as industry standards. Some trainers also offer details about the actions taken by actual participants in the case.

Vignettes and short scenarios also provide employees with the opportunity to actively engage in decision-making exercises about specific ethical and legal problems. These are relatively brief, generally just one paragraph, and put the reader in a situation that requires a decision. Companies using scenario-based training typically develop vignette situations that are common in their respective industries. Some scenarios offer a number of options from which the reader can choose. Although these options are useful for making class comparisons, they impose predetermined responses on readers, which can stifle more honest and creative responses.

Case analyses can motivate employees and even change attitudes. These approaches teach problem solving, though some employees may not be comfortable with their inherent ambiguity. Cases and scenarios require the ability to express opinions and to listen to other's diverse perspectives. Despite the importance of case studies and vignettes in communicating ethics, they can be narrowly focused and require little accountability on the reader's part. Trainers must balance the strengths and weaknesses of cases by ensuring that solutions to the issues are realistic under policy, the law and organizational life.

Role-Playing and Simulation Exercises

Role-playing exercises are interactive because they require at least some participants to adopt the perspective of an individual facing a dilemma. This technique can be quite insightful as it draws out participants' emotions and attitudes as they experience the role. A perceptive trainer can carefully observe the attitudes and emotions exhibited during the exercise and offer some mechanisms for using them to refine policy and communications. A number of studies have supported the effectiveness of role-playing and simulations as part of ethical and regulatory compliance training.

Behavioral simulations are another interactive training method that asks an individual participant to take on a role in a simulated organization, understand the complexity and pressures to which that role is subject and then make choices based on problems and opportunities presented by the simulation designers. The exercise can be enhanced by the dynamics of group participation. As a tool, behavioral simulations can put participants into hyper-realistic scenarios that help employees recognize the challenges of incomplete information, role pressures and relationship pressures in an ethical decision-making situation. This method is growing in use in ethics training in part because it permits trainers to incorporate content-specific issues and to assess employee characteristics such as leadership, group cohesiveness and problem-solving ability.[14]

Video

Most large businesses are using video presentations as one component of their training systems. These are often used at the beginning and end of seminars for sending an overall corporate message about the importance and scope of ethical compliance. Public Service Company of New Mexico, for example, purchased training videos from Pacific Gas and Electric, which feature vignettes of employees confronted with an ethical choice.[15] Videos can be used to present scenarios and cases that are used for group discussion, effectively support many elements of a training program and add a touch of realism, emotion and even humor to very serious subject matter. Smaller firms that lack the resources to develop their own videos may be able to obtain them from other sources, such as industry associations or state and federal government agencies. For example, the Massachusetts Commission Against Discrimination offers a low-cost training video for small businesses about sexual harassment. The video examines why sexual harassment is a problem, what it involves, its causes and resolution. Videos are especially useful for training employees of the TV Generation, and trainees are generally positive toward this method because it is fun, action-oriented, and easy to understand.

Games

A number of companies, including Sony, Wells Fargo, Harris Corporation and Lockheed Martin, have created games as part of their ethics training programs. As with videos, games can be an enjoyable means of supplementing other ethics training content or assessing employees' understanding of company policies and standards. Lockheed Martin's *Gray Matters* game has been adopted by more than 100 organizations and is very helpful for discussing specific ethical dilemmas and the appropriate corporate response. With *Gray Matters*, teams respond to various scenarios and are awarded points based on how well their responses correlate with the best answer as defined by the company. Lockheed Martin recently revised the game, which is now entitled *The Ethics Challenge*. Like other training methods, games are beneficial for generating discussion, increasing employee involvement and reinforcing company policy.

Interactive and Computer-Based Training

Through the use of computer-based training, interactive video and company intranet systems, new vehicles are available for reinforcing ethics training, especially in very large corporations with numerous facilities around the world. Interactive training may be computer- or video-based and is designed for employee involvement and decision-making, content consistency and flexibility. Computer-based training is relatively easy to implement and provides a high degree of control and consistency because every employee receives the same messages and explanations. From a compliance perspective, this is especially useful when employees are required to log in or otherwise record their training time. In addition, computer-based training gives employees considerable flexibility in squeezing the training modules into their work schedules. Companies with field personnel find computer-based training to be an efficient use of resources.

Characteristics of Effective Ethics Training Programs

Trainers and planners often ask what works best for ethical and legal compliance training programs. Although there are no sure bets that are guaranteed to eliminate all unethical or illegal behavior, there are a few things that can help. First, recognize the importance of planning and training in minimizing the potential for misconduct. Boost the focus on these aspects and make preparation and training commitments a high priority. Educate yourself and your company about the risks of employee misconduct and unethical behaviors.

Second, gather up-to-date educational resources on ethics training as well as pertinent regulation information. Using dated information and training materials can itself create a contingency risk. There are resources available from many private-sector sources, as well as several government agencies. The Equal Employment Opportunity Commission (EEOC), for example, provides a range of training support resources, informational materials and assistance to companies with responsibilities under EEOC enforced regulations. Most materials and assistance are provided to the public at no cost, such as posters advising employees of their EEO rights, pamphlets, manuals, fact sheets and enforcement guidance on laws enforced by the Commission. Additional specialized training and technical assistance are provided on a fee basis under the auspices of the EEOC Education, Technical Assistance and Training Revolving Fund Act of 1992. Another excellent source of training resources is the Open Compliance Ethics Group (OCEG), which is a nonprofit organization that can help companies to develop an ethics training program (see Appendix A).

Third, revise and update training techniques, methods and approaches. Evaluate the success of your in-house training efforts and revise as necessary to make them effective. Ineffective training approaches can render the best-designed ethics program impotent if they do not make a difference in employees' actions and choices on a daily basis. In particular, it is important to ground training into realistic scenarios and specific applications. Simply reviewing the code of ethical conduct or pertinent regulations is inadequate.

Fourth, consider outsourcing some training tasks to consultants or third-party firms that specialize in this type of training. *The New York Times*, for example, hired LRN, a Los Angeles-based firm, to supply the publishing firm's legal and ethics training program, including a customized course on its ethics policy.[16] There are many resources available that can be imported and integrated into your in-house training efforts. The EEOC, for example, has developed half-day, one-day and multi-day Technical Assistance Program Seminars (TAPS) that focus on how to prevent equal employment crises from developing and how to resolve discrimination complaints effectively when they do arise.

Activating the Ethics Crisis Management Team

Even the most successful ethics program and cutting-edge ethics training may not deter a determined rogue employee from going against your company's organizational culture to further his or her own selfish interests—although its enforcement mechanism should certainly reduce the probability of such an occurrence. Should such an ethical breach occur, your monitoring and reporting system should detect it and alert you that a problem exists long before it has the potential to escalate into a disaster. It is at this moment that you should convene your ethics crisis management team (ECMT) based on the parameters and definitions set out in your crisis management plan. The team must then meet, coordinate the investigation, evaluate the threat potential and actively oversee the firm's response. During this process, team members should delegate their routine work to subordinates and make overseeing the firm's response to the misconduct their highest priority. As we've emphasized throughout, lapses of ethics must be regarded as serious potential disruptions to business continuity and long-term success. It is not prudent to dismiss the significance of these events.

The ethics continuity plan discussed in Chapter 5 should have defined the role of an immediate supervisor of an employee who has been discovered to have engaged in a breach of ethics or legal misconduct. The ECMT should monitor, document and oversee that immediate supervisors have, in fact, followed the procedures outlined in the plan. The team should not supplant the legitimate roles and duties of managers and supervisors, but rather should serve as independent observers and as a safety net to ensure that all relevant policies and procedures are being followed and effectively implemented. In most cases, the team supports and facilitates the role of the immediate supervisor and managers.

The continuity plan should have listed the critical tasks and objectives for the team. As a general rule, the team should assess the potential impact of the misconduct from every perspective, including legal, public relations, employee morale, business operations, labor and compliance program efficacy. The ECMT needs to make carefully considered decisions to allay any potential negative impact of the misconduct. It must stick to the plan regarding questions of notification of external authorities, public disclosure, as well as messages to employees, stakeholders and the news media. The team also needs to oversee the implementation of all the planned responses. In other words, the ECMT needs to actively manage the situation to prevent it from escalating into a true disaster.

Some situations resolve themselves within a matter of hours of discovery. Other situations deteriorate into scandals that can take years to resolve—if ever. The continuity plan should define your standards for resuming normal operations and de-activating the crisis team. This may seem like common sense, but it is often difficult to recognize when an event has been successfully managed and mitigated or when it continues to present the threat of mushrooming into a true reputation disaster. In any case, it is not helpful to remain in a perpetual state of crisis. Thus, the continuity plan should provide some criteria to be used to indicate when things have returned to normal and when the team members can go back to their normal duties.

The plan should provide the team with guidelines for limiting the damage and successfully recovering from every type of misconduct. The ECMT may have the responsibility to respond to regulatory requirements for documentation of proactive efforts by the company to prevent misconduct and to assess data for the effectiveness of ongoing training programs.

The primary duty of a team approach to managing occurrences of misconduct is the double-loop decision-making response. The team is responsible for ensuring that everyone follows the plan and for simultaneously assessing the appropriateness of the outlined procedures in the context of the given crisis. The team is also accountable for being flexible enough to deviate from specific steps of the plan, depending on the changes in the environment, circumstances, or other unanticipated aspects, yet remaining focused on achieving the plan's overall goals while remaining true to the firm's values and culture.

Another important function for the ethics crisis management team is to conduct a thorough debriefing and post-mortem assessment of how effectively the plan worked, how well the team performed, and how well the overall problem was mitigated and handled. The team should assess its double-loop decision-making and identify weaknesses and potential problems that did not materialize but might have become problematic under different circumstances. It should make recommendations for changes in ethics programs, disciplinary policies, training, enforcement systems and in the plan for handling these events. The team should also address the future training needs of the team itself.

It is very useful for the team to practice and run through the plan implementation in drills, exercises and simulations. These exercises give the team an opportunity to test the plan, identify areas for improvements in the plan (and planning process) and gain experience in quick and effective functioning as a team when these events are detected by the monitoring system. Mock exercises are a useful tool to find hidden problems and areas that should be revised in plans.

The Effectiveness of Ethics Programs

The effectiveness of most ethics programs relies on the degree to which they can be fully integrated with the overall organizational culture. Furthermore, the reasons, methods and nature of such efforts must be aligned with the strategic business operations goals. The collective culture of an organization is an important foundation on which ethics programs should be built. Organizational development and training programs that promote ethical conduct are essential aspects of any ethics program.

It might be useful in a comprehensive ethical assessment or audit to look for manifestations of these underlying values, standards and expectations. Recognizing that actions speak louder than words, what priority would an employee in your company understand to be expected in a choice between maximizing the bottom line versus doing the right thing? Would an interview with your employees reveal any feelings of being pressured to sacrifice ethics in order to make quarterly earnings reports? Do employees have the knowledge, skills, ability and motivations they need in order to make ethical choices in every instance? Do the choices and actions of managers indicate a willingness for openness and self-criticism or is the culture one that is defensive, where a shrewd employee can learn the value of blame-shifting or covering up to survive in the organization? Is it culturally acceptable to ask for help when confronted with difficult ethical decisions? Are the underlying reward and disciplinary systems designed to foster growth, compliance and motivation for acting with ethics? In very simple terms, would an employee in your company believe that unethical behavior will be disciplined and that ethical behavior will be rewarded? Do senior managers talk frequently about the importance for behaving ethically?

It is important to keep in mind that leadership's motivation in designing and implementing an ethics program is directly related to the effectiveness of such programs. Ethics programs must have a commitment from the highest levels of management—a core mission comprehensive business strategy.

The goals for most ethics programs are to prevent and detect criminal conduct, to make a commitment to comply with the law, and, more broadly, to promote an organizational culture that supports ethical conduct and empowers employees to act in ways that are consistent with the company's ethical standards and values. Such program should be reasonably designed, implemented and enforced so that the program is generally effective in preventing and detecting misconduct.

The failure to prevent or detect every occurrence of unethical conduct does not necessarily mean that the program is not generally effective in preventing and detecting misconduct within the organization. Even the best programs will have instances of misconduct. It is, therefore, imperative to have a plan in place to detect the occurrence of unethical conduct and to quickly and appropriately respond to the occurrence in ways that will mitigate the potential for such conduct to escalate into an EMD.

Chapter

7

Answering Negative Publicity and Surviving News Media Scrutiny

Although it is important to develop an ethics and compliance program with training, there will inevitably be ethical lapses that require a quick response to prevent them from turning into full-fledged ethical disasters. Most ethical issues will be relatively minor, internal and will not necessitate any outside communication or involvement. Yet, how your company handles such internal lapses is an important part of the organization's culture, which sets the foundation for handling the more public events. Values and codes of conduct should be followed without unnecessary delay, and each lapse should be studied and reviewed for lessons that can be applied to revising plans and policies. There is no doubt that the development of an organizational culture that responds effectively to lapses is far more important than a code or rule in a manual that no one ever reads. Therefore, ethical lapses are learning opportunities providing cases, scenarios and informal conversations that can be integrated into employee training programs.

If an ethical disaster does occur, the ethics continuity plans, ethics program and ethics training should provide a clear path for a quick and decisive response. It is always important to follow planning and procedures in a consistent yet flexible manner. If ethics continuity planning has occurred, there will be documents to guide the response and all steps for answering questions about the ethical misconduct will be clear. Rest assured that every step taken (or not taken) will be scrutinized by all stakeholders and, eventually, by the media. In

Chapter 3, we underscored the need for understanding stakeholder concerns and risks in order to focus on important ethical issues.

This chapter provides a hands-on approach for dealing with communication responses to ethical lapses or a potential ethical disaster. We will first take a brief look at crisis communication. We shall consider the unique challenges of news media coverage of your ethics scandal. Next, we explore the role of one of the most important people during a crisis—the company spokesperson. We also review a number of details useful in creating and managing your message. Finally, we survey some different communication technologies available for delivering that message to key target audiences.

Corporate Communication during an Ethics Scandal

At the moment that you first learn of ethical misconduct you should be prepared to follow all of your internal procedures related to reporting, investigating, disclosure and follow-up. At the moment that you first understand that the misconduct has the potential to escalate into a scandal or ethical misconduct disaster (EMD) for your company, you have to be prepared to act quickly to manage the potential impact to your business. There are a number of first steps that are required. Activate your crisis management team. Implement your crisis plan and your crisis communication plan. Manage the investigation and disciplinary policies internally. Follow your procedures for notification of law enforcement or regulatory authorities. Prepare yourself to actively respond to the scrutiny of the news media of both the misconduct and almost every aspect of your company and management practices. Remember that the misconduct is only the first aspect of your company that is suddenly vulnerable to intensive news media investigation.

Your first communication act should be to listen. This is one of the most difficult challenges for effective communication. All too often our defensive instincts overcome our ability for self-restraint. Too many executives have attempted an impromptu "message strategy" without taking the time and making the effort to understand the concerns of their audiences. While it is true that you will be expected to respond quickly, it is both possible and reasonable for you to focus your immediate comments on the basic message points that you have developed in advance as part of your crisis communication planning.

It is universally acceptable that, no matter the nature of the allegations or rumors of scandal, you express your concern for those affected as well make a commitment to follow through in a rapid and appropriate manner. It may also be universally acceptable to reiterate both your own and the company's commitment to integrity continuity. If you do not have a specific response message plan in place, you should utilize the basic talking points that have been developed in advance in consultation with your planning team. These comments may include a review of corporate codes of ethical conduct, compliance policies, training programs and the efforts for monitoring and assessing ethical conduct.

It may take some time before your team is able to develop a clear, coherent and specific message response to the particular aspects of an emerging scandal. This will require your team to come together and make decisions about the issues, isolate the challenges and create a comprehensive and cohesive overall message strategy (as well as a plan for getting this message out to the key audiences). Before you brainstorm the themes and specifics, your team will need to conduct reconnaissance on the perceptions of your key stakeholder audiences. This message creation phase will require you to fully understand the impact of the issues as well as the expectations of your various audiences.

Crisis Communication Best Practice Guideline #1: Listen First, Then Craft Your Message

- Before taking action, find out what constituents believe, know, think or want done regarding the issue.
- Use a variety of techniques such as interviews, facilitated discussion groups, information exchanges, availability sessions, advisory groups, toll-free numbers and surveys to help understand what issues your message should address.
- Consider the perspective of all your stakeholders, constituents and key audiences.
- Provide feedback to the expressed concerns of your stakeholders.
- Follow through on all promises made (whether explicit or implicit) that your audience expects.
- Use "perspective taking" (empathize with your key audiences; try to put yourself in their place and understand the impact of the scandal form their point of view).
- Acknowledge the validity of reactions (emotions, feelings, etc.) of your stakeholders even if you believe them to be

unjustified.
- Emphasize communication channels that facilitate two-way communication (your listening, feedback, participation and dialogue).
- Recognize that competing agendas, symbolic meanings, and broader social, cultural, economic or political considerations may complicate crisis communication.

Know Your Audience and Dialogue with Them

You must know who the key stakeholders are for your company. You will need to prioritize the stakeholders in terms of those most impacted by the issue at hand down to those who would be the least impacted. A scandal is not the time to pull back and retreat from your relationships with your stakeholders. If you have successfully laid the groundwork in advance of an ethical breach with your audiences, then you should now utilize that positive relationship. This may allow you to mitigate the impact on your company of negative coverage in the news media.

You should accept your stakeholders as partners in responding to the issue. It is helpful to involve them and allow them to share the survival strategies. If you audiences have been harmed or fear that they might be harmed by the issue, then it is imperative that you demonstrate your concern for them as well as your commitment to ensuring their security. This is where two-way communication plays an important role. Later in this chapter are a number of emerging communication technologies which can expand your capabilities for engaging in two-way dialogue with your stakeholders. Each of these should be considered to determine the best choices for your particular situation. You should find ways to have a dialogue with your stakeholders (particularly those who are most affected) and involve them in the process of the corporate response.

Crisis Communication Best Practice Guideline #2: Accept and Involve Stakeholders in Two-Way Communication

- Connect with stakeholders in two-way communication.
- Demonstrate your willingness to listen to their feedback and input.
- Demonstrate respect for stakeholders affected by the crisis situation by involving them early, before important decisions are made.

- Involve all constituents that have an interest or a stake in the particular crisis.
- Include in the decision-making process the broad range of factors involved in determining public perceptions of risk, concern and outrage.
- Use a wide range of communication channels to engage and involve stakeholders.
- Adhere to the highest ethical standards; recognize that stakeholders hold you professionally and ethically accountable.
- Honor your commitments and promises; stakeholders will hold you most accountable on issues where you have made (implicit or explicit) promises for action or behavior.
- Strive for mutually beneficial outcomes.

You may not consider the news media a stakeholder for your company. Nonetheless, it is important not to overlook the importance that the news media will have on the public (and your constituents') understanding of an ethics scandal. The news media will also play a major role in setting the tone, providing a context and establishing evaluation backgrounds for how your messages, actions, and the dimensions of the ethics scandal are judged. Do not overlook the importance of effectively communicating both to and through the news media. During an ethical crisis, the media are especially important, with unique needs that must be carefully addressed.

News Media Questions about Ethics Disaster

During an ethical crisis, the media are especially important, with unique needs that must be carefully addressed. Who are your main contacts at local news stations? Do you have an area specifically set aside for media access? In times of crisis, it will be important to be proactive in providing media with information, to allow the media a certain level of access, and to provide them with the necessary support so they can get the necessary information—and your message—out to the public.

Members of the press view themselves as corporate and government watchdogs who are obligated to tell the truth and point out misconduct. They are required to report the truth, but can become wrapped up in a compelling story. They return to their offices with stories that will either please or dissatisfy their bosses. If the story is catchy, even scandalous, guaranteed to grab the audience's attention, then the editor is happy. If the story is dull, the editor may not only be unhappy but may choose not to run it.

It is especially important to recognize that the media is looking for brief, concise sound bite excerpts within an interview or press conference that sum up the story. Many business people who claim that they were misrepresented or misquoted are actually victims of the media's tendency to seek succinct sounds bites from a longer interview with an employee. This tendency to edit by sound bite must be recognized and understood by anyone giving a statement or comment to the media. Spokespersons, therefore, need to be prepared to offer short and concise summary statements as well as detailed answers. These sound bites are representative anecdotes, which should be consistent with and encapsulate the larger themes of the message. These phrases should be used consistently and frequently in public communication settings. The crisis communication team should pay careful attention to each part of a crafted response. It is essential to consider how messages or aspects of a message might be perceived if taken as an isolated sound bite.

Crisis Communication Best Practice Guideline #3: Meet the Needs and Expectations of the News Media

- Be accessible to reporters; acknowledge and respect their deadlines.
- Prepare a limited number of key messages before interacting with the media; take control of interviews and repeat your key messages several times.
- Keep interviews short. Establish specific topics of the interview with the reporter in advance and stick to these topics during the interview.
- Say only what you want the media to repeat; everything you say is on the record.
- Tell the truth.
- Provide background materials about complex issues.
- Provide information tailored to the needs of each type of media. For example, provide sound bites and visuals for television.
- If you do not know the answer to a question, focus on what you do know and tell the reporter what actions you will take to get an answer.
- Be aware of, and respond effectively to, media pitfalls and trap questions.
- Avoid saying "no comment."
- Follow up on stories with praise or criticism, as warranted.

- Work to establish long-term relationships with editors and reporters.

Surviving News Media Scrunity

Many business executives believe that there is a bias among journalists that could be described as antagonistic or even anti-business. The assumption is often that this bias will lead reporters to skew, by selective consideration and coverage of events, facts, opinions, perspectives and points of view of ethics scandals and possibly even be subjectively biased in their reporting. Can you expect the news media to be objective or biased in their coverage of your ethics scandal?

Obviously there are practical limitations to the objectivity of a journalist. There are information gaps in what they do or can know to include in their stories. There are time and space limitations of the mass media that are utilized to transmit their story to the public. There is an expectation from editors and audiences that reporters' stories will be reported in a coherent narrative that may not be the most accurate format for reporting a complex and complicated multi-factored ethics scandal. News media reporters can subtly reflect the agenda of the primary audiences whom they serve (for example, compare the questions a reporter writing for the *Wall Street Journal* might ask of you during an ethics scandal compared with those asked by a reporter from the FOX News Network). Don't overlook the implications of ownership and economic influences on major news media outlets that may implicitly shape perspectives and tone of reporters' stories. Nonetheless, believe it or not, most journalists consider themselves to be objective or neutral in their coverage of major corporate scandals.

Reporters, however, may not have a completely detached objectivity in covering breaking scandals. In the post-Enron (more precisely post-Watergate) world of news media journalism, most reporters pride themselves on a perspective of detached skepticism or cynicism in coverage of breaking ethics scandals. With so many different ethics scandals over the past few decades, there is regrettably a willingness (eagerness) among many journalists to investigate even minor allegations and to pursue hints of ethical misconduct in the business world, as well as government, religious organizations and other complex social institutions. The bottom line is that investigative journalists won't go away and abandon a potential ethics scandal story simply because you tell them once that there is no story there.

Once a scandal breaks, journalists will consider it their obligation to continue to pursue and investigate the story. The news media would feel some obligation to balance their reporting, so they may interweave any statements that you make with those from victims of the misconduct or critics of your company.

So, what do the news media want from you or your company as the news about an ethics scandal unfolds? Reporters want a quick response to their inquires. They want you (your company) to be forthcoming as quickly as is reasonable and appropriate with the details of a scandal. This includes answers to the classic questions including: what happened; who was involved; when did it happen; where did it happen; how did it happen; and why did it happen. Further, journalists expect to know the impact of the unethical conduct, what are you doing now and what happens next. Journalists want spokespersons to be candid and honest in answering questions. They want access to those who have primary knowledge of the situation, including ethics compliance officers, managers or others who are directly involved with the scandal.

Role of the Spokesperson

During an ethics crisis or scandal, it is best to have a single voice from your company presenting the facts as accurately, quickly and credibly as possible to create and maintain an image of professionalism and integrity. In most scandals there is an expectation that the senior management or the chief executive will personally speak to the media. It may be possible to designate a spokesperson for some situations; however, surviving a scandal will ultimately require senior management to speak to the media, be interviewed, and communicate to key audiences through multiple channels.

The spokesperson is the point person who communicates the message to the public, whether that message is an apology for wrongdoing, an announcement of a dangerous product recall or instructions on how to communicate with the company during an ethical crisis. He or she becomes the face of the company at press conferences and interviews. This person represents the business to the public and the media and concentrates the message into one voice to ensure its accuracy and effectiveness. Every employee should know to whom to refer questions in order to ensure the consistent repetition of a coherent message.

Choosing and Preparing Your Spokesperson

Generally, there is one spokesperson speaking for the company at a time, although that person may be accompanied by others who can provide the spokesperson with specific details of the situation. However, this does not mean that only one individual should be designated as the spokesperson. Crises can extend for weeks and months, and it is impractical to assume that a single person could withstand the stress of a sustained 24/7 operation week after week. Additionally, it is possible that key team members could be out of position when a crisis breaks, so it is advantageous to have one or more backup spokespersons. In any case, it is prudent to designate and train multiple spokespersons ahead of time. It is also wise to coordinate among spokespersons to ensure that all messages sent to stakeholders are consistent.

A spokesperson can be a member of the crisis management team or a chief executive of the company. Analyze your situation and identify the person who is the best match for your circumstances. The spokesperson's level in the business should be appropriate to the seriousness of the crisis. Obviously, if the CEO or chairman serves as the spokesperson, his or her presence would validate the magnitude and the sincere concern that the company places on the issue. The CEO is also the most highly visible and recognizable member of your business. Further, there is a need to get your message out in a very personal and authoritative manner. This may be most easily accomplished by a statement and comments from the most senior managers in a timely and appropriate setting.

There is an expectation from both your stakeholders and critics that senior management will speak during a crisis to explain what happened, what impacts resulted, what is currently being done and what will happen next. This exigency will also exist in the assumptions that news journalists and reporters bring to covering the scandal. Consider that after the *Exxon Valdez* ran aground, spilling 240,000 barrels of crude oil that eventually covered 2,600 square miles of the pristine Prince William Sound, Exxon chairman Lawrence Rawl was roundly criticized for not commenting on the disaster for nearly six days—and then choosing to make the company's apology from New York.[1] Many crisis communication experts believe that Rawl's tardy response and failure to appear on the scene further infuriated the public and harmed the company's credibility, which may have allowed public resentment to linger more than a decade after the highly publicized disaster.[2]

Characteristics of an Effective Spokesperson

You may be the most appropriate spokesperson for your company. You may be one of several senior managers who are the most appropriate spokespersons for your company. You may be a manager who has been designated as a spokesperson for your company. You may be in a support position to help prepare and support a senior manager or designated spokesperson for your company. In each of these roles, it is important for you to have an idea of the characteristics of an effective spokesperson. If you choose to delegate the responsibility of understanding these characteristics, then you risk a strategic failure in getting your message out in a timely and appropriate manner.

An effective spokesperson should have experience in public speaking and be able to remain calm under stressful situations. Long before a crisis strikes, the spokesperson(s) should have extensive media training. If there is no one in-house who can train personnel, look for consultants or companies that perform media training.

Never forget that the spokesperson is the voice of your business and can thus exert significant control over the process of maintaining, repairing and restoring your firm's image and reputation. The spokesperson must be knowledgeable about the crisis management plan, the crisis communication plan, as well as all of the underlying policies, mission and business operations. He or she should have a rich understanding of the overall business objectives and strategies. The spokesperson should have extensive training in public speaking, argument, question answering and media relations. He or she must hold the confidence of all of the senior managers and executives of the company. The spokesperson is entrusted with tremendous responsibility and needs to act with confidence and support. He or she should be highly motivated and willing to engage in this challenging role.

Crisis Communication Best Practice Guideline #4: Spokesperson Tips

- Speak in personal terms whenever possible.
- Word choice is important–carefully choose specific and precise words.
- If you don't want information or a statement reported and attributed to you, then don't say or provide it.
- Simple, clear and concise phrases are most likely to be reported.
- Use sound bite phrases that encapsulate larger themes.

- If issues are complex or complicated, then it is important to say so (frequently).
- Use a relaxed and conversational tone (avoid appearing confrontational).
- Never lie–tell as much of the truth as you can.
- Explain why you can not disclose confidential information.
- Appearance and non-verbal signals are as important as words–meta-messages can speak just as loudly as your words.
- Never say the phrase "no comment".
- If you not know the answer to a question, it is permissible to say so (but it is better to promise to find the answer and get back to the reporter).

Managing the Message

When an ethical lapse or incident of misconduct occurs, it is important to get your response and the facts out quickly. Your message will need to be crafted, coordinated and communicated in a variety of channels. The message will need to be appropriately timed and delivered. The message that you create should be consistent and coordinated. All of your individual messages need to be consistent and complementary. Messages need to be managed.

The most important facts should always be included in the very first part of any public message. Never exaggerate the situation in your message. The message should attempt to build or retain trust with your audience. Because scandals are a direct threat to your firm's image and reputation, the message should be crafted with a view towards retaining or reestablishing aspects of image and reputation. Word choice is also vital when communicating during the crisis to ensure the message is presented clearly and does not cause overreaction. Literal, precise and specific words are always preferred.

As we have emphasized, make an effort to understand the expectations and information needs of all key stakeholders. Do not underestimate their general need to know and for reassurance that you are acting ethically and with professionalism. It is very important that your message is perceived as honest. Within the constraints of legal requirements and proprietary business concerns, your message should be as forthright and honest as is legally and prudently possible. Even if the news you report is negative, it is always better for stakeholders to learn negative information directly from the company rather than to have it discovered and presented in the news media. In such cases, the negative impact of the information is amplified by the implicit impression of a possible cover-up or reluctance to disclose the information. Efforts to stall, hide bad news and stonewall in the midst of emerging scandals are at the root of many of the most damaging and disastrous ethics scandals over the past quarter century.

Your message should create an image of your company taking action and not simply passively enduring the crisis. Statements should be phrased in ways that are action-oriented, stating what you are doing about the scandal and crisis. It is even helpful to use general phrases when you have nothing else to disclose—you should be "taking all appropriate measures, working around the clock, involving all critical personnel, devoted fully to resolving or learning more, and moving without delay or hesitation."

Your message must consistently define your business, personnel and operations (including company polices) in positive, professional and ethical terms. It should draw upon the themes and values expressed in your corporate mission statement and adhere to your existing statements of ethics, codes of conduct and ethical norms expected of all employees, managers and executives.

If the scandal or misconduct harmed individuals or groups in some way, then your message should be one of compassion for those who have suffered or been negatively affected. Your message must express concern and empathy for anyone who has suffered as a consequence of the misconduct, without necessarily assuming blame or responsibility. Many people who do not have the same knowledge and experience as you will hear what you communicate. Do not craft a message that may be perceived as insensitive or appearing to lack compassion or concern.

Your message should be created with wording that describes the scandal or crisis from the viewpoint of public interest and social norms, not just from that of your company or your company's legal counsel. While there is an appropriate time and place for analysis from a business or legal standpoint, your public messages must clearly demonstrate your understanding of and commitment to expected social standards of ethical conduct from a greater social good standpoint.

Many aspects of your message can be prepared in advance. Have some general scripts of messages that endorse your core values and reaffirm your commitments. It may help to have pre-planned scenarios, detailed response action plans and pre-made statements ahead of time. The crisis communication team may want to create a pool of possible ethical problem scenarios that can affect your business and prepare sample press releases, statements, possible questions and answers, and pertinent background information sheets. It may also want to create videos samples or sound bites ahead of time that can be used as templates when actual events explode in the news media or as training materials during practice drills.

Although some basic messages can be prepared in advance, a coordinated comprehensive message strategy appropriate to a specific crisis will only emerge with active teamwork and attentive management. The specific selection of when, where, and how to get the strategic messages to your audiences is an essential aspect of surviving the impact of a scandal on your company. There are some key aspects of handling a public scandal that may increase your capability to successfully weather the storm.

Be Available

Your first instinct when news of a scandal in your company breaks is to go into seclusion and hope that it all just goes away. Unfortunately, this first instinct is a strategic mistake and should be resisted. No one likes the thought of Mike Wallace and the *60 Minutes* news crew, let alone a Michael Moore type of aggressive "gonzo" style of interview journalism, waiting to interview us in our office lobbies, but it is important to make yourself available. Avoiding the press will itself become another aspect of the scandal that will further enlarge the impact of the public image disaster for you and your company. Obviously, you should be prepared and practiced at answering difficult questions. You should also understand the nature, role and function of the journalist interview.

Always get on top of an emerging story. It is always better to be proactive rather than reactive. This may be your best opportunity to frame an emerging story and to define your company's character and reaction to news of the ethics breakdown. Immediately after a story breaks or your business issues a press release about an ethical lapse, people will begin knocking on your doors looking for more information. Someone from the crisis communication team needs to be available at every hour of the day to answer to stakeholders, particularly the press, who may be on different time schedules, office hours or time zones, than the rest of your business. Even if your team is doing something outside the office, there should always be someone knowledgeable available to answer the phone with statements and detailed information. In addition, this person should have all necessary contact information for other personnel who can address the situation.

It may also be necessary for you to take a series of proactive steps to make yourself available to the news media and public. Your stakeholders want to hear from you as the news of the ethics scandal reaches them. Getting on top or ahead of the story in the news cycle may be an effective means of de-escalating the potential threat of the scandal. Further, if you remain silent while your critics and antagonists are vocal with negative perspectives about the scandal, you risk an escalating disaster.

An emerging scandal creates an information vacuum that needs to be filled as soon as possible. If you do not fill the void, someone else will, and they may not have your firm's or your stakeholders' best interests in mind. Withholding information can cast a guilty shadow. In contrast, openness can increase positive perceptions, even during times of crisis.

Find Allies: Join Forces with Others Sharing Your Crisis

If an ethics crisis involves partner organizations or other stakeholders, it may be beneficial to combine your efforts for press conferences instead of holding separate ones. Is the problem an industry-wide concern as opposed to a company-specific question? Find allies and others who share your boat in this issue. This will help ensure that there is agreement in messages being sent out rather than fractured or inconsistent messages. For example, the Guiliani press conferences held after the anthrax scare following the initial terrorist attacks included the health commissioner, the police commissioner, the president of NBC and Tom Brokaw.[9]

Crisis Communication Best Practice Guideline #5: Coordinate, Collaborate and Consistently Communicate

- Devote effort and resources to the slow, hard work of sustaining partnerships and alliances with your stakeholders.
- Coordinate all of your "voices" so that you have a consistent holistic message package.
- Keep listening: pay attention to feedback.
- Practice message repetition (this includes restating, reiterating, multiple voices, redundancy and repeating messages frequently).

- Use credible and authoritative intermediaries between you and your target audience.
- Be proactive in anticipating the questions that will arise from the crisis.
- Respond quickly when unanticipated questions arise.
- Cite credible sources that believe what you believe.
- Attack, blame, or scapegoat others as a defensive strategy cautiously and understand the backlash risks of such messages.

Handling the Press and News Media

The news media has evolved into a 24-hour information event, which brings with it both greater time constraints and greater demand for compelling stories to compete with the entertainment media. In this environment, your crisis communication team must become the reporter's reporter. It is the team's job to make the reporter's job easy and to supply him or her with needed information before the deadline. Thus, someone from your crisis communication team must be available at all hours of the day. The news media comprises a diverse group of individual reporters who, for the most part, work hard to communicate objective, accurate information. They are looking for concise sound bites in order to edit their stories into the time given them, often under a few minutes. Supplying them with the correct information, doled out in the right amount at the right time, will contribute to a successful public relations campaign during an ethical crisis.

The Journalist Interview: A Basic Survival Guide

When being interviewed by a news journalist there are a number of different conditions that are all too often misunderstood by interviewees. From the journalist's point of view, an interview is an interview no matter the setting or circumstances. It does not matter to the reporter whether the interview is a formal or scheduled session in your office, a sit-down session at a business location, conducted over lunch (either a five-star restaurant or local dive), riding in the adjacent seat of an airline flight or an encounter on a city sidewalk. Most journalists feel an obligation to identify themselves as a news reporter and almost all of them will tell you that you are talking to a reporter. Anything that you say to them is considered fair game for their news report. Sometimes they may also ask if they may take notes or make an (audio/video) recording of the interview, but this is not always a requirement for the conversation to be regarded as an official interview by the journalist. Even if the journalist does not take a detailed transcript or make a recording of the interview, the journalist may report anything you say as a direct quote (perhaps only recalled from the journalist's memory). If you do not wish to talk to the reporter there is no legal obligation that you do so; however, there are a number of public communication and crisis communication reasons why you might want to do so.

It may also be the case that you want to talk with the journalist but you want the interview to remain confidential. Confidentiality during interviews with journalists is one of the most misunderstand constructs that most interviewees face. There are a number of concepts that may prove confusing and disastrous to you if you fail to recognize the context under which you are speaking to the journalist. Here are some commonly used, but frequently misunderstood, terms related to issues of confidentiality during journalist interviews.

For Attribution

Conducting an interview for attribution means that the information may be used in a news report and that the source will be fully identified.

Not for Attribution

Conducting an interview not for attribution means that the information may be used in a news report, but that the source will not be identified.

Background

A background interview usually means that the reporter considers any information obtained as appropriate for including in their news report, but not for attribution. Some journalists also use this term when asking a source to educate them about technical, procedural, product, manufacturing or other issues related to the context of the scandal without seeking anything that would specifically appear in a news report.

Deep Background

This is a term that is used by some journalists when asking for information that would not be attributed and not reported unless another source that is willing to have the information attributed to them provides the same information. Typically, the existence of the original source would remain confidential, but the information provided would find its way into a public news report if there were a second source who would allow attribution.

Embargo

In journalist jargon, an embargo (often called a "press embargo") is an arrangement where a journalist is provided access to information under the provision that the information will not be released to public or included in a news report until after an agreed upon specific date or time. In many circumstances, journalists are willing to agree to information embargos in exchange for exclusive advance access to information to help them enhance the quality of their reporting and to assist them in meeting deadlines by allowing them to write some of their reports earlier than would otherwise be possible. News media (either deliberately or accidentally) periodically break embargo agreements and thus embargos should never be considered an absolute guarantee that the information shared will not appear in news reports. This is particularly probable when the nature of the scandal increases competitive pressures on journalists to scoop other reporters.

On the Record

This typically refers to any interview conducted by a journalist when he or she is taking notes, making a transcript, making a video or audio recording, is subject to being publicly reported in the news, and attributes the source of any information to the interviewee.

Off the Record

Many people misunderstand what the term off the record means to many reporters. It usually means that the reporter will not quote or attribute particular information to the interviewee. However, that information itself may still appear in news reports either un-credited or un-attributed or, perhaps, attributed simply to anonymous sources. In fact, reporters sometimes use off-the-record information to convince other sources to go on the record to corroborate the story. The important point for crisis communication is that off the record is not retroactive; it cannot be invoked after the fact. It must be stated before offering the protected information. The best advice, of course, is never to share confidential or proprietary information with a reporter—even if it is understood to be off the record.

There are times, however, when it can be useful to provide a reporter with deep background information off the record. With mainstream news reporters, you need only to state explicitly that the following information is off the record and, unless the reporter makes a mistake, the information will usually not be attributed to you as the source. With less mainstream news media, such as alternative weeklies and blogs, reporter commitments to keep your name off the record as the source of information are less reliable. Off the record information can be valuable to journalists and, unless you specifically and clearly state the terms of your disclosure, you should not be surprised to see anything you say to a reporter appear in a subsequent news story. Some news media have explicit policies prohibiting their reporters from accepting off the record information. Some journalists will use off the record and deep background information to discover the names of other potential sources who they will then seek to have go on the record for attribution of the same information.

No Comment

Some spokespeople may be tempted to respond to reporters with no comment, especially in the heat of intense questioning. Nothing can be more damaging to a business's image. Crisis communication experts universally agree on the fact that most audience members believe that the phrase "no comment" implies guilt. For many, this response insinuates that the spokesperson is either trying to conceal something or is avoiding the issue (either due to incompetence or because he or she is disorganized and unprepared to respond). None of these perceptions will help you repair your reputation and image. There may be rare instances where it is strategically necessary to not comment on a question or statement. However, even in those cases, it is better to simply not comment rather than speak the words no comment.

Crisis Communication Best Practice Guideline #6: Be Truthful, Honest, Frank, and Open

- Present facts in a sympathetic and forthright style.
- Say what you can and want to say.
- Say why you can't say what you can not say.
- Monitor meta-messages to avoid the appearance of deception, avoidance or reticence.
- Disclose risk information as soon as possible; fill information vacuums.
- If you can not answer a direct question state why.
- If information is evolving or incomplete, emphasize appropriate reservations about its reliability.
- If in doubt, lean toward sharing more information, not less—otherwise people may think something significant is being hidden or withheld.

- If you do not know or are unsure about an answer, express willingness to get back to the questioner with a response by an agreed upon deadline.
- Avoid speculation.
- Never lie.
- Discuss data and information uncertainties (strengths and weaknesses).
- If errors are made, correct them quickly.
- Answer every question in the most appropriate manner.

If the spokesperson does not know the answer to a reporter's or other stakeholder's question, instead of saying, "no comment," he or she should say something to the effect of, "I don't know, but I will find out for you." The spokesperson should record the inquirer's contact information and then re-contact that person quickly with an appropriate response. If the spokesperson makes a promise to find out information, then he or she must follow through.

Handling Misinformation

Occasionally you will face a situation where misinformation has found its way into news reports or public opinion. It may even be included within a question asked directly by a reporter. Misinformation can be especially damaging as it tends to be the basis for rumors and escalating negative publicity. Obviously, you will need to be prepared to handle instances of misinformation. This requires you to have accurate, up-to-date and relevant information to provide in exchange for the inaccurate information.

You may perceive misinformation in almost every media story. A news report can never give the entire story to your satisfaction. This is an inherent reductionistic aspect of the process of reporting. You need to focus on specific instances of inaccurate or misinformation and not surrender to the temptation to disagree (and try to rewrite) every sentence of a news story. Pick your battles carefully, otherwise you may become mired down in a depressing cycle of arguing every minor point and issue with every news story (an inevitably losing proposition). However, sometimes there will be specific factually inaccurate information that is significant enough (having a substantial influence on understanding the issue or perhaps impacting your overall message strategy) that you may choose to clarify.

At times you will want to respond and correct misinformation (and perhaps ask for a retraction), but not all misinformation calls for immediate alarm and effort-seeking correction or retraction. There are a few rules of thumb to keep in mind. If it is not vital information, sometimes it is best to just let it go. It may be sufficient to call the news station or the reporter and ask that the information be corrected in their files so that it is not reported incorrectly again. Remember that when you ask for a printed or broadcast correction, it may make audiences remember the error more or remind them of aspects that do not serve your interests. Thus, it may be better to just ignore some instances of misinformation.

When you contact the media, remember that the reporter and/ or editor may get defensive if he or she feels it is an insult to his or her journalistic abilities. Sometimes it is appropriate to write a letter to the editor to get the facts straight. On rare occasions, you will want to have a correction printed, such as when incorrect numbers may affect your stock price. However, it may be the best strategy to incorporate the accurate and correct information in your message strategy and use the strategy of repetition to more gradually ensure that the correct information is reported.

Presentation Tips

Your business's future reputation lies in the choices made by your spokesperson. Your spokesperson cannot over-prepare. Like most managers, your spokesperson may have achieved great career success, may effectively handle a significant amount of responsibilities, and may believes that he or she does not need advice or coaching, or need to practice presentation skills. However, like any specialized skill, everyone can benefit from supplemental coaching and training with presentation skills. Do not resist the advice and assistance of trained communication professionals and consultants to ensure that your communication skills are at their peak performance readiness. Consider supplemental training for communication skills. Remember, the presentation of the message is just as important as the content of the message. Thus, it is important to ensure that one's communication skills are superior at all times.

Crisis Communication Best Practice Guideline #7: Communicate Clearly and with Compassion

- Use clear, non-technical language that is appropriate to the audience.
- Use graphics and other pictorial material to clarify messages when appropriate.
- Use stories, narratives, examples and anecdotes to make

technical data come alive.

- Avoid embarrassing people, if possible.
- Respect the unique communication needs of special and diverse audiences.
- Express genuine empathy when appropriate.
- Avoid using distant, abstract and unfeeling language.
- Acknowledge and respond in words, gestures and actions to emotions that people express, such as anxiety, fear, anger, outrage and helplessness.
- Acknowledge and respond to the distinctions that the public views as important in evaluating risks.
- Always try to include a discussion of actions that are under way or can be taken.
- Be sensitive to local norms, such as speech and dress.
- Strive for brevity, but respect requests for information and offer to provide desired information within a specified time period.
- Promises only what you can deliver, then follow through.
- Understand that trust is earned—do not merely ask or expect to be trusted by the public.

Answering Questions

Your spokesperson should know how to handle tough questions, provide appropriate answers, use his or her voice effectively, and be aware of his or her nonverbal communication. It is important to attempt to anticipate what might be asked. This should be done before the interview or conference with members of the crisis communication team. It may be useful to repeat or paraphrase a question to ensure it is understood. Always maintain direct eye contact with those who are asking questions. It may be necessary to diffuse hostile questions by rewording the statements in more objective terms, clarifying misstatements, breaking multiple-part questions down into a series of questions and creating an answer that is not merely a yes or no. An effective and credible spokesperson is never afraid to say "I don't know" if, in fact, he or she does not know the answer to a given question. It is important to keep answers short, direct and to the point. A skilled spokesperson can handle non-questions politely and use these as opportunities to keep pushing the central message.

An effective spokesperson uses his or her voice successfully to create a conversational and credible presence when interacting with news media. An effective spokesperson understands the implications of various nonverbal communication cues and how stakeholder audiences might interpret various nonverbal behaviors. For example, a monotone style coupled with rigid non-verbal expressions may create an image that is interpreted as being insincere and conveying a lack of compassion and, perhaps, even deception. Furthermore, failure to establish eye contact (in electronic media interaction as well as face to face interaction) may be interpreted as a sign of deliberate deception. It is important to note that interpreting nonverbal symbols as well as expected norms for nonverbal behaviors vary from culture to culture around the world. These differences can lead to serious instances of misunderstanding and context-specific inappropriate behaviors.

It is essential to understand your audience, their expectations and interpretative rules, and the limits of your ability to adapt to expectations that are beyond your capabilities. In North American culture, for example, direct eye contact implies trust and sincerity. Lack of direct eye contact (indirect) implies untruthfulness. In other cultures, eye contact is a highly intimate act that would be inappropriate in a public information setting such as a press conference. In a press conference held within the context of the dominant North American culture, the spokesperson should approach the lectern, then turn and look directly at the audience and the cameras to signal that he or she is ready to begin talking, and maintain that eye contact for the duration of the conference. There are also variations in non-verbal norms and expectations for body motion, use of time, use of space, and appearance. Even on a fundamental level, the spokesperson needs to speak in a conversational style (avoid simply reading whenever possible) and use movement strategically to maintain the audience's attention. Body movement can distract or sustain the audience's attention.

Handling Difficult and Challenging Questions

Reporters tend to ask lengthy questions that contain an assertion or conclusion and then ask the spokesperson to respond with a yes or no answer. This tactic enables them to put the words they include in the question into the voice of the respondent. By affirming "yes" to these lengthy questions, the spokesperson must understand that he or she has essentially become the source for any words, phrases or opinions that are included in the wording of the question. Likewise, a response of "no" may be taken by the reporter in many cases as a denial of all or part of the assumptions embedded in the question.

Therefore, it can sometimes be tricky to simply answer a question with a simple yes or no and not inadvertently say things that one did not intend to say. As a general rule, try to respond to questions with an answer that states facts, your message, and is generally responsive to the intent of the question. If a question is simple, straightforward and direct, then it may be possible to respond with an equally simple yes or no answer. However, the longer (usually with assumptions and conjecture) questions are usually more appropriately answered with a statement that responds but does not affirm or deny embedded assumptions of questions.

Look Out for Implied Questions

Some questioners will insist on yes or no responses and others will offer a multiple-choice response of the questioner's choosing. For example, a reporter might ask, "Did procedural flaws cause the ethical lapse or was it poor management that led to the scandal?" The proposed responses unfairly limit the discussion of possible causes of the scandal to procedural flaws or management error, neither of which might be appropriate. Spokespersons must critically assess whether the response choices offered are fair and appropriate before answering.

Correct Erroneous Information and Assumptions

If a question includes an erroneous statistic or statement of fact as part of the presumption on which the question is based, make sure that it is clear in the response. The errors implicit (or explicit) in the question must be challenged and corrected. Merely answering such questions without challenging or correcting the erroneous information may be taken as acquiescence and agreement with the facts as presented in the question.

Break Down the Multi-Part Question

Sometimes a reporter will put forward a long, complicated, multi-part question. In this instance, the best approach is to ask the questioner to rephrase the question or to break it into separate questions. It also may be effective to specify which part or parts of the question the spokesperson is responding to. At the very least, the spokesperson should label or number the parts of the answer corresponding to the various parts of the question.

Be Aware of Passive-Aggressive-Type Questions

Some questions are inherently tricky in presenting double-bind dilemmas, meaning that no matter how you answer them, you will appear to be guilty of malfeasance. The question, "When did you stop dumping chemicals into the river?" illustrates the problem. It is appropriate to provide a tactful preface to answering such questions, perhaps taking the opportunity to note that there are no simple answers and a longer than usual response may be necessary to fully and fairly respond to the inquiry. It may be the case that the question cannot be answered as asked with a simple answer and, in this case, it is imperative that the response explains why.

The final part of your message plan should include effectively responding to difficult questions in a manner that demonstrates poise and creates a sympathetic spokesperson for the business. Do not avoid or mishandle questions simply because of stress or limited time and information constraints. This is an opportunity to demonstrate effective leadership by communicating with the news media and public during a difficult and trying time.

A spokesperson must appear in control yet concerned about the events of the scandal. The spokesperson should always tell the truth. Statements should be concise and clear. The spokesperson should seize every opportunity to correct errors and misinformation stated in questions or comments. He or she should appear sensitive, organized and demonstrate respect for the various audiences. A spokesperson should offer sympathy and concern for those who have been harmed. He or she must appear pleasant on camera. A spokesperson should offer to find out information that is unknown and must follow up on all promises made.

Answering challenging questions involves the ability to listen, process and then respond strategically. The spokesperson must be able to identify the implied, passive/aggressive or multi-part question. If a speaker cannot recognize these questions, he or she is more likely to admit to something that is not true. Your spokesperson should answer only direct questions and should be able to break down or rephrase indirect, implied and multi-part inquiries. He or she must focus on both delivery and content when answering questions from the public. Delivering important and truthful information to the public is as important as the manner in which it is delivered. Also, the spokesperson must keep the needs of the company's multiple audiences in mind.

The ability to recognize and effectively answer challenging questions are valuable skills that will help your business communicate with the public in a responsible and positive way. For example, in the event of breaking news of a scandal, an immediate appearance and presentation that communicates all relevant information as quickly as possible to affected stakeholders will help address their concerns. This also creates a meta-message of decisive action, cooperation, control and commitment to a corrective solution as attributes of you and your company. In fact, one of the biggest tasks that you will face in the days, weeks and months ahead is to get your message out to your key audiences. Determining how you can most effectively reach those audiences is part of implementing the crisis communication plan.

Getting the Message Out: Choosing the Best Channels

To successfully survive an EMD requires you to speak out and get your message act together. To repair or restore damaged reputation, reclaim your brand and image, and to heal the wounds inflicted on your relationships with stakeholders, constituents, employees, customers, suppliers, neighbors and investors, it is imperative that you craft a message that will address all of the concerns and appropriately position your company for recovery. However, even the best-formed message strategy is worthless if you can't reach the key audiences that you need to reach. You cannot rely on the news media (alone) to get your message out to your key audiences. You have to choose from a variety of communication technologies that will allow you to directly reach out to critical audiences with your well-crafted message plan. These technologies may be cost effective and enable you to get your message directly to specific audiences without the gatekeeping mediation of the news media. However, not all of these channels can reach all of your target audiences. Therefore, it is important to understand the options and to make strategic choices as to how best to get your message to your target audiences.

It is essential to get your message out rapidly without delay. There is often little time to reflect, so decisions about messages should be prepared in advance as much as possible. There is a vast assortment of methods for communicating with stakeholders. However, only you can decide what is best for your business and your audiences. It is also important that your message is consistent and compatible across all of these channels because many of them overlap and all of them will be subject to media scrutiny–looking for inconsistency among your messages. After a crisis breaks, routine forms of public communication should be implemented, such as sending out press releases and/or mass e-mails, updating your website, and setting up 800 numbers with a call center. In addition to these primary channels, you can expand your initial communication with press conferences, online conferences, backgrounders, briefings, seminars, interviews, talk shows, satellite media tours, personal conferences, or dinners. There are also a number of new communication channels blossoming, such as blogs, chat rooms, instant messaging and text messaging, that can be explored. Finally, sometimes the media is the best way to communicate to your employees, shareholders, customers and other stakeholders. Newspaper and television ads, op-ed pieces, and letters to the editor can also be used to communicate to your stakeholders.

Traditional Press Conferences

If the crisis affecting your business is large enough, a press conference (a "presser" in journalist jargon) may be expected. A presser is one of the most traditional and expected events to be held after a major exigency has occurred. Since these exigencies are easy enough to recognize, you should have no problem in getting the press to attend. (In the event that you call for a press conference and no news media is sufficiently interested to attend, you probably are not facing an exigency sufficient to sustain a press conference format). However, remember that press conferences have been disparaged by many businesses, and editors do not appreciate spending reporters' time at press conferences for trivial matters that could easily have been handled with a press release.

Utilizing a press conference leaves you still dependent on the news media to get your message out to key audiences. Therefore, there are potential risks of gatekeeping and message filtering that you must consider. Also, remember that the news media are on the lookout for sound bites or small samples of your message presented at your press conference to report to their audiences. This sampling process will result in only a small part of what you provide directly reaching audiences. With that in mind, make sure that you are scheduling a press conference for something worthy, and that there are no better ways to contact your audience efficiently and uniformly.

Location

First, choose a location for the press conference. It does not need to be in a fancy ballroom, but it does need to be convenient for the members of the press who are expected to attend. The locations should be a large enough space to accommodate the number of people you are inviting, as well as press equipment and camera crews, tables and chairs, and a few booths. It should also have a sufficient power source for the broadcast media needs.

Time

If your public relations department has already established relationships with the media, they should know their time schedules. Make sure you are holding the press conference at a convenient time, such as late morning, right after the camera crews have been given their assignments. It also gives them time to prepare the information for the evening newscast. However, if your business is undergoing a crisis that is affecting a broad range of people, it may be necessary, at least in the first days, to have daily, or even twice-daily, press briefings if information needs warrant.

Layout

The room should have areas for coats and belongings, chairs and/ or tables (depending upon time constraints and abilities), an area for camera crews, refreshment tables, booths for information and a greeting area. All this information should be made available to the guests so they know where everything is. It can be incorporated in their invitations or in information packets upon arrival.

Invitations

If you are planning a conference a few days ahead of time, instead of a few hours, you want to send out invitations to all media contacts. Do not invite some and not others—an action that could create animosity. On the date of the conference, greet each guest as he or she comes in the door. There should also be a booth with personnel handing out press kits that include all vital information and resources. These should be specialized for their recipients—varying for radio vs. print, national vs. local, etc.

Accommodations

Accommodate media crews as much as possible, including providing power. If preparing an ad hoc press conference, it might be in a remote location. After a plane crash off the Pacific Coast near Oxnard California, authorities set up a communications center in the parking lot of the Coast Guard station. In situations like this, you may not be able to accommodate power and other needs. However, if possible, you might be obliged to provide somewhere for them to sleep and/ or refreshments.

Online Press Conferences

A new, developing form of conferences is the e-conference, or web-based conference. While these are costly and require just as much prior planning as a traditional conference, they do not require you to rent an actual facility, supply refreshments and address other physical needs. They can be set up by professional businesses skilled in this area or by websites that host conferences, (e.g. WebEx™). Instead of supplying guests with a physical address, you supply them with a web address. The online conference can include voice, text, data, including graphics and video content.

The e-conference can function as a traditional press conference. There is opportunity for questions and answers, follow-up, and presentation of company statements. To access the e-conference, a reporter needs only internet access, making attending the e-conference easier and increasing the likelihood of media exposure.

E-mail, Instant Messages, Web Pages, and Podcasting

As technology inexorably continues to advance in the coming years, this discussion of communication channels and technology will become obsolete. At some point in the future, many of these technology rich communication channels will merge into a unified and interconnected real time network that will broadly expand the options for disseminating information and perspective to your various constituent audiences. This will enable the interconnecting of streaming video, voice, electronic text, digital data packets, video/tele-conferencing, internet web content, podcasting and new emerging communication devices. Rather than viewing these options as separate and de-coupled, future corporate communicators will be able to get their information and point of view out faster, with fewer gatekeepers and message filters, and targeted to very specific (and narrow) constituent audiences. However, for the next few years until this integration occurs, corporate communication decision-makers will have to select specific channels for reaching specific audiences in a more piecemeal fashion.

Many nontraditional forms of communication are sprouting to form a patchwork of different communication technologies, each with specific advantages and limitations for getting your message out to your target audiences. Your business may want to consider using them in the event of a crisis. Your company's website should be updated regularly during a crisis with information for employees, community members, customers, shareholders, and the media. Your website can also be an excellent backup source during a crisis as the telephone lines can quickly be jammed with people looking for information.

If your employees or other stakeholders are avid users of chat rooms, instant messaging, text messaging, or blogs, then these might be appropriate medium to communicate with them. There are millions of blogs, or web-based journals, on a variety of topics, including companies, brands, and products. Companies are increasingly establishing blogs to interact with their stakeholders, and these can be harnessed to repeat consistent messages during a crisis. Companies can even create internal blogs for communicating specific information to employees and external blogs to communicate other messages to the press and the public.[3] During a crisis, it may also be beneficial to monitor what individual bloggers are saying about your company through services such as *technorati.com*. This monitoring may reveal that stakeholder perceptions about your company and its situation are worse (or better) than feared and the service provider may suggest ways to modify your messages to make them more effective.

Podcasts are audio files available through the Internet or MP3 players, which provide another opportunity to communicate with stakeholders. A podcast is simply a web feed of audio, video or data files that is placed on the Internet and made available for download. One can manually download the files directly from the website to allow for the pull of information by audience members. There are also programs that let users preprogram their devices in order to automatically download and store the digital files at predetermined scheduled times so that they are available when the user chooses to access the information. Podcasts are particularly useful for recording emergency instructions for employees, such as what critical documents to grab or where to assemble after an evacuation.[4] These podcasts provide a way to distribute audio as an addition to existing text (or mostly text) web, fax or other text-based products. There are several services available for publishing podcasts, including *ipodder. com* and *odeo.com*.

In the event of a crisis, mass e-mails or instant messaging may be the simplest way to contact a large number of people at one time. There are a number of products on the market that can be utilized for this function. Instant messaging offers a real time communication exchange capability that utilizes a specialized program that immediately enables interactive communication. Unfortunately, the attempts at creating a unified standard for instant messaging have failed and each of the major providers uses their own proprietary technology and protocols, which render them essentially incompatible. This may change in the future. Instant messaging has grown in availability and popularity particularly among teens and young adults. Many companies have established instant message portals to provide FAQ information and to answer specific questions. These features might be valuable during an emerging scandal to provide a fast, consistent, and reliable channel for communication with specific key constituents. Instant messaging is now interconnected with the telephone network, allowing interaction with target audiences via computer, mobile phones or landline phones.

Automated Message Systems and Toll Free Telephone Numbers

Automated message and notification systems give organizations the ability to broadcast voice, text or data to any number of people within seconds using a variety of different communication channels. The advantages of such a system include ready availability, high reliability, security, capability to target select audiences with specific messages, ease of use and cost effectiveness. These systems utilize a combination of electronic mail, text messaging, internet, telephone and alternative channels to rapidly and accurately disseminate a specific message to targeted audiences.

A toll free number already reserved can be activated or converted to use to answer questions from employees, customers, the public and the media. If possible, connect this number to a call center with trained personnel briefed on the situation and how to handle questions. Make sure they know not to say no comment, to refer press questions to the crisis communications team, and that it is okay to say, "I don't know, but I'll find out for you." Then, they must make sure to get back to the caller. One California university has a call center set up in Texas to answer parent and public inquires in case there is a crisis situation on their campus. A call center or 800 number should be distributed well in advance of any crisis and clearly inform users that, in the event of a crisis, your regular telephone lines may be overwhelmed and this source of information can be relied upon for consistent and accurate messages. It might even be possible to target various stakeholders and constituent audiences with variations of access codes or extensions to even more precisely target specific messages and information to specific groups. While you can push the information and instructions for using these technologies, it ultimately relies on the knowledge, skills, and abilities of your callers to pull the messages and information from you.

A personalized message from a CEO or other top management voice may be directed to employees, stakeholders, customers, vendors, and other key constituents. Such a message can be pushed by means of an automated message system or available for pulling from a dedicated toll-free informational telephone hotline.

Backgrounders, Briefings, and Seminars

Backgrounders, briefings and seminars are informational sessions to inform reporters and other stakeholders about issues relating to the crisis. They help to increase the knowledge surrounding a specific issue or topic. A backgrounder is an informal and often extended session with one or more reporters. A backgrounder allows you the opportunity to explain the variable factors, context and more complicated issues that would be essential to understand, comprehend, or, more to the point, report the story. These can be conducted over the telephone, via e-mail, or face-to-face.

A briefing is a session that is most often used following an initial wide-cast press conference. If the press conference is the big event where important statements, disclosures, and events are reported, then briefings are the lower key and more modest sessions that follow in the aftermath. Briefings, by definition, typically update facts and statistics, report on developments, and are invariably handled by lower level personnel. Your senior management may be expected to be in attendance at a press conference, but it is unlikely that even the most junior reporter would expect to see your senior management attend the periodic briefings.

Seminars are extended sessions where you bring in professionals, commentators, scholars, researchers, analysts and other experts to meet with the news media and reporters to provide additional (and perhaps unbiased) insight, applied expertise and knowledge that would be helpful to reporters to understand, comprehend, and report the story. In an ethics scandal, you might want to bring business ethics scholars, employee behavior researchers, training experts, or experts from the Integrity Institute to help educate the reporters, as well as to provide more extensive analysis and information about employee ethical behaviors, the efficacy of ethical compliance programs, types of ethics training programs' success rates, or even the consequences of an EMD.

One of the faster growing applications of the seminar approach with the news media is the advent of "webinars." Webinars allow your company to put select experts on-line via a company website and promote their availability through a wide variety of promotional means. Reporters, as well as interested member of the general public (including your stakeholders and various constituents), can access the web page at the designated time and watch and listen to presentations by the experts, as well as engage them in real time interactive question and answer sessions. Such webinars are a great attraction to reporters who can access these conferences while remaining at their work desks and seamlessly integrate the materials and comments from the experts into their reporting stories. In addition, such technology can allow you to bring the expertise of a wide variety of worldwide experts into contact with reporters and the public in very short order. Such webinar technology solves the challenge of gathering your experts from across great distances and makes them instantly available and easily accessible to a worldwide audience.

Like the advent of on-line webinars, communication technology has changed rapidly in the past decade and continues to do so. There are many ways of getting your message out directly to your target audiences without relying on the news media to filter or scrutinize your message. It is critical to expand your thinking to keep pace with the new emerging communication channels to get your message out. The webinar is one of many important ways to circumvent the spin of the news media coverage of your EMD and get your message out to the public.

As you assess the rapidly emerging communication technology, there are two important principles to keep in mind. These two key principals are the push and pull communication factors. The push dimension includes the need to get your information (or corrected information) out to the public and media and typically follows the traditional approaches of outgoing messages. Usually, the audiences are fairly passive in this dimension and you must take all of the initiative to get your message out to them. You should evaluate the best channels and technologies to help you quickly and efficiently push information out to all of your targeted audiences. The pull dimension is the desire and ability for all of your constituent target audiences to come and find the information and messages from you. This relies on the motivation, skills and abilities of your various audiences to find the information that they need. Some key audiences will be compelled to seek some information out and may visit your websites, call your offices, and search out information on accessible databases on their own initiative. It may even be possible to create both the incentive and means by which key audiences may come seeking information from you. Good crisis communication plans incorporate both push and pull dimensions as part of the overall strategy of getting messages out to the targeted audiences.

News Show Interviews and Talk Show Appearances

Another means to speak directly with the public and your constituents is to use interviews and local or national talk shows. If the scandal is only local news, you should consider regional broadcast opportunities to get your chief executive speaking in a personal way to the public. As the size of the scandal grows into a national news focus, you should consider other options to get a personal appearance scheduled in national platforms. One tactic to survive a major scandal and repair your company's reputation may be to schedule an appearance on *The Larry King Show* (CNN) or on *The Today Show* (NBC). If the scandal has become a major national story, you might consider an appearance by your chief executive on a Sunday morning news/policy analysis show.

These options can be used to inform various audiences about what is going on and to bring more light to a topic. Both local and national media offer a variety of unedited (or sparsely edited) avenues to speak to the public. Do not underestimate the power of a national (or local) television or radio interview where you have the opportunity to get your message out without extensive censorship. It is amazing how important a visit to the *Larry King Show* might be for your company CEO in the midst of a major ethics scandal if you feel that your side of the story is not otherwise getting out to the general public. There are a wide variety of radio and television opportunities that should be considered.

Although most senior executives may not like this advice, it is important for the person at the top to come forward and speak directly to the media and the public. Particularly during an ethics crisis, a personal touch is needed. Impersonal messages and impersonal channels for reaching audiences may only exacerbate the negative fallout from the scandal. Delegating talk show and news conference appearances to lower level public information workers may itself become a part of the news cycle, with reporters raising questions about the absence of senior executives or top management voices during the throes of the scandal. Adequately prepare senior executives and then get them talking in ways that personalize them and provide a sense of direct access to both the media and the public.

A successful talk show or news program interview requires a lot of work and coordination. It is necessary to brief the interviewee and, if needed, the reporter before the interview. The company spokesperson should be briefed about the reporter, what he or she wants, when and where the interview will take place and possible questions that may be asked. The interviewer or reporter should be briefed as to how the spokesperson prefers to be addressed, including pronunciation, and important background information on the business. This can be done in advance, before the day of the interview.

Tips for Effective Talk/News Show Appearances

- Do not use technical jargon. Use simple language that anyone can understand.

- Prepare talking points related to your message.

- Make information relevant and familiar to the audience by using specific facts or analogies.

- Refute any incorrect information or statements immediately.

- If the interviewer tries to butt in, the spokesperson should raise his or her voice slightly and finish his or her statement.

- During the interview, the spokesperson should look at the reporter, not the camera. Looking into someone's eyes implies integrity and honesty.

- If an appeal or statement to the audience occurs, then the spokesperson should look directly at the camera.

- Speak fluently and at a consistent pace.

- Ideas should flow together in appropriate sequences. Long, awkward pauses also cause listeners to question integrity and intelligence.

- Pauses can sometimes be used strategically, but they may also be taken as a conversation switch indicator.

- The interviewer may try to use pauses in the conversation to make the interviewee feel like he or she needs to speak more. Do not let this conversation squeeze cause you to say something that you might regret saying.

- It is the interviewer's job to keep the interview rolling. Do not feel obligated to fill the gaps in the conversation.

- Information should not be volunteered that is not already known, requested by the interviewer or part of your strategic message plan.

- The spokesperson should be polite and conversational, yet firm and assertive.

These appearances are high stakes opportunities to humanize your company and get your message out to the public. A bad performance can likewise become a major setback to your reputation survival.

Satellite Media Interviews

Like the webinar, a satellite media tour allows a spokesperson or select experts to connect with various reporters for live interviews around the country or the world in a few hours. Unlike the webinar, these are not inexpensive options. Although they are very costly, they are likely more cost-effective and certainly more time-effective than sending the spokesperson in person to various media broadcast locations.

Live feed uplink broadcasting studios require basic television camera(s) and audio equipment, production equipment, studio lighting, sound dampening walls/floors, special air condition ing systems and a small television set. The audio is typically two-way interactive, which allows an interviewer at a remote location to conduct the interview first-person with the interviewee. The video and audio data can be transmitted via fiber optic cable, internet connections, telephone lines, or broadcast in microwave feeds to a regional receptor. It is feasible to produce a live broadcast interview and record an interview for later (and repeated) playback in the broadcast media news cycle.

The choice is to either have an in-house or leased satellite live feed uplink studio. Some large corporations, universities, foundations and agencies build live feed uplink broadcasting studios inside of their existing facilities. To build and equip such a studio in your facility requires a great investment and there are on-going costs. Rental costs are not inexpensive, but at least you can choose when and how to use these services. However, it is important to note that the explosion of 24/7 cablecast news media channels and the need of local stations to have news content has created an opportunity for firms that have the capability to provide live feed uplink telecast content to reach a vast audience.

It is a fairly simple matter, once the logistics and facility choices have been made, to make your spokesperson or senior executives available. While this method does not completely eliminate the issue of news media editing, filtering and gatekeeping, the high demand for live feed commentary provides a great opportunity to get your message out to a wide variety of audiences no matter how poorly you are faring in the editorial process regarding the scandal that has rocked your company. After that, the same basic principles for successfully giving interviews to the news media should ensure an effective representation of your message in widely distributed media outlets.

Personal Conferences

All of the above strategies can be used to inform a wide variety of constituents. Part of the problem with modern public relations is the lack of relationship between those in charge of the company and those in the public. The management who believes that they can simply hire a PR agency to effectively communicate to the company's constituents has (perhaps fatally) overlooked the basic rule for effectively communicating: make it personal, sincere and genuine. Even Aristotle in ancient Greece acknowledged that the most powerful form of persuasion was *ethos*, or the character and personal credibility of the individual. Particularly during an ethics crisis, a more personal touch is often needed. Impersonal messages and impersonal channels for reaching audiences may only exacerbate the negative fallout of your scandal.

You can contact the news media and your constituents directly if it makes strategic sense to do so. It may be an option to schedule a personal one-on-one session with particular individual stakeholders. This may be useful if the particular stakeholder is an opinion leader who would subsequently influence others. Talking personally to union leaders, mutual fund managers, state pension management officers, news editors, political and regulatory voices, lobbyists and even corporate critics, is a communication option that should not be left unconsidered.

In some cases, it may be appropriate to consider hosting a dinner or event for corporate shareholders or employees to inform them about what is happening, what you are doing in response, and to simply ease worries and fear.

Newspaper and Television Advertisements

It may be a useful option to consider purchasing advertisements in print and broadcast media to communicate during a scandal without interference from journalists and editors. Such advertising is usually accepted by mainstream media as long as the text is clearly labeled as a paid advertisement. Such advertisements are expected to be non-deceptive and accepted in good faith that the information content is accurate and reliable.

These may be expensive and require outside expertise to produce. Furthermore, it is rare than paid advertisements alone can be effective at getting your message out to your constituents. Nonetheless, when used prudently, paid advertising can be a part of an effective communication strategy.

Such advertisements may provide an opportunity to get your primary message out to a wide audience in an unfiltered medium. These advertisements can address issues or aspects of the scandal; however, in most cases they provide an opportunity to communicate your regret for the scandal and commitment to fixing or repairing any harm that has resulted.

Opinion Pieces and Letters to the Editor

Opinion (Op-ed) pieces can be used to inform the public about a topic related to your business that they otherwise may not be adequately informed about. Most editors, however, will insist as labeling the essay as an opinion point of view. Most of these essays are limited to approximately 750 words, so you will need to be concise and specific.

Editorial essays (opinion pieces) can be an effective means of getting your side of the story into the press without filtering by individual reporters. If the scandal is newsworthy, most major media editors (print as well as broadcasters) may be receptive to a point of view essay that is offered for perspective. Often, these pieces will need to carry the by-line of authorship by your most senior or chief executive to provide sufficient merit for inclusion in the (limited) space of the media. In scandals that last beyond a few weeks in the news cycle, this approach may be a significant strategy to communication your point of view concisely to a large audience. Be prepared for counter-perspective or counter-point essays to appear along side or nearby your opinion piece. Many editors will feel obliged to find one of your critics, victims, opposing parties or detractors to write an opposing editorial essay to coincide with your advocacy.

If you have access to a live feed update broadcast facility (these can be built in-house for larger corporations or leased from third party vendors on a short term basis when needed), then you may consider making editorial video recordings and make them available to news media. You may also be able to more readily respond to requests to appear on news broadcasts, news media interviews, and as a talking head for a variety of cable and broadcast news media.

Letters to the editor should be used sparingly and typically only when responding to specific news reports that have previously appeared. A calm and well-reasoned letter to the editor can be useful for corrections of misinformation, for clarification, or for filling in blanks that appear in a new story. Letters to the editor are always subject to editing (for style, grammar and length, among other things) and there is no guarantee that your point as a whole will be made in what is published/broadcasted. Letters to the editor might also be a tactic to raise a topic or issue on which reporters/editors have not heretofore focused.

Communication the Key for Surviving a Scandal

Crisis communication with key stakeholders and effectively working with the news media is key to corporate survival of an ethics disaster. Effective communication doesn't just happen. Success depends on adequate preparation and management of your advocacy messages to key constituent audiences in the most effective means possible.

Communication must occur before, during, and after an ethical disaster strikes your company. Effective communication is an aspect of successfully surviving the hit that a major scandal or EMD will have on your company. The bottom line is that a well thought out and detailed communication is essential to managing both a crisis and the consequences of a crisis for your organization.

Chapter

8

Recovering from an Ethical Misconduct Disaster

A major ethical misconduct disaster has rocked your business. Your reputation has been damaged. Your company may face charges and fines. Your customer base may have been eroded. Can you ever get back to normal again? How does a company strategically plan to recover from such disasters? A major task is to get your people back to normal after the distractions and disruptions of the disaster have subsided. There may well be broken systems, processes, rules and structures that have been exposed (or destroyed) during the disaster that will have to be repaired. This is no small task in the overall process. Outside assistance may be essential. There will be many questions in the minds of your employees, customers, vendors, investors, and neighbors about your company's future (as well as future of their jobs, their pension funds, their contracts, their investments and/or the economic impact to the community, and so on). Every action and message you send will be scrutinized for signals of what might come next. You must understand that every movement of your internal disciplinary process, entanglement with the legal system, and news report about the nature of your operations will influence the motivation, morale, and expectations of all of your stakeholders—and it will do so with an intensity that was not present before the crisis occurred. Recovery may depend on accurate assessment of underlying cultural norms, ethical decision-making, reward/disciplinary structures, communication content, implicit/explicit rule systems, loss of respect and trust that will need to be restored, and understanding what went wrong and what can be done to prevent a recurrence of the event.

Consider what happened after the *Exxon Valdez* ran aground in Prince William Sound, Alaska spilling 240,000 barrels of crude oil in an environmentally-sensitive area. The company spent billions of dollars over several years cleaning up after the accident, and chairman Lawrence Rawl apologized to the public for the accident in full-page newspaper ads and in a letter to Exxon shareholders. Nonetheless, the company's well-publicized, belated response, foot dragging, attempts to shift blame and excuses during and after the crisis left its reputation sullied in the minds of some stakeholders more than a decade later.[1] As Journalist William J. Small wrote about the beleaguered company, "No company ever spent more to repair the damages of an industrial accident. None worked harder to marshal an army (and navy) to fight the damages to the environment. No corporation ever had to cover so much territory to repair the result and probably no other company ever got a more damaging portrayal in the mass media."[2]

But it is possible to recover from an ethical misconduct disaster, as we shall see in this chapter. First, we will consider the importance of the post-disaster assessment as a learning and improvement process. Then we will examine the importance of reconciling with stakeholders, including acknowledging the misconduct, attaining forgiveness for the misconduct and compensating or otherwise repairing the harm to stakeholders as part of the process of restoring the firm's reputation. Next, we take a detailed look at communicating to restore a damaged reputation, both tactics that work to restore reputations and common failures that can derail recovery.

Post-Disaster Assessment

It is important to debrief the implications and fallout from the scandal systematically. Using both internal and external resources, you must systematically conduct a thorough post-mortem analysis of everything that happened. This includes accounting for what went right and what went wrong. The objective is not just generating an autopsy report, but producing an analysis that serves as the basis for changes to the ethical climate, culture, and systems that can reduce the probability of such events occurring again in the future.

Consider the disaster endured by HCA (then called Columbia HCA Healthcare Corporation) after it was accused of "patient dumping"—discharging emergency room patients or transferring them to other facilities before they are stabilized—and over-billing the government for Medicare and other federal programs. During the ensuing scandal, HCA ultimately paid more than $840 million in criminal fines and civil penalties, as well as $631 million to settle fraud charges, and both its stock price and its reputation suffered serious setbacks, which took years to recover from. Thomas Frist, Jr., newly hired as chairman and chief executive in the aftermath of the over-billing scandal, oversaw a post-mortem assessment. As a result, he initiated a 100-day plan to change the firm's culture. Among other provisions, the plan included a new mission statement and the creation of a new senior executive position to over see ethics and compliance. (Previously, compliance issues were the purview of HCA's general counsel).[3] Understanding the causes and failures in an ethics disaster can serve as the basis for changes to the ethical climate, culture, and systems that can reduce the probability of such events occurring again in the future.

A post-disaster analysis may take months or even years to develop completely. Of course, you cannot afford to wait for the final recommendations or findings of such a process to begin to recover your operations and reputation. Even while this analysis is ongoing, it is imperative that you move quickly and decisively to restore a sense of normalcy to your operations, to repair your corporate/brand, image and reputation, and to reclaim your integrity. This can be accomplished in a variety of ways—all of which will say something about your company's essential nature and character. HCA, for example, hired Alan Yuspeh as a senior vice president of ethics, compliance, and corporate responsibility to help the firm establish an ethical and accountable culture that would restore its credibility with all stakeholders. Yuspeh immediately went to work to refine HCA's monitoring techniques, strengthen employees' ethics and compliance training, develop a code of conduct, and create an internal mechanism for employees to report any wrongdoing. It is notable that while the resulting mission statement emphasized a commitment to quality medical care and honesty in business practices, it was silent with regard to financial performance.[4]

Reconciling with Stakeholders

In the aftermath of a major ethical crisis, there will always be at least two courts in which your company will be tried: the legal system and the court of public opinion. In the justice system, your actions and messages may have repercussions (i.e., deferred prosecution agreements). The courts may be more lenient if you appear to accept responsibility and take positive steps to restore any damage that has been done—and take steps to ensure that the ethical disaster is unlikely to occur again in the future. Public opinion may likewise be more lenient if you appear to accept responsibility and take positive steps to restore any damage and to ensure that such misconduct is unlikely to occur again. Some recovery strategies may be in conflict or even mutually exclusive in addressing in these two courts. The challenge is to balance the requirements (and pitfalls) of the legal system while reclaiming your image of integrity in the fickle court of public opinion. Sometimes the legal system can provide you with clear options—but not always. Sometimes the public is more lenient and forgiving than we expect them to be—but not always.

Thus, there is a need to make critical decisions regarding both the legal repercussions and public reputation implications of your actions to recover from a major crisis. Decisions should take the legal implications into account, but you must remember that merely doing the minimally required does not ensure that the various stakeholders will be inclined to forgive and move forward. It may be necessary to act specifically in ways that will positively influence your stakeholders. There is a narrow range of actions and messages that strike the perfect balance between legal and reputation needs that you should strive to follow. In the court of public opinion, your actions and messages will be a major factor in determining the perceptions of your reputation and stakeholders' willingness to move forward.

There are some basic actions and messages that may aid your recovery or repair of reputation and image. The recovery may be a long process where gains are achieved in small increments. Nonetheless, the recovery can begin with basic steps. Among the most basic is the need to acknowledge the crisis or ethical disaster. This will be more challenging in some corporate cultures than others. In some cases, a necessary part of successful recovery is attaining forgiveness of those injured by the scandal. It may be necessary to apologize directly and ask forgiveness of specific parties who have been harmed in some way. Such requests for forgiveness are often inherent requirements for reconciliation of stakeholders and organizations (and executives). On the other hand, legal counsel should help the firm avoid setting itself up for damaging litigation that could ultimately put the company out of business.

It is also a legal, ethical and symbolic necessity to move quickly to repair any damages or harms that may have occurred as a result of an ethical disaster. This can include compensating those who (may) have been injured in some way and/or addressing the needs of those who may otherwise be affected, such as shareholders, customers, vendors, employees, neighbors and other stakeholders. It is important to go beyond the bare minimum and take bold and notable actions to seek to restore and repair any negative consequences that have resulted from the scandal. Ford Motor Company, for example, continues to defend itself in cases related to the Firestone/Ford Explorer rollover case litigation despite a lengthy and comprehensive recovery from the immediate impact of the reputation crisis.

You should look both within and beyond the borders of your organization when trying to heal wounds and restore wrongs. The key is to make any recovery efforts meaningful (by accepting blame, apologizing, promising to fix and/or redressing grievances), which can, in turn, mitigate vulnerability to lawsuits, criminal convictions, etc. When lawsuits emerge, a strong defense may be needed just to maintain equity and justice in our litigious society. Your defense efforts too can assist in recovering and making restitution, if considered a part of the overall recovery process. Companies often settle lawsuits before trial to diminish publicity, resolve the conflict and chart a new responsible course for the future. In other cases, the lawsuits themselves provide a public platform to clarify issues and establish facts favorable to a company's image and reputation. Obviously, the decision to avoid or engage in the courtroom is a calculated strategic decision that should be made with prudence and caution.

In many cases there are opportunities to recover image and reputation among your key stakeholders by going beyond just the minimum obligatory requirements. These are opportunities to act in such a way that will shape perceptions as to the nature of the company, your motivations, and the underlying ethical fabric of your corporate culture. Every statement and every action will create both subtext and interpretative clues (i.e., meta-communication, framing or spin) in the minds of stakeholders. It is essential to demonstrate that you are going the extra mile, working on the issue 24/7, committed to ensuring that this never happens again, and taking decisive action (even if it is focused on investigation or repairing any harm done). How you are perceived as handling the crisis will itself become a message about the nature of your company.

Your recovery should directly relate back to and connect with the primary theme or message about ethics and ethical expectations in your company. Show the world what an ethical company would do when faced with the scandal or image crisis. It is vital to remember that, at least in this respect, actions speak louder than words.

The worst case occurs when your pronouncements about the high ethical character of your company are juxtaposed with symbolic images of executives' stonewalling, foot-dragging, insensitivity to the plight of those harmed, or over-reliance on legal tactics that may work well in a court of law, but that may ultimately hurt your firm in the court of public opinion. Every action (or inaction) sends a subtle message that stakeholders will interpret in order to judge your company's character. Therefore, it is important to find ways not only to say, but to demonstrate symbolically, that you are an ethical organization, that you are committed to acting with integrity, and that you will go beyond the required or minimum expectation in order to show the world the true nature of the organization.

One recent example of a symbolic action that went above and beyond occurred when the Walt Disney Corporation experienced a potential crisis of public concern about amusement park ride safety after a series of incidents involving Disney theme-park attractions. An elderly woman died in February 2005 after riding the Magic Kingdom's "Pirates of the Caribbean." In June, a 4-year-old boy died after riding Epcot Resort's "Mission: Space" attraction, and several other riders were treated for chest pain after exiting the same ride. That same month, a 16-year-old girl almost died of cardiac arrest after riding the "Twilight Zone Tower of Terror" attraction at the Disney-MGM Studios theme park. By early July, news media outlets were reporting seven incidents of "Mission: Space" riders being taken to the hospital for chest pains, fainting or nausea. The growing news media attention on ride safety issues prompted Disney to respond.[5]

Disney's corporate culture is inherently reticent to discuss publicly any incidents of ride mishaps. However, Disney is also fundamentally sensitive that growing concerns about ride safety among customers and others stakeholders could become a disaster for the amusement park giant. Disney used the upcoming operational inspection of the "Tower of Terror" attraction as a strategic message, meta-communication, and framing opportunity to address the generalized fears about attraction safety.

The initial Disney response was predictably appropriate and expected. Disney released a written statement to the press and various stakeholders stating that Disney engineers deemed the "Twilight Zone Tower of Terror" ride safe and reiterated its concern for the girl and her family. Walt Disney World, like Florida's other major amusement theme parks, is not directly regulated by the state, and instead has its own inspectors as permitted under Florida law. (Florida's Bureau of Fair Rides and Exhibitions regulates and inspects the smaller amusement attractions, traveling carnivals and other venues within the state for ride safety, but large, permanent amusement parks that have their own safety inspectors are exempt from this requirement.)[6]

Nonetheless, in an unusual and surprisingly public move, Disney invited officials from Florida's Bureau of Fair Rides and Exhibitions to monitor the Disney engineers' inspection of the ride and to independently inspect the ride. This step clearly went beyond the required legal or regulatory compliance steps that Disney was mandated to follow. The action was not motivated by Disney's need for the expertise of the state inspectors. Rather, this public move by Disney was clearly perceived as a symbolic action to allay public anxiety about Disney's attractions' safety. "I think they felt, in an abundance of caution, they wanted to help the public understand they're doing everything necessary to make sure the rides are safe," said Liz Compton, a spokeswoman for the State of Florida Bureau of Fair Rides and Exhibitions.[7]

What Disney officials knew, but the public may not have known, is that Disney's attraction ride safety record was excellent. Disney's own engineers and inspectors had already ensured that the operating mechanisms and attraction functions were all within the prescribed operating parameters. Disney had an extremely high level of confidence that the state inspectors would confirm publicly—and as an outside authority with no connection to the company, objectively— that the "Twilight Zone Tower of Terror" was operating as designed and with a good safety record.

In a statistical context, the publicized incidents involving medical emergencies for patrons on Disney attraction rides are particularly low for a high-use ride. In almost any comparison, the rate of mishap on the Disney attractions would be substantially below any relevant comparison basis.[8]

Therefore, at a very small risk and cost, Disney's invitation to state inspectors to inspect its rides sent a message that the company was going beyond the minimum (legal) requirement in its response in order to recover ground in the perception crisis over ride safety. Disney also pointed to its onsite informational campaign to alert patrons to the risks associated with various attractions and its detailed attraction warnings to discourage those most at risk for negative health impact from riding particular attractions.

There are other ways to both symbolically and legally demonstrate your corporate culture's commitment to and prioritization of integrity. One obvious action (with legal, practical, and symbolic benefits) would be to bring in an organization such as the Integrity Institute. As discussed in Chapter 2, The Integrity Institute can help arrange steps to assess ethics compliance and training programs, measure the underlying ethical status of the corporate culture, identify high-risk aspects of your operations, align policies with ethical criteria, respond specifically to problem issues, arrange training, provide certification of your efforts and demonstrate to both the courts and stakeholders that you are taking steps to recover from the scandal. The goal of The Integrity Institute's certification process is to become proactive in understanding and benchmarking your firm's ethical culture and, if necessary, to take corrective action to address any deficiencies. In this way, a company can begin to reconcile any gaps between stakeholder expectations and company actions.

Communication for Repairing Reputations

Crisis communication is a broad area of research and application that includes pre-crisis decision-making, planning, goal setting, training, teamwork and gaining coherence for crisis management plans. Public crisis communication focuses on the verbal, visual, and/or written interaction between the organization and its stakeholders (often through the news media), before, during and after a negative event. It seeks to minimize damage to a firm's reputation. Public crisis communication must include conveying the facts surrounding the event (e.g., accurate information on personnel, policies, steps taken in response to behaviors, or even disclosure of misconduct). There will inevitably be questions in the minds of key stakeholders regarding responsibility, blame, consequences and remedial actions, which must be addressed during and following a crisis.

During and after a crisis, then, maintaining or restoring the corporate or organizational reputation and image is crucial, and relies on effective use of language and symbolic appeals with an organization's stakeholders. A rhetorical perspective to crisis management and image restoration acknowledges the symbolic nature of crisis responses and, in particular, views all crisis actions as messages which various stakeholders will attempt to interpret and assign meaning.

One important aspect of image recovery is to remember that perception is everything when your corporate reputation, image or brand is on the line. It is imperative that you carefully analyze and understand the perceptions that various stakeholders hold. Oftentimes it is the degree to which the perceptions of your corporate acts either conform to or violate the pre-existing expectations of these stakeholders that will determine how well you recover from an ethical misconduct disaster.

Effective communication is inherently more complicated than simply getting the facts straight and fulfilling all of the procedural expectations in getting your messages to targeted constituents. Two important concepts must be taken into account to fully understand how your audience will interpret your message: meta-messages and framing.

Meta-Messages

Meta-messages are literally messages about messages. More generally, they are (usually implicit) interpretative clues that provide the audience with cues to guide their understanding of messages. Perhaps the most basic meta-message can be illustrated with the language function of irony. Irony is revealed by context and/or non-verbal behavior that alerts the audience that the message is something other than/more than what the words themselves portend. Irony can transform a salutation of good morning into a belligerent confrontational challenge. Meta-messages are more generally the messages that exist between the lines that guide audiences' interpretation of what they are hearing or reading. Meta-messages usually exist as either intentionally positive or unintentionally negative. Meta-messages may include the setting (location, context, etc.), non-verbal communication behaviors (tone, timing, appearance, movement, etc.), the presence/absence of specific individuals, topics/issues discussed (or not discussed), or any other aspect that can be taken as a hint of something more than what is literally being said.

Obviously negative meta-messages can undermine your message strategy and perhaps even have the reverse persuasive effect on your audience than what you sought with your communication. Thus, on one hand, it is essential to exercise caution to potential negative meta-messages that can undermine your communication goals. Critically evaluate how elements of the message or the medium could be (mis)understood and (mis)interpreted by your audience.

On the other hand, you can consider the strategic use of meta-message to bolster the effectiveness of your communication. Consider how you can embed meta-messages that are consistent with your message. Be attentive to the setting and timing of your communication.

Framing

Framing refers to the process by which selective words, narratives, or terminology subtlety influences the way in which otherwise objective information is interpreted or evaluated by audiences. Framing includes labels and embedded words as well as how information is packaged. In political contexts, framing is related to the idea of spin and spin control. Words function as a form of label that defines the reality for the audience. The classic illustration is the maxim that one side's freedom fighter is the other side's terrorist. In this case, the specific word choices determine the persuasive interpretation of all other elements presented, as well as carry with it the implications of guilt, which are embedded in concepts associated with one word or the other.

Framing also sets the parameters of defining the issue for the audience. One common illustration of this principle is in the social controversy over abortion rights. It is significant that each side of this debate self-describes their position with one-sided polarized terms, which in turn implicitly (negatively) define their opposition. Therefore, the pro-life position is juxtaposed by implication with the anti-life position.

Here is a dramatic example to illustrate the concept in the context of communicating in the midst of an ethics scandal. One could use different words to describe the action of misconduct; calling it an ethical lapse, misdeed, illegality, criminal act, violation of policy, poor judgment, bad decision or a mistake. Each term carries with it a set of implications that frames the nature of the act under question. The reality is that many, if not all, of these terms are correct at some level for describing the act in question. It is imperative, however, for the framing implications of these word choices to be understood and recognized.

Communicated frames facilitate the interpretative process and guide the audience towards a particular conclusion. In its most basic manifestation, framing can influence the agenda of the expected communication topics and information. In its strongest manifestation, framing can serve as a subtle aspect of persuasion that is capable of changing opinion, shifting attitudes, and motivating specific action among the audience.

Tactics for Image Repair and Reputation Restoration

What should you say and what is the best way to say it when your company's reputation has taken a serious hit? There are a number of basic communication tactics that should be followed. In addition, there are a number of rhetorical message strategies that may help guide the creation of your basic message during these events. Initially, you should adhere to some key tactics in order to survive (see Table 1).

Stress, strong opinions about ethical issues, political concerns, distraction and sensory overload—all of which are found during a crisis situation—can have devastating effects on your audience's ability to understand and comprehend complex messages about your company. It is important to carefully consider how, what, where, when and why you will seek to communicate with all of your stakeholders.

Table 1
Recommendations for Crisis Communication
1. Implement your crisis management plan and activate your crisis communication team.
2. Do not panic.
3. Do not be hasty in confessing blame nor in blaming others.
4. Be reflective.
5. Communicate all the steps (investigative, disciplinary, remedial, etc.) proactively being taken.
6. Your crisis team and crisis leader should be in full control of managing the crisis.
7. Create your core messages quickly and stay on message consistently.
8. Recognize the needs and agenda of the news media.
9. Act in a way to bolster your credibility and trustworthiness.

First, implement you crisis management plan and activate your crisis communication team. Provide decisive leadership as your plan is set in motion. Get your people on task per their roles as detailed in your plans. Conduct a rapid assessment of the challenges and threats as well as the opportunities available in the emerging crisis. This is not the time to stall or be indecisive. Do not wait until you have all the facts because that will be intolerably late. Get your spokesperson and senior managers visible and show them focusing on task. Hiding your executives or senior managers is often interpreted as evidence that the company is trying to hide something, thereby making the news media more aggressive in covert investigations.

Second, do not panic. When the news of a scandal is racing along the company grapevine, and a news camera crew has staked out your corporate headquarter's lobby, it is essential to remain calm and to logically strategize. When confronted by a crisis, it is crucial not to overreact or shoot from the hip. It is essential to maintain control and remain calm. Do not speculate, but proceed with informed reasoning. Understand the nature of your existing reputation and image in the minds of your key stakeholders. Continue to monitor and measure stakeholder perceptions both during and after the scandal to see if there are lasting implications for your image and reputation, to fine tune your message strategies and to make tentative assessments as to whether your strategies are succeeding or require further adjustment.

Third, do not be hasty in confessing blame or in blaming others. Take responsibility to follow up, investigate, act appropriately and express your commitment to a thorough and honest examination of the emerging situation. Demonstrate that the issue is being handled at the highest levels of senior management and that it is being treated as a serious and salient issue. Take ownership for acting (not necessarily accepting blame for the misconduct at this early point). Do not pass the buck or blame others. Do not make premature speculative assertions.

Fourth, be reflective. Try to understand the implications of the emerging scandal from the perspective of key stakeholders. They may not have access to inside information and thus may not always give you (or the company) the benefit of the doubt. Remember to look at issues from an external, not an internal, viewpoint. Contemplate the potential reasoning processes that your audiences may use to interpret and understand what they have heard. Recognize how certain information may be used to justify erosion of positive reputations and image even if you consider it unfair or unjustified. This is a dimension of thinking worst-case or pessimistically, and then taking the steps necessary to respond. Occasionally, this will be unnecessary and perhaps even over-kill in terms of your response. However, failing to anticipate how some of your audience may be interpreting the information to which they have been exposed is a dangerous and high-risk tactic.

Fifth, communicate the steps (investigative, disciplinary, remedial, etc.) being taken. Demonstrate that you are acting. Everything that you say and do should contribute to the image that you are being proactive and moving forward in appropriate ways. You should not appear passive or merely reactive. As a general guide, it is best to be honest and forthright in all of your communications. If there are proprietary limits or legal restrictions that constrain what you can appropriately say, then it is better to say nothing than to communicate anything which may (subsequently) regarded as misleading, deceptive or manipulative. It is also useful to be transparent in all of your communication interactions. Never lie, distort, misrepresent or exaggerate the facts of the situation. If you do not know the answer to a question, then it is best to state simply that you do not know the answer rather than to speculate, stonewall or guess at the facts. You need to thoroughly investigate what happened. Accept collective accountability for doing what is appropriate given the information that is available.

Sixth, your crisis team and crisis leader should be in full control of managing the crisis. Your spokesperson should be regularly and consistently briefing the news media. Your emergency notification network and alternative communication channels should be pushing your message to all key stakeholders. You should also establish an effective communications network to enable the rapid flow of information both internally and externally. Remember that information must be available in both push and pull media channels and targeted to your key stakeholders.

Seventh, create your core messages quickly and stay on message consistently. You need to have a single voice and single message that consistently puts forward the facts and interpretation that is in your strategic interest.

Eighth, recognize the needs and agenda of the news media. Respond to the media in a professional, sensitive and helpful manner. It is important to communicate your message. Do not leave an information gap or message void. Utilize nontraditional communication channels to get your message directly and rapidly to all of your stakeholders.

Ninth, act in a way that bolsters your credibility and trustworthiness. Every action and message that you produce will be critically scrutinized within a framework of expectations held by your stakeholders. Past failures to sustain credibility will create challenges in subsequent crises. Your messages and actions must contribute to the perception of a fast response. Communicate in a way that inspires trust. Create an image consistent with your actions and messages that conveys that you are taking action. Action images are very positive tools. "We are responding, acting, moving and acting appropriately" is a very important message. If you say little else, let the audience know that you are working 24/7 and doing everything reasonably appropriate to move quickly in response to the scandal. Serious damage to your reputation and credibility may occur if the audience perceives that you are slow to respond, delaying, avoiding action" or, in the worst case, ignoring the issue. Proactive, doing, and fixing behaviors are usually associated with positive perceptions of corporate motives, intentions and trustworthiness.

Whenever possible, provide information in anticipation of the information needs of news media and other stakeholders. Many of their questions are quite logical and thus should be fully anticipated. Do not forget that effective communication requires engaged listening and openness to other perspectives and opinions. Demonstrate that you are following up on issues and requests for information. Keep all of the promises that you make. Communicate frequently and periodically, even when the only new information you can present is that you have no new information.

Do not underestimate the power of hunger for information among your key stakeholders. It is natural and normal for people to have strong expectations for information. Scandals invite both curiosity and quests for self-preservation. It is normal for stakeholders to wonder whether this scandal affects their jobs, their retirement, their local community, future hiring, production, suppliers, sales, etc. One of the reasons that rumors run rampant during escalating EMDs is the natural and normal need for information and the desire to make sense of things among all those who are touched (or feel threatened) by the events. Remember that these events disrupt the routine in stakeholders' lives. When there are breakdowns in the flow of information, it is only natural that anxiety and uncertainty will erupt.

Common Communication Failures that Derail Recovery

Communicated messages are complex and dynamic. It is a mistake to think only in terms of information being communicated in a message. Every message has implicit meta-message meanings and is subject to interpretation. In addition, it is inherent for mistakes, omissions, additions, and distortions to appear in messages as they work their way sequentially from your spokesperson through a reporter to the reader and then to secondary audiences. It is a well-known communication concept that messages tend to distort the longer the sequence (chain) of message relays. Think of the childhood game "telephone," in which the goal is to pass the message from the beginning of a line or in a circle of people. The entertainment of this game is that the message is never the same at the end. It is inevitable that messages will grow in their distortion the more people involved in the sequence. This is amusing when the game of telephone is played, but it's not so funny in real life when the reputation of your company is at stake. By the time that Jay Leno or David Letterman has selectively focused on some part of your message as part of a humorous monologue for the millions of viewers in their audiences, you should not be surprised at the strange perceptions about your company and the scandal that are revealed in a public opinion pool.

There are some considerations to try to keep your recovery messages on tract. Consider these as a partial list of considerations that are focused on specific aspects of your spokesperson and interaction with the public. You can't control all aspects of your message as it works it way across the public opinion landscape. You can, at the very least, try to avoid the most common gaffes. Communication failures run rampant in corporations' responses to ethical scandals. Even a crisis communication plan does not ensure a failsafe response in the event of an ethical disaster. Communication problems come in every shape and size; some are obvious, while others silently lurk around the corner. The more that you and your team are aware of their existence, the more you will be ready to disable them. The following are a few common failures to keep in mind.

Messages are sent to the receiver through both verbal and nonverbal behaviors. Every message has meta-message dimensions as well. Some of these meta-messages are very subtle and expressed in things as minor as non-verbal cues. Nonverbal messages may be a simple nodding of the head in agreement or the rolling of the eyes in disbelief or annoyance. During a crisis, it is imperative that misunderstandings from verbal and nonverbal behavior are minimized. The burden is on both the source (generally, the spokesperson)—to verify that the message is understood correctly—and on the receiver—to clarify understanding with questions. This requires both clarity and succinctness. Poor word choice also hinders the receiver from understanding the message correctly.

Failure to Have Proper Concern and Care for the Media

Do not dismiss the news media as simply a pesky nuisance or attempt to physically keep them outside the facility. This approach is rather shortsighted and ignores the simple fact that the media has the potential to be the loudest voice to the public throughout the crisis. As we saw in Chapter 7, every business should develop a customized communication plan for working with the news media and have in place messages and methods of disseminating information to various forms of the media (such as print and television). In addition, the crisis communication team should develop fact sheets and talking points for relaying information to the media and the general public. Potential questions and appropriate answers should be developed beforehand in anticipation of their need and use.

Leaving Information Voids

Silence is not always golden, and waiting for the press to break the story—or hoping that no one will discover the story—is never the best practice during a crisis. Instead, an effective measure called "stealing thunder" can be utilized. This may mean that the best communication strategy is breaking the news about a crisis by contacting the media before the media contacts you after they have learned about the story from other sources. Failure to communicate (at all) is one of the major communication failures at the emergence of crises.

Not communicating at all to the public or the press, or not responding immediately when a crisis occurs, may seem the most prudent course of action given a situation where information is sporadic and incomplete at best. However, there is a strong public need to know and they will expect you to speak out without understanding the challenges of inaccurate and changing information. Furthermore, the news media will bring scrutiny and consistent demands for your comments or disclosure. If you do not communicate, you essentially create an information void. A general rule in both physical science and reputation disasters is that a void is both an opportunity and an invitation to be filled. Voids have no ability to discriminate between good content and bad content. If you leave voids, you have relinquished control of how and with what the void will be filled. Therefore, it is essential that even though you may not yet know all the facts, have not completely resolved the issues and have not even completed an investigation and inquiry, you must be prepared to quickly and decisively respond to such crises with well-crafted messages containing as much information as you can prudently provide, and make yourself available for conversation no matter how uncomfortable it is for you to do so.

Failure to Understand the Stakeholder Audiences

Failure to understand and analyze the target audience can be best illustrated by analyzing Enron's initial and sustained responses to mismanagement claims. The executives at Enron argued incessantly that nothing illegal transpired. What they failed to understand and act upon were stakeholders' concerns. Employees, stockholders and the public didn't care that Enron's actions were technically legal. They were concerned that Enron had lost thousands of families' life savings. Enron executives failed to understand the differences and the impact of public concern versus legality.

One of the biggest aspects of crisis communication that is frequently overlooked is to understand completely the agenda and critical posture of your key audiences. To be effective, you must be able to analyze and understand the nature, assumptions, perceptions, opinions, biases, expectations and concerns of you audiences. This must be more exhaustive than most demographic analyses that are routinely conducted. You need to have an in-depth, reliable and valid assessment of the nature and characteristics of your audience. Failing to understand or appropriately adapt to the nature of your key audiences is likely to derail your communicated attempts to restore or repair the reputation and image damage from ethics scandals. Mis-analyzing your key audiences and/or failing to completely adapt to audiences that you do understand will prevent your successful recovery and impede your efforts to repair your corporate image in the post-scandal period.

Failure to Be Honest

Deliberate deception in the event of a crisis is self-explanatory in its error. The ease with which information can be discovered through employees, journalists, web pages and such mediums as blogs (weblogs) should discourage any business from believing that it can pull the wool over anybody's eyes. Instead, the use of deception often leads to increased uncertainty, lack of trust and feelings of negativity.

Very often, telling the truth may create risks, but you must provide a complete account and what you are willing to do to correct the problems that were the cause or result of an ethical disaster. Understand that doing this creates legal risks, but these can be mitigated—in telling the truth, you send the message that "we didn't intend to harm, harm happened, here are the steps taken so that it never happens again, we want to fix our harm." In this scenario, the legal risks can be minimized because telling the truth shows a good-faith effort to correct the injustice. This does not eliminate the risk, but can serve as a positive factor down the line. A classic example of decisive action to deal with risk by telling the truth was Johnson & Johnson's recall of Tylenol laced with cyanide that was discovered on store shelves. The company's honest and responsible approach to the crisis resulted in consumers and other stakeholders having even more confidence in the company today.

Failure to Be Compassionate

Most people will evaluate your response during and after a scandal in very personal terms. At a time when you may be frustrated, under stress, and facing severe information and time constraints, you must maintain your composure and be sensitive to the needs and concerns of others. Two important concepts in crisis communication are attribution and compassion.

Attribution centers on the assignment of blame, guilt or responsibility for problems that have emerged. Typically, attribution takes the form of either blaming someone else (scapegoat), taking the blame and responsibly yourself or blaming no-one in order to turn the focus on the discussion to solutions and moving forward. On another level, attributions may simply fall into either internal (us) or external (them) categories. While the actual causes of most of these scandals is various and the reasons for the scandal numerous, listeners may focus on key statements to try to ascertain whether they believe that you are either blaming someone or taking responsibility for the problems. Putting aside the question of actual causes for the moment, in the public's mind the appropriateness of the source blamed will be combined with pre-existing attitudes, beliefs, and values to determine whether any attribution other than acceptance of responsibility will be regarded as positive or an indictment of the character and integrity of the organization itself. The danger of blaming external causes (rather than taking responsibility) is that, regardless of any real or actual connections, there is a tendency in the public perception to discredit any strategy that seems to evade responsibility. Although this may not be a good legal strategy for the court of justice, the court of public opinion often provides a favorable verdict for companies that are perceived as taking responsibility and handling the scandal. Furthermore, offers of reparations or restoration made in the sprit of being compassionate towards individuals who (may) have been harmed is usually a positive step towards image repair. It is a high-risk strategy to craft an attribution that may appear to evade ownership of the problem. On the other hand, blame the victims strategies usually create additional reputation issues. One study has found a positive benefit of using messages of compassion rather than messages of external attribution.[9] Unwarranted blame can easily turn against the accuser and should be avoided.

The above communication failures may seem overt and obvious. There are other communication problems that are much more subtle and take many forms. The following diagram (Figure 1) illustrates what they are and how they can interact to cause even more mayhem. Each must be acknowledged and dealt with on a case-by-case basis.

Figure 1 Communication Problems

Information Flow

Underloaded–overloaded

Blocked

Delayed

Messages

Communication

Misunderstandings

Processes

Poor word choice

Groupthink

Nonverbal misinterpretation

Decision-making breakdowns

Communication apprehension

Perception Psychological

Idealization

Stress

Misinterpretation

Family

Distraction

Sensory overload

Noise

Incorrect Information Flow

It is critical that information flow freely to and from the communication crisis team and other participants. Unfortunately, this information flow can be hindered by miscommunication. Information can be blocked by a number of factors such as people (gatekeepers or filters) or other intermediaries. These blocks can change the message, serve other people's agendas, or misdirect an audience. The information flow should be protected against such possibilities. You must have an active system to determine what information should be sent to which audience and how.

You can use redundant messages, active feedback systems and double-checking to better ensure that the correct information is reaching the intended audience on a consistent basis. This is an area where the guidance of a communication expect may help you measure and monitor your information target. It is useful to assess, measure and gauge both the information needs of your various constituents as well to have a precise grasp of your message and information delivery to key constituents.

Underloaded and Overloaded Messages

Messages that are underloaded are ineffective because there is insufficient or inadequate information for any meaningful or accurate communication. The information flow is so slow (timing problem) or small (adequacy problem) that it reveals little useful information, which results in frustration and perhaps even retaliation. Incomplete, insufficient or truncated messages are counter-productive. These messages create more questions and speculation. There is a high correlation between underloaded messages and misunderstandings. Such messages actually do more than just fail to persuade or inform. Underloaded messages can be counter-productive and create negative reaction on the part of audiences. On the other hand, overloaded messages contain every available piece of information, both relevant and irrelevant. The audience is left to sift through all of the information and make complex choices to discover the truth, and the probability of misunderstanding and misinterpretation is extremely high. You should not make your audience work to understand the central fact or depend on them to sift accurately through large amounts of information and to choose what they think is important or relevant. You should choose what is important and relevant and make sure they get that point consistently.

Overloaded messages are just as problematic as underloaded

messages. Most of us can easily understand why a message or series of messages that is incomplete, incoherent, and inadequate is a communication problem. However, it is a bit more subtle point to grasp that overloaded messages are equally bad. Think of this analogy from our routine communication interactions. Every day we are inundated with an enormous amount of information, including junk mail, e-mail spam, fragments of conversations, written correspondence, mass media messages (radio, TV, etc.), information from the internet, newspaper text, etc. We have to filter and selectively choose which messages to perceive and process and which ones to ignore or discard without devoting analytical energy. We then have to further choose the messages to which we will devote analytical energy to actively consider and evaluate. Can you image how effective any message would be if it were buried in an avalanche of messages, information and communication and the audience was unable to recognize which parts or pieces were important? Actually, unmitigated overload results in an impoverished underload situation for any given decision-making in your audience. The bottom line is that you must communicate the messages and information that are most relevant to your message strategy and not dump everything but the kitchen sink into your communication channels. Otherwise, your important messages will be lost in the clutter. The politician's mantra of "stay on message–stay on message" is useful to remember as we rise to speak on behalf of our companies during reputation crises.

Expectation Violations

The public (including you and me) holds expectations about what a situation or an interaction should and will be like. Whenever there is an event of social symbolic significance, people have expectations for what should be done and what should be said. In historic terms, there are events in society for which we share an assumption that someone should say something. Beyond the occasions of newborn babies and office retirement functions, these assumptions are more complicated and explicit whenever there is perceived damage, injury, or harm. We hold expectations for not only when, but also for what and how someone should communicate in these situations. For example, a subordinate may expect an executive to take the lead in a crisis situation and make a quick and reasoned response. Instead, the employee finds that the disaster and its associated stress have left the executive ineffective, unable to lead and wavering on even predetermined decisions. This response leaves the employee disappointed and frustrated–as measured against what was expected in terms of performance compared to actual performance.

The general expectation across society presumes that the conduct of corporations (and employees of corporations) will adhere to the accepted norms for appropriate conduct (both legal and ethical). The news of an ethics scandal creates a disruption of this expectation of appropriate behavior. The violation of this generally held expectation is itself a factor that must be addressed in the messages and communication that is forthcoming from an organization entangled in such a scandal. Furthermore, the violation of this expectation creates the further subsequent expectation of a justificatory response. Society wants an explanation, an apology, and a promise to make amends from those suspected of breaking this trust.

A stronger expectation is demanded when there are issues of accountability to the public or greater society involved, or in situations where there is a sense of betrayed trust or widespread harm. Serious violations of these expectations result in a greater exigency that must be communicated to the public. This means that there is a greater expectation of a communication response from the owners of the scandal. In a real sense, the public feels that you owe them an explanation. The assumption is widely held and there is a general expectation that in ethical scandals those involved should be forthcoming and provide a satisfactory explanation and solution to the problems. When someone bumps you in the hallway as you walk by, the expectation is for an apology or at least a request to excuse me. When a corporation (or employees of a corporation) disrupts the implicit contract with the public of appropriate conduct, there is an expectation for both and apology and an act of restitution (repairing the harm). The concern with a violation of expectations in a crisis situation is that it often provokes excitement, which results in a response that diverts attention away from the purpose of the interaction. Using the example of the ineffective manager above, the subordinate may focus on his or her disappointment in the manager instead of dealing with the problem at hand that needs a quick decision.

Ethics scandals violate the social contract and create a sense of accountability of the company in the minds of the public. There is an expectation that companies embroiled in ethics scandals should say something. The something expected to be communicated is most often both apologetic and remedy-oriented. If your messages fail to meet these expectations, you have little chance to repair your image and you risk further damage to your reputation.

Failures in Group Processes

Groupthink

Groupthink refers to a mode of thinking that people engage in when they are deeply involved in a cohesive group, such as a crisis communication team, when members—striving for unanimity—override their motivation to appraise alternative courses of action realistically.[10] In other words, someone has to question the decisions being made as a form of checks and balances on decision-making within the communication crisis team. For example, your team quickly resolves that your chief executive officer should be interviewed during the developing phase of a scandal and the members of the team uncritically go along with that idea, despite knowledge among some present that the CEO lacks the requisite skills and is unwilling to be coached for an effective interview. This may be a strategic mistake of great proportions.

Noise or surrounding over-stimulation in your meeting room may impact the occurrence of groupthink. Ringing telephones, multiple television news channels, blaring noises and general commotion that is correlated with a major scandal can hamper the ability to think clearly when confronted with difficult decisions. Further, your corporate culture may be such that disagreement is discouraged and the need to stick together might motivate someone to stay quiet and go along with the team rather than to risk breaking the harmony and speaking up and out when questioning a course of action that has the appearance of consensus. You need to be aware of groupthink and to request honest opinions–perhaps anonymously–in order to analyze all possible alternatives.

Personality Dominance

Another more subtle communication problem is the dominance of a particular personality that causes communication apprehension among a team's membership. Communication professor James McCroskey has defined communication apprehension as "an individual's level of fear or anxiety associated with either real or anticipated communication with another person or persons."[11] As this definition suggests, communication apprehension is not limited to public speaking situations. An individual may feel apprehensive about almost any kind of communication encounter, especially in the highly charged environment of an ethical misconduct crisis. There are several anxiety-producing factors that affect nearly all of us, including poor preparation, self-expectations, a fear of being evaluated, anxieties that grow from specific audience characteristics such as size and power, and fears that arise because of misunderstanding the physiology of communication apprehension (energy, nervousness, and anxiety). Some strategies will help managers cope with communication apprehension and be less susceptible to the dominant behavior of an aggressive personality. Such strategies might include developing a positive mind set, being prepared, anticipating the situation, practicing active listening, exercising, acknowledging the potential benefits of apprehension and maintaining the proper perspective.

Inaccurate Group Perceptions

The old quip that possession is nine tenths of the law underscores the idea that perception is nine tenths of the truth. Misperception and misinterpretation of messages have the potential to lead a business to ruin. Management science professor Jerry Harvey believes the problem is grounded in group dynamics. He calls this the Abilene paradox, which is the idea that groups frequently take actions that are contrary to what their members really want to do and thereby defeat the purposes the group set out to achieve.[12]

Principles from which Harvey draws are:

1. **Action Anxiety:** This concept is based on the premise that each of us, when confronted with a potential conflict in a group, knows the sensible action we should take, but when it comes time to take action, we become anxious and can not carry through with the action we know is best.

2. **Negative Fantasies:** We often conjure up disastrous fantasies as a result of acting. Such dire predictions give us an ironclad excuse for inaction when action is called for. Real risk is a condition of human existence. All actions have consequences that are potentially worse than standing still.

3. **Separation Anxiety—Fear of the Known:** Oftentimes we fear known consequences more than the unknown. In a group, we fear being ostracized or being branded a non-team player. In short, we fear separation.

4. **Psychological Reversal of Risk and Certainty:** The more unwilling we are to risk separation, the more likely we are to experience the separation we so fear. Our negative fantasies

become more real than the consequences of pursuing what we think are hopeless courses of action.

Each of us has a choice. We can remain silent or we can confront the group—not with new information, but with what the group already silently agrees upon. Each individual has to calculate the real risk of taking an action, as well as the risk of taking no action at all. Avoid scapegoating. A group setting needs individuals to own up to their own beliefs and feelings without attributing them to others. It is up to the individual to own up to his or her distinctive, and often contradictory, point of view. It is when we remain quiet that failure and problems ensue.

Another type of perception problem is idealization, in which false impressions can be related to another person. Gaps of knowledge in regard to the situation or person are completed by personal preferences or generalities that can ultimately lead to mistaken impressions. Constrained environments such as those created by a crisis situation foster the use of projection and the development of transference, which can lead to incorrect impressions. To counter this tendency, it is necessary to include a number of systematic reality checks in your procedures. Soliciting and incorporating feedback from your audiences in your standard operating procedures and external sources may help check this negative tendency. Extensive audience analysis and self-critical assessment is also a prudent

Image Restoration Strategies

Communication professor William Benoit has developed a widely-cited theory of image repair strategies employed in post-crisis communication. His theory posits that because reputation is so important, when an individual is accused of wrongdoing, he or she is highly motivated to develop and use various strategies in an attempt to restore that reputation.[13] These strategies for restoring sullied reputations after an ethical misconduct disaster include denying the misconduct, evading responsibility, reducing offensiveness, taking corrective action and expressing regret/asking for forgiveness. These strategies are summarized in Table 2.

Table 2 Benoit's Image Restoration Strategies	
Denial	
Simple denial	Shifting the blame
Evading Responsibility	
Provocation	Lack of information/control
Accident	Good intentions
Reducing Offensiveness	
Bolstering positive feelings	Minimizing negative feelings
Differentiating the misconduct from more offensive actions	Putting the misconduct in a more favorable context
Attacking accusers	Compensating victims
Taking Corrective Action	
Expressing Regret/Asking Forgiveness	

Denying the Misconduct

Persons or organizations attempting to recover from charges of wrongdoing may deny the misconduct, or even deny that any wrongdoing occurred.[14] Alternatively, they may admit to committing the misconduct, but deny that it resulted in harm to others.[15] Regardless of whether the company's spokesperson denies that the wrongdoing actually occurred or denies that that the company did it, if stakeholders accept this denial, it should absolve the company of culpability. One strategy for dealing with attacks, then, is simply to deny the undesirable action. Of course, this strategy can occasionally backfire. Former Tyco CEO Dennis Kozlowski's decision to testify that he did not engage in misconduct at his trial for grand larceny and fraud failed to work. The jurors did not believe his denial and found him guilty on all but one of 23 charges.[16]

Many CEOs have used denial of awareness of specific misconduct, such as discrimination or financial mismanagement, as their defense when accused of wrongdoing. Former HealthSouth CEO Richard Scrushy denied all criminal charges stemming from a $2.7 billion accounting fraud. Although Scrushy was acquitted of all charges, he had to pay $25 million in legal fees to defend himself, and his former company, HealthSouth, issued a statement that he would not be welcomed back.[17] One consistent problem with denial as a strategy is that to simply deny one's culpability or guilt leaves the question of who is to blame unanswered. This open-ended mystery is problematic for most audiences and renders simple denial message strategies as typically unpersuasive.

Another option related to denial is scapegoating, or attempting to shift the blame to another person or organization.[18] This strategy can be considered a variant of denial in that the accused organization could not have committed the wrongdoing if another person or entity can be proven responsible. Often when an unethical activity occurs, there is a tendency to blame a lower-level manager and then to fire them "for not following company policy." At Wal-Mart, for example, Jared Bowen, a junior vice president, was asked by vice chairman Thomas Coughlin to approve some expense payments without any receipts. Bowen took his concerns about the questionable expenditures to a higher-level executive, triggering an internal probe. That investigation ultimately led to Coughlin's resignation over allegations of expense-account abuses, but not before Bowen himself was fired for not being forthcoming.[19] However, blame shifting may well be more effective than simple denial for two reasons. First, it provides a new target for any ill will that stakeholders may feel. Second, it provides an answer for the question, "Who did it?" Shifting ill will away from the company to a specific person or entity fulfills stakeholders' need to have someone to hold responsible.

Evading Responsibility

Organizations trying to recover from an EMD may attempt to evade or reduce their apparent involvement in misconduct.[20] One tactic for evading responsibility is to claim that the misconduct was provoked by someone (or something) else's transgression.[21] Another tactic for evading responsibility is citing a lack of information about or control over important factors in the situation.[22] For example, although Richard Scrushy was acquitted of wrongdoing, 15 former HealthSouth executives plead guilty to misconduct, which suggests that Scrushy's defense that he was not personally involved in misstating financial results was accepted.[23] Rather than deny the act occurred, the accused might suggest that he or she should not be held completely responsible for the offensive act.

This tactic rarely works unless, in fact, the situation was truthfully beyond one's control. This strategy is least effective when false because once the preponderance of evidence emerges that one was or should have been responsible, there is a tendency for the use of this tactic itself to be regarded as an ethical breach (a form of lying).

However, in cases where there is a clearly delineated boundary between individuals' degree of responsibility, then this is a strategy that has been used successfully in a limited number of instances.

Reducing Offensiveness

Persons or organizations trying to recover from an EMD may attempt to reduce the perceived offensiveness of the act in the minds of key stakeholders.[24] An accused firm may attempt to bolster or strengthen stakeholders' positive feelings toward the firm, thereby mitigating the negative effects of the misconduct.[25] Politicians under fire often respond by claiming their opponents have done something even worse than what they are accused of doing. This tactic, when unjustified, is often regarded as a weak form of defense.

It is also possible that attacking one's accuser will divert stakeholders' attention away from the original accusation. However, this would appear to be a weak strategy except in the cases where there is widespread misunderstanding of the nature of the offense. If the scandal in the public mind is much greater than the reality of the ethical breach, it may be desirable to focus your communication efforts on explaining that the true nature of the offense was much less significant than generally believed.

Taking Corrective Action

One significant tactic to help mitigate negative feelings arising from the wrongful act is to offer to reimburse any victims.[26] Such restitution may take the form of valued goods or services rather than or in addition to financial reimbursement. If the victim accepts the compensation and it has sufficient value, any negative effects from the misconduct may be outweighed or even eliminated, restoring reputation. These are attempts to lessen unfavorable feelings toward the accused organization by enhancing stakeholders' esteem for the firm or by decreasing negative feelings about the wrongdoing

Taking corrective action as an image restoration strategy may be a major means of repairing damaged reputation. This strategy requires the company (or individual) to vow to correct or fix the problem.[27] It does not have to inherently imply guilt or responsibility. This correction may take two forms: restoring the situation to the state of affairs existing before the misconduct and/or promising to mend one's ways by making changes to prevent a recurrence of the wrongdoing. If the problem is one that could recur, the firm's reputation may be enhanced by demonstrating a willingness to take steps to prevent it from happening again (e.g. revising a code of conduct, improving employee training).

This strategy may be one component of or coupled with an apology message;[28] however, the accused may also take corrective action without admitting guilt, as Johnson & Johnson did when it introduced tamper-resistant packaging after the Tylenol-poisoning incidents. This strategy differs from compensation in that the corrective action addresses the actual source of injury (offering to rectify past damage and/or prevent its recurrence), while compensation consists of a gift designed to offset, rather than to correct, the injury

This strategy is most effective in cases where constituents have been harmed and you have the capability to make them whole again. The message and meta-message conveyed by this strategy is that your are taking proper and appropriate steps to repair damages that may have occurred due to the ethics disaster. This may also help with the repair of your corporate image.

Asking for Forgiveness/Expressing Regret

The accused may admit responsibility for the offensive act and ask for forgiveness. This strategy may also include concessions, in which one may admit guilt and express regret.[29] If the apology is believed to be sincere, the wrongful act may be pardoned. For example, after an America West Airlines passenger was removed from a flight for joking about a drunken-pilot episode at the airline, Joette Schmidt, vice president for customer service, went on the *Today* show to ask passenger Sheryl Cole's forgiveness. Given an opportunity to defend the airline, Schmidt instead declared, "I'm here primarily to apologize to Ms. Cole. We overreacted." Caught off guard, the victim in the incident later said, "I'm sympathetic to America West right now. I know they're going through a tough time."[30] Indeed, research suggests that companies may be underestimating the benefits of a heartfelt apology. Apologies may defuse victims' anger, and juries may take a firm's apology into account when considering punitive damages.[31] It may be wise to couple this strategy with plans to correct (or prevent recurrence of) the problem, although these strategies can occur independently.

Recovering Your Corporate Reputation

Recovering or repairing your corporate reputation after a scandal is possible. It takes focused effort and a comprehensive message strategy. While numerous critical assessments have been offered regarding the desirability and/or effectiveness of image restoration strategies, some researchers have examined the degree to which these strategies are utilized by organizations and their crisis managers when confronted by crises.[32] The results suggest that regardless of the type of crisis, four message strategies have consistently been regarded as most promising for repairing damaged reputations in the perceptions of stakeholders:

1) taking correction action;
2) compensating;
3) expressing regret; and
4) bolstering your reputation with positive messages.

Thus, these four communication strategies would seem to be the most effective at helping a firm recover from an ethical misconduct disaster. Research also suggests that denial strategies (simple denial and blame shifting) and silence consistently have the least effectiveness and are among the most likely to backlash. In the case of unethical, illegal or even criminal activity, the research literature suggests that there are no sure-fire image repair strategies that can assure you of restoring your reputation completely.

It would seem prudent to recommend that, in the aftermath of ethical scandals, the most likely strategies to move toward repair of your image would be to quickly speak out to take corrective actions and move to prevent any future reoccurrences, compensate those harmed or injured by the misconduct, express regret without necessarily assuming blame and get positive messages about your company out to all of your stakeholder audiences and the general public as quickly and effectively as possible. The worst things to say or do in the aftermath of the scandal would be to issue communication with the central message of simple denials or blame shifting (scapegoating or external attributions), or to fail to communicate about the issue (silence) altogether.

OCEG 2005
Benchmarking Study
Key Findings

The recent wave of corporate scandals in the United States and across the globe has resulted in widespread reform and activism. These scandals were met with responses from all sectors: lawmakers, regulators, investors, the public, employees and the companies themselves.

In the United States, for example, numerous initiatives have been implemented to protect against corporate misconduct: legislation such as Sarbanes-Oxley; new guidelines from the United States Sentencing Commission; rules from the Securities and Exchange Commission; rules from the Public Company Accounting Oversight Board; rules from the Government Accounting Office; revised listing requirements from NYSE, NASDAQ, and AMEX; revised broker dealer standards from NASD; revised guidance from the Office of Inspectors General; new ratings criteria related to governance coming from existing analysts; and entirely new ratings agencies dedicated to governance. Individual and institutional investors, and other stakeholders, are raising the bar and voicing a host of new expectations about ethics in business practices. Similar reforms are occurring in Europe and Asia.

While not every organization with lacking governance programs or compliance problems ends up on the front page of the newspaper, many companies are paying a heavy price in terms of increased cost of capital and increased insurance premiums. Organizations that are unable to demonstrate that they comply with minimum legal requirements on a variety of fronts are being regularly dropped from investment and insurance portfolios. Those organizations with identified governance weaknesses, or ambiguity with respect to compliance, pay a penalty in terms of increased insurance rates or reduced coverage. Investors, especially institutional investors and pension plans, are demanding more disclosure and more influence in directing good corporate governance.

Ratings agencies and analysts are convinced that there is a cognizable difference in business performance between organizations that exhibit good corporate governance and those that exhibit poor corporate governance. Stock pricing is beginning to reflect this belief. On a positive note, those organizations that demonstrate excellence in ethics and governance are benefiting by receiving better insurance coverage and rates, higher bond ratings, and improved stock performance.[1]

Increased Enforcement & Risk

Lawmakers passed the Sarbanes-Oxley Act in 2002, in large part, to hold executives of public corporations more accountable for their financials and financial controls.

Since 2000, data from the Securities and Exchange Commission (SEC) shows a marked increase in the amounts of fines and disgorgement (see Figure 1). As SEC actions and fines continue to grow, the SEC continues to increase its ability to apply more resources to enforce rules and regulations.

Today's public corporations–and the executives running them – are at far greater risk of criminal and civil liability than at any other time before.

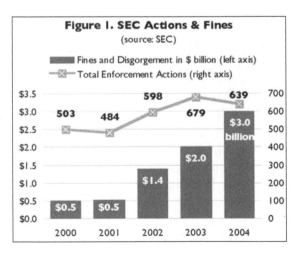

Figure I. SEC Actions & Fines
(source: SEC)

Fines and Disgorgement in $ billion (left axis)
Total Enforcement Actions (right axis)

Total Cost of Compliance

In the past few years, several studies and surveys have focused on the costs of implementing Sarbanes-Oxley compliance, and opened up debate about whether the Sarbanes-Oxley requirements are fair to companies of smaller size and stature. While this debate is certainly of importance and merits attention, a movement is already underway by many of today's companies – both large and small – to implement improvements to lower the costs of Sarbanes Oxley compliance.

However, Sarbanes-Oxley is just the tip of the iceberg. While total costs to comply with SOX are estimated between $500 thousand-$1 million per $1 billion in revenue, compliance with all other regulations can cost as much as five to six times that number. In October 2001, before passage of Sarbanes-Oxley, total regulatory compliance costs were estimated to be $450 billion - $843 billion annually (about $4,500 per employee in a large company and almost $7,000 per employee in a small company).[2] These costs are almost certainly higher given the new environment.

Given these large numbers, it is easy to understand the importance of addressing not only the visible issue of the day (financial compliance), but also the ever growing patchwork of total regulatory and legal compliance requirements. While each legal domain / area has its own specific requirements, the best organizations use a consistent "meta process" to maximize the effectiveness of a Compliance & Ethics Program.

Some of the most sophisticated Compliance & Ethics Programs go well beyond the fundamental legal and regulatory requirements of compliance. They integrate both compliance and a culture of ethics into core business processes, impacting how everyone thinks and acts every day – from the board and CEO to every employee and agent that represents the company.

Far from being a burden, the best Compliance & Ethics Programs provide the company with a better way to look at their business. These programs enable a company to identify opportunities for improving processes; and a culture to enhance reputation and achieve enterprise objectives.

What are These Principles? What Does It Cost to Put Them into Pactice? Is Your Organization's Program on the Right Path?

In early 2005, the Open Compliance & Ethics Group (OCEG), in sponsorship with Aon, undertook a comprehensive study to evaluate key elements of Compliance & Ethics Programs. In addition to collecting extensive data on how companies structured and funded their programs, OCEG asked companies to indicate whether they suffered reputational damage from compliance and ethics "lapses" in the past.

Seventy nine respondents completed the survey, thereby providing valuable directional analysis and guidance. The power of the research is in its depth of knowledge about the inner-workings of how companies are implementing, managing and evaluating Compliance & Ethics Programs.

Summary of Key Findings

A key question within the OCEG 2005 Benchmarking Study asked "In the past 5 years, has your entity suffered reputational damage as a result of a compliance or ethics-related matter?" Four answers to the question were provided: 1) No, 2) Yes, but not very visible to the public, 3) Yes, moderately visible to the public and, 4) Yes, highly visible to the public. Respondents were grouped by those answering No (option 1) and those answering yes (option 2, 3 or 4).

- **Key Finding 1–Crisis Can Help the Cause**.
  Companies that have experienced reputational damage in the past see themselves as much further along in terms of program maturity and in relation to their peers – both today and in the future.
- **Key Finding 2–Pay Now or Pay Later.**
  Companies that have experienced reputational damage invest three TIMES MORE than their non-damaged peers in specific Compliance & Ethics processes.

Another set of questions aimed to understand the degree to which the program was reactive versus proactive – and whether or not the program focused on the "rules" versus the values and principles behind the rules.

- **Key Finding 3–Preference for Proactive and Values-Based Programs.**
  Compliance & Ethics Programs are becoming more proactive and values-based, allowing companies to prevent ethical and compliance violations before they become a crisis.
- **Key Finding 4–Proactive Skills Training May Need**

More Emphasis.
To reach the objective of more proactive programs, companies must provide training to the people who are accountable for the Compliance & Ethics Program - training that focuses on more proactive disciplines.

OCEG was particularly interested in understanding the degree to which these programs are integrated into the fabric of the enterprise – and the degree to which these programs are aligned with overall business strategy.

- **Key Finding 5–Set/Align Objectives for More Benefit.**
  Companies that set explicit objectives for their Compliance & Ethics Programs rate the benefits of their programs more highly and ascribe them more importance than companies that do not set explicit objectives.
- **Key Finding 6–Integrate/Cooperate for More Benefit.**
  Additional benefits and performance can be realized when an organization integrates the Compliance & Ethics program with other aspects of the enterprise–and when the program has a good working relationship with other business functions / processes.

Additional Findings

Experience
- 54 percent of the companies in this study have implemented a Compliance & Ethics Program relatively recently (within the last five years).

- ZERO companies in this study with a program in place for 10 years or more experienced highly visible reputational damage in the last five years–a testament to the important impact these programs can have over time.

Oversight & Organization
- In 82 percent of the large companies in this study, oversight of the Compliance & Ethics Program is done by a compliance committee or some other board committee. For small and medium sized companies, the split is about 50-50 between a board committee and the board or executive management team.
- The Chief Compliance Officer or a compliance executive is,

more than 50 percent of the time, responsible for both the strategic and operational tasks of the Compliance & Ethics Program.
- On average, the number of direct full time equivalent employees (FTEs) in the Compliance & Ethics department is 46. Large companies have on average 82.1 direct FTEs while medium and smaller companies have fewer than five direct FTEs.

Strategy & Challenges

- Companies in this study believe that the major challenges for their programs in the future will be board support, C-suite support and Investor expectations.

Code of Conduct & Training

- 78 out of 79 respondents employ a Code of Conduct and 75 percent of those that have a Code of Conduct make it available on their website.
- Success of training is largely measured via completion of a course or a basic test. Very few organizations use performance observation (only nine out of 50) as a means of evaluating the success of training.
- Despite the additions to the Federal Sentencing Guidelines, organizations are still behind the curve when it comes to distributing a code of conduct to agents of the organization (only 16 percent)–let alone training them (only 8 percent).

Budgeting & Costs

- The 59 companies that responded to budget questions spend an average of approximately $5.8 million on TOTAL compliance and ethics processes (including Sarbanes-Oxley, Employment, Safety, Anti-Corruption, Ethics, etc.) for every $1 billion in revenues. This amount appears consistent with information gained through selected telephone interviews with Chief Compliance Officers of several major organizations and data presented by other sources, including the Small Business Administration.

About this Research

During the first quarter of 2005, OCEG administered an extensive study of Compliance & Ethics Programs. The study was conducted via a secure web-site and all participants were provided assurance of confidentiality.

OCEG posted an open invitation to any organization with a compliance & ethics program to apply and participate. 500 organizations expressed initial interest. After receiving the questionnaire and a clear communication regarding the amount of time required to complete the survey, 300 organizations (60 percent response) requested login information. Ultimately, 79 (15.8 percent response) surveys were completed and submitted for analysis by the deadline and are included in this sample. An additional 25 responses were received and will be included in a future report.

Respondents include 30 percent of the "Fortune 50", five of the "10 Most Admired Companies" and represent some of the world's "Best Companies to Work For."

There was no cost to access the survey, and every respondent receives the aggregated results along with a separate report that allows them to benchmark their answers against the results. The survey analyzed over 125 attributes of governance, Compliance & Ethics Programs such as organizational structures, processes, program metrics, planning and budgeting information.

Due to its comprehensive nature, OCEG estimated the time required by participants to complete the survey would be five hours to 15 hours. To help organizations navigate and effectively respond to the survey, OCEG conducted training in late January 2005.

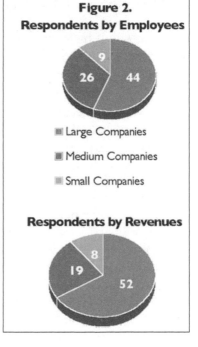

Figure 2.
Respondents by Employees

9
26 44

- Large Companies
- Medium Companies
- Small Companies

Respondents by Revenues

8
19
52

Completion of every question was not required, although organizations were informed that they would only receive aggregated results for the questions to which they submitted a response. For most respondents, the survey was completed by the person, or the person's assistant, who is in charge of the Compliance & Ethics Program.

OCEG conducted follow-up phone interviews with several respondents to clarify responses and to explore best practices with those respondents who reported that they had more "mature" and "optimized" programs than their peers.

Companies were categorized based on number of employees, revenues and industry. In this "Key Findings" report, we group respondents into three basic categories:

- Small Companies, less than 500 employees or $50 million in annual revenue.
- Medium Companies, 500 to 9,999 employees or between $50 million and one billion dollars in annual revenue.
- Large Companies, 10,000 or more employees or over one billion dollars in annual revenue.

Key Finding 1–Crisis May Help the Cause

Companies that have experienced reputational damage in the past see themselves as much further along in terms of program maturity and in relation to their peers–both today and in the future.

Companies suffer when ethical and/or legal issues surface. The level of exposure and visibility to the public can affect the degree to which a company's reputation is damaged.

In this study, companies were asked if they suffered reputational damage as a result of compliance or ethics related matter in the last five years. We then segmented the responses into "Yes," which included any form of visibility from low to high, and "No." High visibility reputational damage includes problems where the organization or its executives were regularly featured on the front page of the newspaper (e.g. the Wall Street Journal). A low level of visibility includes when a government investigation is disclosed, but not generally known outside of the industry.

Overall, companies with reputational damage rate their programs further ahead of the curve than their peers (Figure 3). In terms of program maturity, they also rate their programs as more optimized than those companies not experiencing any reputational damage (Figure 4).

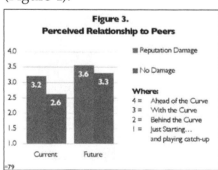

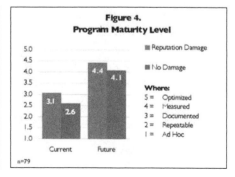

When considering the number of years companies have had their program in place, the most optimized programs are in companies with reputational damage whose programs are seven years or older (Figure 5).

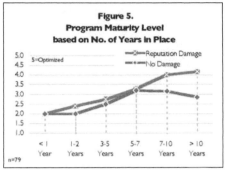

Figure 5.
Program Maturity Level
based on No. of Years in Place

While no company wants to experience reputational damage, the good news is that they appear to install superior programs to their peers after the event. And when looking to the future, these companies seem to be placing a higher level of expectations for themselves as well (Figures 3 and 4).

Key Finding 2–Pay Now or Pay Later

Companies that have experienced reputational damage invest *Three Times More* than their non-damaged peers in specific Compliance & Ethics processes.

Companies that experience some sort of reputational damage are certainly more likely to spend more on outside counsel. Allocation for External Legal fees increases from 28 percent to 39 percent according to Figure 6. Yet, companies do not significantly increase (Audit-Internal) – and in some cases actually decrease (Legal-Internal, Audit-External) their other budgets typically associated with compliance.

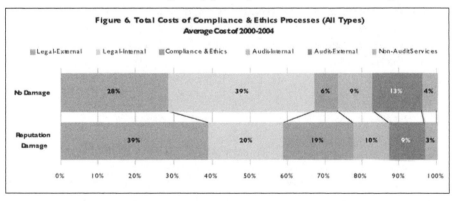

Figure 6. Total Costs of Compliance & Ethics Processes (All Types)
Average Cost of 2000-2004

Most interesting, though, is the substantial increase that companies place in their general Compliance & Ethics Program budget. These budgets represent all monies that are not included in external audit numbers and SOX 404 compliance.

Budgets shift from 6 percent in companies with no damage to

19 percent for companies with any sort of reputational damage, representing a more than three-fold increase. This additional investment is even more significant when considering that total budgets for companies that have experienced reputational damage are, in absolute terms, significantly higher.

No doubt exists that Compliance & Ethics Programs that are more effective require a substantial investment in formal control structures–including the policies, procedures and standards that document expected conduct.

In phone interviews, OCEG found that those organizations that reported programs that were more "mature" and "ahead of the curve" when compared with peers, tended to also focus on the informal, cultural aspects – including leadership, the ethical climate, mindsets and perceptions of employees about senior management.

An important message here, however, is that while a "crisis may help the cause," it also tends to treble costs.

Key Finding 3–Proactive Programs are Preferred

Compliance & Ethics Programs are becoming more proactive and values-based, allowing companies to prevent ethical and compliance violations before they become a crisis.

Compliance & Ethics Programs can differentiate themselves based on two primary characteristics: Rules-Based / Values-Based and Reactive / Proactive. Of course, programs must be able to deliver on both of these dimensions, but HOW companies build and extend their programs today can have a dramatic effect on their benefits.

A *program style* tends to be either values-based or rules-based. Values-Based programs tend to focus on the principles behind rules and regulations as well as their intended outcomes. Rules-Based programs tend to focus on controlling business activity to ensure it operates within legal and voluntary boundaries. Figure 7 shows that most companies rate their program's style as more Rules-Based. As they continue to develop their program's style though, companies intend to move towards a Values-Based program.

A *program stance* tends to be either proactive or reactive. A proactive program spends more time and budget in the planning and design aspects of their program, looking for ways to prevent non-compliance and encourage proper behavior. A reactive program focuses more resources on discovering the violations and finding the authority responsible.

Figure 7 shows that most companies believe their program stance is reactive. Yet, when examining a company's motivation for starting a program in Figure 8, the two top motivations–"Good business practice" and "Right thing to do"–are certainly more proactive than the other motivations.

Companies see their future program stance as more proactive – and are in the process of making it happen.

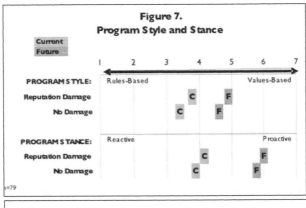

Key Finding 4–Proactive Vs. Reactive Skills

To reach the objective of more proactive programs, companies must provide training to the people who are accountable for the Compliance & Ethics Program-training that focuses on more proactive disciplines.

Although most companies strive for proactive programs, the vast majority of training for the individuals charged with strategic and operational responsibility of the Compliance & Ethics Program continues to revolve around legal compliance and reactive (or neutral) disciplines.

Figure 9 identifies the type of training provided to employees with strategic or operational responsibilities. Today, more training

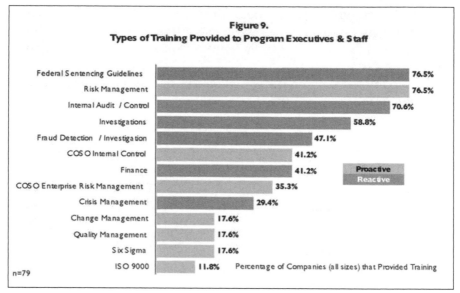

Figure 9.
Types of Training Provided to Program Executives & Staff

Federal Sentencing Guidelines	76.5%
Risk Management	76.5%
Internal Audit / Control	70.6%
Investigations	58.8%
Fraud Detection / Investigation	47.1%
COSO Internal Control	41.2%
Finance	41.2%
COSO Enterprise Risk Management	35.3%
Crisis Management	29.4%
Change Management	17.6%
Quality Management	17.6%
Six Sigma	17.6%
ISO 9000	11.8%

Proactive
Reactive

n=79

Percentage of Companies (all sizes) that Provided Training

is focused on areas such as Federal Sentencing Guidelines, internal audit / control and investigations. Company use of proactive training modules that address the human capital aspects (such as change management) is much less common. As well, training that focuses in business process quality and integration (ISO 9000, Six Sigma, Quality Management) also stand in the clear minority.

To further their efforts towards a more proactive and values-based program, companies need to emphasize new skills. Based on phone interviews, the curriculum for these proactive skills should include:

- Strategy Development / Measurement
- Communications / Change Management
- Human Capital Management
- Quality Management / Six Sigma
- Compensation / Incentives
- Fraud Prevention (vs. Detection)
- Corporate Reputation-Building

Focusing on these skills will help to bridge the gap from today's program stance to a more proactive one that addresses human capital and business process quality issues.

Key Finding 5–Set/Align Objectives and Realize More Value

Companies that set explicit objectives for their Compliance & Ethics Programs rate the benefits of their programs more highly and ascribe them more importance than companies that do not set explicit objectives.

Over one-quarter (21 of 79 respondents) of the companies report that their organization does not explicitly state objectives for their Compliance & Ethics Program. Large companies tend to be better at setting objectives (over 80 percent set objectives), whereas their small counterparts (44 percent) do not set any objectives.

However, Figure 10 shows there is a clear benefit for companies to set objectives for their programs. When companies rate the overall benefit of their program, companies with stated objectives consider their programs 15 percent more beneficial on average.

As most would imagine, the number one rated benefit is "Compliance with the Law" for Compliance & Ethics Programs. The next two most important are "Ethical Culture" and "Better Reputation."

Defining and aligning objectives takes time away from other activities. In Figure 11, senior executives of companies with stated objectives spend significantly more time (44 percent more) creating a strategy and overall design of their program.

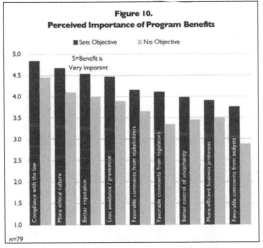

Figure 10.
Perceived Importance of Program Benefits

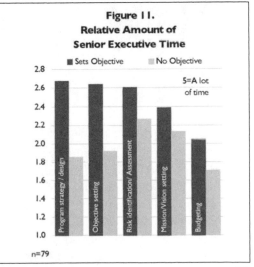

Figure 11.
Relative Amount of Senior Executive Time

However, those who spend this extra time clearly view it as beneficial.

Key Finding 6–Integrate/Collaborate and Realize More Value

Additional benefits and performance can be realized when an organization integrates the Compliance & Ethics program with other aspects of the enterprise–and when the program has a good working relationship with other business functions / processes.

The Compliance & Ethics program produces greater benefit when it is better integrated with certain departments of an organization. Integration can be analyzed along two dimensions.

On the one hand, integration can be considered as a function of *frequency of interactions* between the Compliance & Ethics program and the other departments of the organization. Especially interesting are the results from a more interactive relationship between the Compliance & Ethics program and the board of directors (figure 12). Frequent interaction produces a program 16% more beneficial overall. Noteworthy are the gain in benefits for loss avoidance/prevention and the better control of uncertainty.

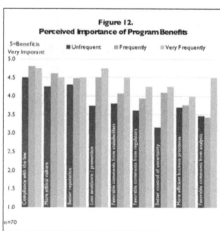
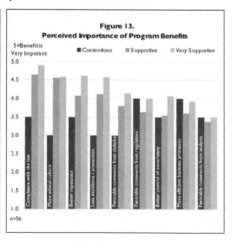

On the other hand, integration can be considered a function of *quality of relationship*. The relationship between the Compliance & Ethics program and other departments in the organization can vary from contentious/counter-productive to very supportive/ productive.

Special attention should be given to the relationship between the Compliance & Ethics program and the department in charge

230

of business strategy. Developing a very supportive/productive relationship with the department in charge of business strategy allows the executive implementing the program to generate a program 24% more beneficial overall. Most notable are the benefits regarding compliance with the law and realizing a more ethical culture.

Conclusion

OCEG would like to thank those organizations that participated in this study. The Compliance & Ethics function and executive position is relatively new. This project is intended to help frame issues that face this function and the executives accountable for its success.

As with all good research, benchmarking studies often generate additional questions to be answered in the future. Future research questions include:

- How do these patterns change across industries, geographies?
- Is there correlation between program outcomes and internal processes?
- To what degree do CEOs, other C-Level executives and chief compliance officers share the same vision about the Compliance & Ethics program?

Appendix

B

Capitalizing on the Value of Integrity: An Integrated Model to Standardize the Measure of Non-Financial Performance as an Assessment of Corporate Integrity
–Lynn Brewer–

Redefining Integrity

The corporate scandals that began in the early 2000s with Enron revealed business ethics as a key element of corporate responsibility. Investors were suddenly faced with the realization the underlying integrity of financial statements and their ability to make good investment decisions requires a better understanding of non-financial performance and its impact on financial performance. The burden now is placed upon corporations to find a meaningful way to measure non-financial performance as a means of communicating corporate integrity.

Despite the immense changes in regulation following the corporate scandals, a recent survey of executives and board directors found nearly three-quarters were under increased pressure to assess non-financial performance. Most, however, struggle to find a way to quantifiably measure their non-financial performance.[1] Why? Because no standardized measure of non-financial performance exists that provides for the increased transparency the regulatory changes were expected to provide and investors demand.

To transcend regulation as a means of transparency, we must begin by redefining "integrity". Initially seen as synonymous with business ethics, the focus was on values, providing for, at best, a qualitative assessment, which cannot be standardized. However, by shifting the focus from values-based to structural soundness, wholeness and incorruptibility of the corporation, we can meet the needs of both investors and board directors by providing a quantifiably measure of the corporation's ability to withstand market forces.

Measuring Integrity

The regulatory focus on the Sarbanes-Oxley Act[2] ("SOX") has placed an undue burden on corporations in the area of compliance but does little to provide real shareholder value and certainly has not reassured investors as the markets remain "flat" three years after the passage of perhaps the most sweeping changes in corporate securities law since 1933. SOX focuses on the punitives facing a company that engages in questionable accounting but does not provide predictive insight into the "markers" that have proven to ultimately destroy a company's shareholder value.[3]

Models such as Six Sigma[4] and the Balanced Scorecard[5] seek to understand and refine an organization to achieve better results. However, these models, and others, fail to meet a "wholeness" test necessary for a more complete understanding of corporate integrity. Even the Triple Bottom Line[6] falls short. To quantifiably measure the integrity of an organization, the measures must be integrated to determine the correlative values of the key indicators.

The purpose of an integrated model that measures the wholeness, soundness and incorruptibility of an organization is two-fold: (1) To provide leaders and directors with a broad spectrum understanding of the organization in order to effectively enhance the bottom line without increasing risk; and (2) To provide a predictive ability to create long-term shareholder value for investors. Although residual benefits exist beyond these two objectives, the long-term opportunity exists to transcend regulation by providing an alternative—assessment and certification of corporate integrity. Companies could capitalize on the value of integrity and realize a financial "return on integrity".

The goal of a broad acceptance of a standardized model that assesses corporate integrity, which can used as the basis for certification, is that we could end the need for regulation, and more specifically SOX, as a means of transparency. However, to achieve this goal, two things must occur: 1) A movement away from the current means of myopic measures of governance, risk and compliance to a standardized model that not only assesses key non-financial performance indicators but integrates those measures to understand the correlation between the measures; and 2) Avoidance of the inherent problems facing the accounting of financial performance by multiple commercial firms interpreting generally accepted accounting principles, the assessment and certification of corporate integrity would need to be administered by a single public policy institute to maintain the integrity and provide the greatest value proposition for companies and their investors.

Similar to the Underwriters Laboratories Model.[7], assessment of a company's integrity would be independently and objectively certified, similar to the Good Housekeeping Seal of Approval.[8] This approach provides the organization with the ability to communicate its adherence to a standard of integrity and also provides investors with the ability to trust the quality of the communication.

It is not the intent to suggest that companies stop using the various models currently used in an effort to understand their business. Rather, employing a standardized method to objectively assess and certify the structural integrity of a company will help leaders and board directors better understand the impact non-financial performance is having on their financial performance. It also reassures investors that integrity exists beyond the quality of financial reporting.

Integria™[9]–The Integrated Model to Standardize the Measure of Integrity

Similar to mapping the DNA of an organization, the unique Integria™ Model, (the "Model") integrates ten components, or drivers, to determine the "markers" that can weaken the overall structural soundness of the organization. The components measured include: (1) communication; (2) compensation; (3) compliance and ethics; (4) corporate citizenship (environmental and social responsibility); (5) culture; (6) earnings; (7) governance; (8) leadership; (9) risk; and (10) stakeholder perceptions. While institutional investors already use many of these drivers, the Model, for the first time, integrates them to establish a standard that can predict the sustainability and success of the organization. This measurement to an established standard is then used as the basis of certification of integrity by The Integrity Institute.

The measurement of each specific driver is based upon widely accepted and acclaimed models that have been validated and contributed to The Integrity Institute by its Founding Members, each a renowned expert in their respective field. The independent models are used to assess the integrity of each intangible driver and the results are then measured and weighted relative to the other nine components. To protect the integrity of the Model, the specific weighting of each integrated component is proprietary and therefore will not be discussed in detail. Using business analytic technology and a weighting similar to that of Fair Isaac[10] credit scoring, the Model dynamically predicts the likelihood of future events that can increase or decrease shareholder value, raise or lower the cost of capital, impact employee retention, and determine the impact the organization's non-financial performance is likely to have on the risk profile established by the company.

Overview of Methodologies

Standardizing the measure of non-financial performance begins and ends with the quality, transparency, and integrity of communications between organizations and their stakeholders. To that end, we begin with the overview of the individual components of the Model with the measure of communications integrity.[11]

(1) Communication Integrity

The Communication Integrity Assessment Model[12] draws upon a number of organizational communication theories and empirical research findings, as well as business ethics models in the assessment of manifested communication that can be predictive indicators of ethics and integrity. The assessment model and related research method (instruments, procedures, and data analysis process) examines samples of both public (external) and private (internal) communication. There are four communication dimensions measured: 1) communicated information; 2) communicated messages; 3) communicated meta-messages; and 4) communication processes. In addition, the issue of measuring "ethical communication" itself is an additional evaluation assessment of the model and method.

Communicated information includes the presence/absence of specific words, phrases, data, content, or facts/figures in the various communication artifacts sampled. In addition to the presence or absence of specific information, the question of how frequently such words appear, the timing of when, where, and how such information appears in the communication content are analyzed.

Communicated messages are a broader and more thematic communication content. Included in this analysis are the explicit messages about "norms", rules, expectations, climate, and modeling of how to act ethically with integrity and implicit messages (reading between the lines) about these same issues. It is significant to determine the consistency / inconsistency between the explicit and implicit messages. The overt communication to foster ethics and integrity among employees are measured and evaluated.

Communicated meta-messages are messages that are not explicitly (high contest) articulated yet are clear and discernable by audiences. These implicit messages may be about "norms", rules, expectations, climate, and modeling of how to act ethically with integrity. The method seeks to recognize what is being communicated "between or underneath" the lines of the explicit messages.

Communication processes include both formal and informal procedures, mechanisms, reporting rules, policies, feedback channels, participation norms, and communication networks that operate within the organization. Various conclusions about underlying ethical characteristics can be drawn from a snapshot of the communication process that typify (or are absent) in an organization.

One primary method to measure communication integrity focuses on the content of the annual letter to shareholders written voluntarily by, or at least signed by, the CEO or Chairman of the company. Analyzing of the cognitive content of the annual letter measures to what extent forward-thinking statements are realized, as well as the leadership's willingness to be held accountable for any failures to meet the objectives identified in the letter from the previous year. While the financial information contained within the annual report reflects the "results" of the previous year, the letter to shareholders provides "insight" into the future, and yet a unique understanding of the present mindset of the leadership.

According to the studies by Laura Rittenhouse, who has studied CEO letters for the past ten years, companies where the CEO candidly communicates in the annual letter to shareholders consistently outperform those who rank among the bottom.[13] For the year ending 2003, top-ranked companies in Rittenhouse's survey increased the value of their share price over a two-year period by 21.5 percent, while bottom-ranked companies saw only a 7.3 percent increase.[14] Top-ranked firms also beat the S&P 500 Index Fund over the previous two years.[15]

On its face this may seem like an obscure measure of a company's integrity. As a simple example of the importance of this document, we need only review Enron's 2000 letter to shareholders included in its annual report and signed by CEO Jeffrey K. Skilling. It stated Enron had hit "a record $1.3 billion in net income".[16] Yet the audited financials contained in the same annual report were clear—Enron had reached only a fraction of that amount[17]. There were no footnotes or further discussion as to the basis for the discrepancy. Despite this sobering reality, every reference by the media or analysts from that point forward stated that Enron was a $1.3 billion company—no questions asked.

By the mid-1970s, the "Annual Report" had become "possibly the most important corporate marketing device,"[18] as a result of statutory requirements for publicly traded companies. According to Mike Jones, in addition to marketing efforts, accounting narratives are "unlikely to be impartial and . . . likely to be used by management to give a more favorable impression of corporate performance than is warranted."[19] Analysis of the letter to shareholders specifically reveals that "what is omitted from an annual report is as significant as what is included in the narrative."[20]

The Jenkins Report identified 56 detailed items for disclosure outside the financial statements and related notes.[21] Among those items was the need for more information with a forward-looking perspective.[22] Beattie and Pratt also note, "The historical, backward-looking perspective of the traditional accounting model becomes a less useful predictor of the future as the pace of change in business increases. Moreover, financial performance measures have been shown to be lagging indicators of future performance compared to key non-financial indicators."[23]

No single shareholder letter is more widely read than Warren Buffett's, Chairman of Berkshire Hathaway. Mr. Buffett pointed out at the SEC roundtable held in New York, a month after the implosion of Enron, "the CEO [should] regard himself as the Chief Disclosure Officer . . ." and should write his own shareholder letter.[24] Buffett postulates that most letters are probably prepared by investor relations or public relations professionals, but R.D. Hines points out that the chairman's statement (letter) is the most widely read section of the annual report.[25] In fact, the rest of the annual report is too complicated for the average investor to understand; in the case of Enron, it was too confusing even for institutional investors.

Given the importance of this document in ascertaining the cognition and recognition of the CEO, key value drivers are identified through various studies. Key words are used to measure the level of disclosure and then the extent to which emphasis is placed on such things as capital stewardship, strategy, vision, innovation, leadership, compliance, culture, environmental and social issues, corporate governance, and other areas of importance to investors such as executive compensation packages.

Through this process and the examination of "forward-looking" statements, the assessment identifies the level of disclosure and seeks to predict whether a decrease in disclosure relates to the company's effort to hide losses, as loss-making firms tend to decrease disclosure in the year that the loss is reported.[26]

The predictive analysis begins with identification of key words that are often associated with "forward-looking" statements. Then, topics which are generally used for forecasting earnings, such as: earnings per share (EPS), breakeven, budget, contribution, earnings, loss, margin, profitability, and cash flow are considered. The analysis then includes data mining of statements previously made to determine whether the "predictions" became reality. If, over time, "predictions" do not meet reality then it may indicate the leadership is out of touch with reality, as we saw in the case of Enron.

(2) Compensation Integrity

The issue of executive compensation is a particularly hot topic and would seem that the amount of executive compensation paid would be an obvious starting point for assessment of compensation integrity. Of course, the headlines seem to complicate the matter by focusing on stories of Sandy Weill, Chairman of Citigroup, who received $151 million in 2000, or Jack Welch, former Chairman of GE, who received $125 million for overseeing GE's success.[27] Yet little attention is paid to the fact that Warren Buffett, as Chairman of Berkshire Hathaway, in 1993, had an annual salary of $100,000, plus benefits for a total compensation package of $248,000,[28] (far less than the $5 million annual <u>bonuses</u> paid to mid-level executives at Enron).

Compensation, and more specifically executive compensation, is a complicated matter in a free market society. Executives who build the long-term value of a company for investors should be recognized and rewarded. But rewarding an executive (or any employee) with a package based upon false reality or performance that can be manipulated can have a negative impact on the company's overall integrity. For instance, leaders who fail to recognize the disparity between their own compensation package and that of those whom they seek to lead, or promoting employees, just because they seem to provide short term gains for the company, despite the fact they may have engaged in behavior that violates the code of conduct, can devastate an organization's cultural integrity. Or, worse, if the compensation packages are tied to stock performance which calls into question the earnings integrity of the company, then predicatively, shareholder value can be destroyed virtually overnight.

As large institutional investors seek to enforce their rights as shareholders, the issue becomes even more complicated as negative value is placed upon these companies who are seen as paying excessive compensation. Companies that partake in the practice of excessive compensation over the interests of the shareholder will be penalized because appropriate executive compensation is considered a key component of good oversight by the board. Counterbalancing this effort by outsiders to "regulate" compensation based upon various and non-standard assessments is just one benefit of an independent and objective assessment of corporate integrity. Rather than assess the issue myopically, however; The Integrity Institute's analysis seeks to measure the impact the compensation practices have on the overall integrity of the organization.

While the issue at hand for the institutional shareholders is poor board governance, which could have been one of the factors that contributed to awarding excessive compensation in the case of Enron and the New York Stock Exchange (NYSE)'s Richard Grasso, the integrity of the leadership played just as much of a role. The executives at both Enron and the NYSE created compensation packages that were so complicated not even the board fully understood the extent to which the compensation was excessive—leaving the members of the board itself personally exposed for failure to govern.

A board does have a fiduciary responsibility to uphold the integrity of its oversight; but senior executives can go to great lengths to keep facts hidden from the board, leaving directors in the dark. Unfortunately, the directors' lack of knowledge does not remove the liability facing them as courts have suggested that it isn't what board directors know that may hurt them but what they do not know. For this reason, the independent objective assessment of compensation integrity of the organization and its leadership becomes as important for the risk management of board directors as it does for the organization itself and its investors.

Just one example of outside efforts to regulate compensation comes as Moody's Investors Service found that one out of every four companies it reviewed had either excessive compensation or compensation that was not aligned with long-term growth and the bondholder's interest.[29] The largest influence in bringing this issue to light are the two largest institutional investors, CalPERS[30] and TIAA-CREF,[31] who have both created policies for fair and just compensation of executives. However, neither fund would argue that an effort to "standardize" compensation is their intent but rather to ensure their own stakeholders are protected which requires integrity in their own fiduciary responsibilities as capital stewards.

With pension funds, which account for roughly 40 percent of all institutional money[32], increasing their investments in under regulated hedge funds, thereby diverting funds at record numbers (up from $5 billion in 1995 to as much a $300 billion by 2008[33]), companies would do well to heed these warnings. Access to institutional funds is going to get tighter, making it more imperative for companies to find a way to differentiate themselves from their competitors in attracting what now appears to be a reduction in targeted investment dollars. Engaging in compensation practices that lack integrity is bound to draw attention towards a company alright but not in a positive way. However, with no means of counterbalancing the appearance that a company lacks integrity, the investors are likely to continue to dilute their interest in the markets which is cause for concern for our global economy as investment in our capital markets begin to shrink. Short of getting involved in hedge funds (as Enron did), assessment and certification of integrity may be the answer for many companies.

Of course as long as stock options are given to illiquid companies in which hedge funds are investing in the hopes of an IPO, listed companies will continue to heavily use options as a form of compensation to attract new talent. Efforts undertaken by executives to receive excessive compensation when contrasted with the rate of return to investors, or attempting to "hide" the true value of their stock options by assigning artificially low values to expense options using the Black-Scholes model,[34] speaks to the wholeness and soundness of the organization's practices. Properly expensing stock options increases costs and reduces earnings and thus understating the value of options and the extent to which executives will go to hide their compensation package—whether from the board or investors— addresses the incorruptibility of an organization. The mandatory adoption of FAS123R – option expensing – in 2005-2006 will begin to shed more light on this.

Enron's own CEO, Jeff Skilling, brought the issue to light when it came to expensing stock options to create an illusion for investors. "[T]he most egregious [method of receiving excessive compensation] or the one that is used by every corporation in the world is executive stock options. . . [E]ssentially what you do is you issue stock options to reduce compensation expense, and therefore increase your profitability."[35]

According to the *Economist*, stock options accounted for 58 percent of the pay of U.S. CEOs in 2001. That year, the average CEO earned $10.83 million. Something to consider is that every day the stock price of a company that grants options goes up $1.00, the executives who are granted the options (often numbering in the millions), receive enormous benefit—thereby creating a potential conflict of interest in maintaining a level of integrity. Having personally witnessed the widespread acceptance of fraud at Enron, the granting of options played a significant role in the demise of the cultural integrity as many, myself included, chose to "look the other way" for the benefit of those options.

The SEC's recent investigation of Mercury Interactive, where executives clearly granted stock options to themselves and other employees when the stock was at its near terms lows–thus transferring millions of dollars of value from shareholders to employees – is not notable so much for the amounts of pay delivered but for the blatant violation of every facet of the company's stated compensation philosophy and strategy (per its Compensation Committee Report) and for violation of accounting and financial reporting rules and regulations. More than a dozen companies are being investigated for the same, and billions of dollars of value were misappropriated.

As Warren Buffett points out, maintaining integrity in expensing options is important. "When a company gives something of value to its employees in return for their services, it is clearly a compensation expense. And if expenses don't belong in the earnings statement, where in the world do they belong?"[36]

To demonstrate the financial impact of Buffett and Skilling's comments, we can look at just a few examples. Had options been expensed "JDS Uniphase's net loss in fiscal 2002 would increase [by] $564 million. . . . Brocade Communications System's 2001 profit of $3 million would have turned into a $592 million loss. [And] Dell's 2001 earnings would have been reduced [by] 59 percent; Intel's 79 percent; [and] Cisco's 171 percent."[37]

The correlation of compensation integrity and earnings integrity addresses this issue of restatements by these companies after stock options have already been exercised. Stock rises as earnings increase and untold numbers of options are granted and exercised before the rest of the world has time to react. For instance, JDS Uniphase announced a restatement of its 3rd Quarter 2001 results, causing its stock to drop to as low as $7.90 – 94 percent lower than its high of $146.32. The question is how many millions in stock options were granted at a strike price of $15.00, exercised at the $146.32 before the restatement and unsuspecting investors were left holding the bag at $7.90? On the other hand, companies like Brocade restated its earnings when it was revealed the company recorded stock option charges for employees too soon between May 1999 and July 2000. Rather than recording the compensation upon the hire date of employees, the company recorded the compensation when the workers accepted the job offer. The net result caused an increase in Brocade's stock price.

The Compensation Integrity Assessment Model[38] used by The Integrity Institute recognizes the notion of compensation being "excessive" is not based on an absolute number or "multiple", but on the methods by which the compensation is determined; the relationship between compensation delivered and value created; and the periods over which the compensation is determined and delivered. The focus of the model used for assessment of compensation integrity is not a moral judgment as to the amount of the compensation but whether the integrity of the compensation practices can ultimately impact the overall integrity of the organization.

The key consideration is whether a company can be managed in a sound and sustainable manner when it delivers compensation to individuals that to many appears to be excessive. Unfortunately it is not that simple. Some of the highest earning executives have created tremendous long-term value for stakeholders; while other lesser paid executives have been convicted of egregious behavior. However for other companies we must ask two important questions: If the compensation of executives is not excessive, why hide it? And if the company desires to hide their compensation, what else will they hide?

Beyond excessive compensation, we look for other tactics used to motivate employees to take certain actions that can jeopardize the integrity of an organization. For example, paying bonuses to accounts payable personnel for holding payments to vendors; or paying compensation at any level of the organization based upon future outcomes that may be manipulated, such as selling goods before the end of the quarter with a side agreement that allows the goods to be returned at the beginning of the next quarter. These tactics that boost income or compensation signal that a company is weak and while may provide for short term returns will not provide for long term sustainability.

Finally, there are a number of compensation plan design details that until recently have received less attention, partly because of minimal disclosure requirements. Interestingly, it is these features that have created some of the most egregious compensation practices making headlines. Change-in-control provisions–the provisions for "golden parachutes" are responsible for creating some recent furor in executive pay. Among the provisions: cash payments of 3 years' worth of base salary, plus 3 years' of bonus, plus the full acceleration of all vesting schedules on stock based awards, and the list goes on. Perhaps the most questionable, is the "tax gross-up" – an additional payment of cash to cover taxes due on the compensation payments. Of course, this too is taxable compensation so a tax gross-up payment must be large enough that after it is taxed there is still sufficient money to cover the tax on the other forms of compensation. Tax gross-up agreements are in place for 72 percent of CEOs in the top 50 NYSE companies (as measured by market capitalization) and 29 percent of the top NASDAQ firms.[39]

The perverse incentive here is that a CEO may manage a company poorly, resulting in a decline in share value affecting all shareholders and creating a situation where the firm is a takeover target. The CEO then receives several years' worth of compensation, tax-free, as a reward for the poor job he or she has done. Regardless of the past performance of the company, this also raises the question of whether such substantial financial opportunities create and incentive to sell the company regardless of the long-term impact of such an action. One element of the assessment of compensation integrity, in fact, is the analysis of the potential rewards for "failure" compared to the potential rewards for long-term success. To the extent these rewards are even equal but several years' pay can be received for a few weeks or months of sales effort, we believe the compensation system has been structured to the detriment of the stakeholders.

These "hidden" forms of compensation, along with non-qualified deferred compensation, executive retirement agreements, severance arrangements, and others are the source of the nine-figure compensation payments that are increasingly common. These instances, unfortunately, are commingled with cases of executives who have created substantial long-term value and deserve substantial rewards for doing so. It is this complexity that requires a detailed and thoughtful model of compensation integrity to identify – before the pay is given for the wrong reason – those companies with unsustainable compensation policies that will ultimately be to the long-term, or even short-term, detriment of stakeholders.

The assessment model's main purpose is to identify the philosophy, strategy, and processes used by the organization in compensation practices. The assessment focuses on four aspects of pay: (1) *Pay Governance*: the policies, processes, and outcomes for determining and delivering pay; (2) *Financial efficiency*: the extent to which compensation program design optimizes financial outcomes for all stakeholders; (3) *Compliance and disclosure*: the degree to which the Company adheres to the spirit and the letter of compensation disclosures and regulatory requirements; and (4) *Execution:* how compensation programs are actually operated relative to stated philosophies and strategies and plan objectives.

Through the analysis, The Integrity Institute determines the premise for the assignment of compensation and examines its impact on a company's organizational and cultural integrity, as well as the impact earnings integrity is having on the compensation integrity. Then opportunities for and barriers to improvement emerge in the areas of base salaries, annual incentives, long-term incentives, supplemental benefits, prerequisites, severance, deferred compensation or "rabbi trusts,"[40] change-in-control or "golden parachutes."

The resulting data is then measured against: (1) nontransparent compensation and incomplete disclosures; (2) peer comparisons; (3) accounting measures used in bonus plans, restricted stock awards, option pricing and re-pricing; (4) supplemental executive retirement plans; (5) the disclosed or undisclosed perks and benefits; and (6) any golden-parachutes.

Other issues considered include: (1) to what extent the executive compensation is increasing in comparison to the value the stock has decreased; (2) to what extent executives have received payments for short-term achievement of accounting-based goals (e.g., earnings per share) in absence of real economic performance and shareholder value creation; (3) whether equity compensation is being delivered in a manner consistent with the stated objectives of the plan; and (4) the aggregate amount of compensation delivered relative to financial results for the organization.

While none of the compensation factors on their face may indicate that an organization does not have integrity in its compensation practices, it does provide a good understanding of the executive team's alignment with stakeholder interests and their capital stewardship practices. And because the measures outlined are then measured against the other "intangible" factors that drive non-financial performance, we are able to predicatively determine to what extent compensation practices of the organization jeopardize the integrity of the organization and its financial performance, rather than leave the matter to speculation and the influence of non-standard measures.

(3) Compliance and Ethical Integrity

As noted in a recent benchmarking study by the Open Compliance and Ethics Group (*www.OCEG.org*).

Organizations that are unable to demonstrate that they comply with minimum legal requirements on a variety of fronts are being regularly dropped from investment and insurance portfolios. Those organizations with identified governance weaknesses, or ambiguity with respect to compliance, pay a penalty in terms of increased insurance rates or reduced coverage. Investors, especially institutional investors and pension plans, are demanding more disclosure and more influence in directing good corporate governance.

Ratings agencies and analysts are convinced that there is a cognizable difference in business performance between organizations that exhibit good corporate governance and those that exhibit poor corporate governance. Stock pricing is beginning to reflect this belief. On a positive note, those organizations that demonstrate excellence in ethics and governance are benefiting by receiving better insurance coverage and rates, higher bond ratings, and improved stock performance.[41]

In 2001 companies in the United States alone spent $843 billion annually to comply with regulatory requirements. In 2004, the amount rose to a staggering $1.1 trillion annually. Yet over the same time period, whistle-blowing reports to the Securities and Exchange Commission rose from 6,400 per month in 2001 to 40,000 per month in 2004. Enforcement actions went from 484 in 2001 to 639 in 2004 and fines went from $500 million to $3 billion[42]. The question is—if companies spending so much to be in compliance with the law, why are the reports of fraud up?

There can be no doubt there are a number of contributing factors, the least of which is a heightened awareness of the devastation that can be caused by a company's lack of integrity; and yet the government's response has always been to simply pile yet another piece of regulation on top of another with no real benefit. As best said by John A. Thain, CEO of the New York Stock Exchange states, "There is no question that, broadly speaking, Sarbanes-Oxley was necessary"[43]; however, the cost of implementing the new requirements has led some to question how effective or necessary the specific provisions of the law truly are.

According to the Financial Executives International (FEI), in a survey of 217 companies with average revenue above $5 billion, the cost of compliance with SOX Section 404 alone was an average of $4.36 million. The survey also indicated actual costs associated with compliance to be approximately 39 percent higher than companies expected to spend.[44] And yet, according to William H. Donaldson, the SEC's chairman at the time, at the end of March 2005, of the 2,500 companies that filed internal controls reports with the Securities and

Exchange Commission, under SOX 404, about 8 percent, or 200, found material weaknesses[45]. While 200 represents a small fraction of the 11,000 US listed companies and may not be statistically significant; 40,000 whistle-blowing reports to the SEC every month is. Even if 75 percent of the reports are disgruntled employees or frivolous reports, unlikely although, it still means the SEC is receiving more reports of misdeeds <u>every</u> month than there are publicly traded companies. This presents the likelihood that more material weaknesses exist than are being reported. The argument will always be made in the interpretation of "materiality" used by the company. Although as Aldous Huxley once pointed out "Facts do not cease to exist because they are ignored."

To add insult to injury, "to prosecute or not to prosecute" is no longer the question asked by the Justice Department. It has now moved from this two-prong approach to add a third option: Deferred Prosecution Agreements. Rather than undergo lengthy efforts to prosecute a company, which even if successful may be overturned on appeal, as we found with the conviction of Arthur Andersen, prosecution is being deferred. Deferred Prosecution means the company can forego prosecution for a stated period of time; however, they must admit guilt and pay the fines placed upon them by the government. The result is increased civil liabilities as class action lawyers use the guilty pleas as the basis for derivative suits.

The other element of the Deferred Prosecution Agreement requires the company to demonstrate a marked improvement in its practices which lead to the corruption; however, prior to the development of the Integria Model, no standardized measure existed that would provide a company with an opportunity to bargain for baseline assessment and ultimate certification of corporate integrity over admitting any guilt. The Integrity Institute now offers this alternative to companies who are the subject of prosecution.

The Integrity Institute uses the framework developed by the Open Compliance and Ethics Group (OCEG)[46] as the basis for our Compliance and Ethics Integrity Assessment Model[47]. The OCEG Framework enhances organizational value by providing universal guidelines for integrated compliance and ethics programs. By incorporating effective governance, compliance, and risk management into all their business practices, organizations can begin to measure the effectiveness and performance of their programs against an objective, external benchmark.[48] The OCEG guidelines encompass the "full lifecycle of planning, implementing, managing, evaluating, and improving integrated compliance and ethics programs."[49]

The OCEG Framework allows us to assess compliance with salient laws, rules, and regulations, as well as mandated responses that an organization *must* take to reduce legal and regulatory risks. By using the Framework, organizations are provided with tangible actions they should take to address both short and long-term legal risks, as well as related integral, ethical, and reputational risks often associated with the "spirit" of the law.

The OCEG Framework incorporates the Federal Sentencing Guidelines[50] (FSG), 2004 FSG Proposed Amendments,[51] the "Thompson memo,"[52] COSO Enterprise Risk Management,[53] Six Sigma,[54] Australian Standard AS3806-1998,[55] Sarbanes-Oxley,[56] SEC rules,[57] PCAOB rules,[58] PLI Compliance Counselor,[59] ISO 9000- and 14000-series quality frameworks,[60] Malcolm Baldrige Award criteria,[61] HCCA recommendations,[62] and many other governing rules and regulations.

An assessment of the integrity of an organization's compliance and ethics program using the OCEG Framework focuses on 25 high level areas that should be addressed in order to meet the test of integrity. Using the Guidelines created by OCEG, The Integrity Institute can assess the integrity of the culture, the alignment of the strategy with the organization's compliance and ethics program, the ability to respond to the potential lapses in compliance with the organization's established program, and finally, the company's ongoing evaluation of its own program. The assessment of these four areas (governance, risk, compliance and culture) using the OCEG Guidelines allows The Integrity Institute to efficiently understand the soundness, wholeness, and incorruptibility of the compliance and ethics programs of any organization.

(4) Corporate Citizenship Integrity (Environmental and Social Responsibility)

Being a good company is noble, but the purpose of measuring the integrity of the environmental policies and social responsibility practices of an organization is far broader than corporate honor. The focus of The Integrity Institute's corporate citizenship integrity assessment[63] measures the structure—not the morality—of corporate citizenship and identifies the changing landscape of environmental and social responsibility pressure being placed on companies to do the right thing.

Companies that see the "moral" importance to good corporate citizenship long ago adopted environmental and corporate social responsibility policies because it was the "right thing to do." Often these companies have done so quietly. However, a growing number of companies realize that there is financial value tied to being (or at least being seen as) a "good company." These companies are more likely to be a bit more boisterous in their approach—publishing, like Enron, glossy Corporate Social Responsibility Reports. Jeff Immelt, CEO of General Electric, notes, "If this wasn't good for business, we probably wouldn't do it."[64]

The question is: when is it good for business and when is it not? When asked why GE would spend $20 million of its shareholders' money on health care in Ghana, a country where it does almost no business, Immelt points out that his vision for GE is to become known as a "good company," not just in the U.S. but around the world. Immelt recognizes something many leaders fail to recognize, "Good leaders give back."

Beyond giving back, which senior executives are unlikely to accept as an integrity measure, Immelt speaks to the changing landscape of today's business environment:

The world's changed. Businesses today aren't admired. Size is not respected. There's a bigger gulf today between haves and have-nots than ever before. It's up to us to use our platform to be a good citizen. Because not only is it a nice thing to do, it's a business imperative.[65]

The purpose of measuring corporate citizenship integrity of organizations is to predict the extent to which the organization's corporate citizenship policies and practices contribute to or destroy the value of integrity for the organization, including the measure of how the integrity of the company's reputation is tied to its effort to be a "good" corporate citizen.

Commitment to good corporate citizenship demonstrates just how much pressure is influencing business. GE's business operations in Iran is a good example. Immelt notes, "While American firms are barred by law from doing business in Iran, [GE's] foreign-owned subsidiaries are permitted to do so."[66] However, given the political pressure and the US policies on doing business in counties that sponsor terrorism, the legal loopholes appear to have closed in on GE.

A 2003 shareholder proposal from the pension funds of New York City police officers and firefighters, which had investments in GE worth to $951 million, asked GE to review its operations in Iran with respect to the reputational and financial risks.[67] However, GE was not the only company to receive such pressure from the institutional investor. The Pension Fund also had major funds invested in ConocoPhillips and Halliburton,[68] Which both agreed they would no longer do business in the Country in response to the pressure placed upon them by the NYC pension fund.[69] New York City Comptroller William C. Thompson Jr. stated clearly, "as shareholders we are concerned that [each] Company's business dealings in Iran could expose the Company to negative publicity, public protests, and a loss of investor confidence, all of which could have a negative effect on shareholder value."[70] In 2004, GE made about $270 million in business in Iran, less than 1 percent of its revenue;[71] however, the Company eventually succumbed to the pressure and announced on February 1, 2005 it would no longer do business in Iran once its contracts were complete.[72]

Damage to reputation is one of the biggest business risks facing organizations.[73] Unfortunately. a false sense that a company's reputation is secure is the very thing that creates its risk, as was the opinion of those inside Enron and Arthur Andersen.[74] And as companies and investors now realize, a negative event at a single company can trigger a change in share value across the entire industry—based upon market perceptions—as seen in the energy sector after the collapse of Enron—something predicted by Moody's Investor Service relative to Japan's consumer finance industry.[75] As the investing population has witnessed, New York Attorney General Elliott Spitzer is no longer prosecuting companies but industries,[76] causing an immense ripple in the reputational wave that flows between investors and companies and beyond to its vendors and suppliers across the globe.

With the $951 million investment funds of NYC Fireman and Policeman's Pension Fund riding on the GE's social policies,[77] it is fairly easy to understand the value of integrity when it comes to Company's own environmental and social policies. As GE's Chairman Jeff Immelt pointed out, the Company spends billions of dollars protecting their reputation[78]—but "If [it] wasn't good for business, we probably wouldn't do it."[79] This is perhaps why in 2002, GE undertook compliance audits in the labor, environmental, health, and safety standards of its suppliers.[80] Between 2002 and the end of 2004, GE had performed over 3000 supplier audits.[81] With the number of suppliers GE has, it may take the Company a while to complete this task; but it illustrates the leadership's awareness of how their own reputation is tied to that of their suppliers.

However, very few companies have the ability to spend billions of dollars on audits to determine their vendors' integrity. With "81 percent of Global 500 executives rat[ing] environmental and health and safety issues among the top ten factors driving the value in their businesses,"[82] organizations should not underestimate the negative impact a vendors' practices could have on the integrity risk in these areas.

The same emotion that sets the "intrinsic" value of an organization's reputation also drives the need for greater integrity in environmental and social issues if companies are to attract investors. Contrary to the old belief that social investing does not provide the same returns, using environmental performance as a key in selecting companies, can potentially lead to higher-than-average returns, according to Innovest Strategic Advisors, which rates companies on their environmental policies.[83]

It does not bode well for the US as it struggles to compete in the global economy with perhaps the strictest international corporate governance laws, that 44 percent of the public believe the commitment of U.S. firms to corporate citizenship is heading in the wrong direction[84]. Meanwhile 66 percent of opinion leaders surveyed in France, Germany, and the UK, agree that corporate citizenship will be important in the future, and 42 percent agree strongly that corporate responsibility will affect share prices in the future. [85]

Most experts do agree that "environmental issues pose a serious and pervasive challenge to the financial and accounting activities of corporations, while simultaneously presenting a significant concern for the health and welfare of the citizens around the world."[86] The best way to overcome this challenge is for organizations to provide stakeholders with the assurance that their environmental policies and social responsibility practices have integrity.[87]

While Immelt may understand, many other leaders fail to understand the importance of environmental integrity—feeling as though a focus on environmental issues increases costs. However, while "doing the right thing" may raise costs in the short term initially, investment dollars withdrawn by institutional investors who recognize an organization's failure to focus on the importance of things such as climate risk are likely to more than offset expenses.

A survey conducted among fund managers, analysts, and investor relations officers found that 78 percent of the participants opined that "management of environmental and social risk has a positive impact on a company's long-term market value."[88] Only 13 percent felt as though it had "no influence" in the long-term market value of the

company.[89] As institutional investors align their investment dollars, their focus is on the 78 percent "doing the right thing" versus the 13 percent who felt there was no "long-term market value."
California State Treasurer Phil Angelides further explored institutional investors' focus on environmental integrity. Speaking before a summit of institutional investors that controlled more than $1 trillion in assets, he commented,

> *In global warming, we are facing an enormous risk to the U.S. economy and to retirement funds that Wall Street has so far chosen to ignore. The corporate scandals over the last couple of years have made it clear that investors need to pay more attention to corporate practices that affect long-term value. As fiduciaries, we must take it upon ourselves to identify the emerging environmental challenges facing the companies in which we are shareholders, to demand more information, and to spur needed actions to respond to those challenges.90*

The Asset Management Working Group (AMWG) of the UNEP Finance Initiative, which is comprised of 12 financial institutions managing total assets of about $1.6 trillion, recently invited leading financial research institutions from around the world to produce sector-specific reports. The focus of the reports were to: (1) identify the specific environmental and social issues that are likely to be material for a company's competitiveness and reputation in that particular industry; and (2) identify and quantify the Group's power to impact stock price.[91] As a result of the research, the United Nations established Principles for Responsible Investing which recognized that social, environmental, and corporate governance issues are material to investors, especially over the long term.[92]

As of January, 2004, global pension assets in the eleven major capital markets reached $14.2 trillion dollars.[93] Many institutional investors, charged with the fiduciary responsibility to protect those assets, have an environmental and social fund that directs investment dollars to companies that recognize the risk associated with environmental and social changes. The key is to assist companies in their ability to tap into these funds by understanding and communicating their commitment to integrity in the area of corporate citizenship.

To demonstrate, at least the short term economic impact to industries when faced with social and environmental pressure to operate with integrity, we examined the 1999 World Trade Organization meeting in Seattle.[94] As a result of brutal riots in Seattle, the meeting collapsed in a week with no action taken on the agenda.[95] The protests, although emotionally driven, demonstrated the social pressure placed on firms and industries which are perceived as either socially or environmentally *irresponsible*.[96] Apparel, footwear, and toy manufacturers were the firms perceived as lacking *social* integrity.[97] The industries perceived as lacking in *environmental* integrity were mining, oil and gas, paper, chemicals, steel, and utilities.[98]

The results of the study by Schneitz and Epstein demonstrated that the portfolio of *Fortune* 500 companies having a reputation for social responsibility declined by only slightly more than 1 percent, while firms seen as lacking in social responsibility declined by 2.36 percent over the same period.[99] In dollars, that amounted to a $378 million dollar loss of shareholder value for the average firm in the sample. The environmentally and socially irresponsible industries suffered a decline in market capitalization of over 3 percent.[100]

To measure the integrity of environmental and social policies, The Integrity Institute uses information gathered from company literature (environmental reports, regulatory filings, annual reports), along with disclosures made in the letter to the shareholders to determine the organization's commitment to behave in an economically and environmentally sustainable manner, while honoring the interests of direct stakeholders. It is important to note that while the process may appear to be similar to a "social audit", we only measure the integrity of the company's corporate citizenship relative to the other measures of integrity – not as a stand-alone product.

The mission of the corporate citizenship integrity assessment is to understand the process of developing, and advocating by example, corporate citizenship business practices which benefit not only the corporation and its employees, but also the greater community, the economy and the world environment. Companies which operate with integrity in the area of corporate citizenship seek to reshape the way business is done in both the for-profit and non-profit world.

While corporate citizenship is defined at many levels, there is a core of minimum standards for corporate citizenship performance. These standards represent an initial step in the full development of a corporate citizen. The minimum standards are intended to be specific, documented and measurable. They are also achievable and meaningful in terms of impacts on communities, employees, the environment and economic systems.

These standards are not about getting a "passing" or "failing" grade but are assessment tools for the corporation's current level of commitment to operate as a corporate citizen with integrity.

The standards assist in setting measurable and achievable targets for improvement and form the objective foundation for reporting to all direct stakeholders both the "talk" and actual "walk" of its citizenship.

The dimensions covered by the minimum standards incorporate the concepts of community involvement, diversity, employee relations, environment, international relationships, marketplace practices, fiscal responsibility, and accountability. These factors have been defined as: 1) community development; 2) diversity; 3) environment; 4) international relationships; 5) marketplace practices; 6) fiscal responsibility; and 7) accountability: auditing, monitoring & reporting.

Among the things analyzed in the assessment of corporate citizenship are: (1) policies relative to an organization's environmental programs; (2) implementation processes of environmental strategies and consistency in the policies; (3) board structure; (4) environmental audits; (5) environmental reporting; (6) life cycle analysis; (7) senior environmental officer level; (8) compliance and quality ratings; (9) other environmental indicators; and (10) the extent to which the company participates in voluntary environmental programs. This review also includes an analysis of supply chain management, water use, and climate change strategy.

Using information in documents published by the companies themselves or stakeholders (such as industry sector and firm-specific reports; summaries published by international organizations such as Dow Jones Sustainability Index;[101] press reviews; and surveys), The Integrity Institute identifies violations of human rights by the organization or its vendors. The results of the corporate citizenship integrity assessment are then measured against an assessment of clients, vendor, and suppliers to determine the extent to which the soundness, wholeness, and incorruptibility test has been met.

(5) Cultural Integrity

Perhaps it could be argued that at the heart of any organization's integrity is its "human resources."[102] No doubt, the organization stands strong or falls at the hands of human beings, whose collective consciousness and values define the culture of the organization and whether it has integrity. In applying the test of integrity, The Integrity Institute assesses whether the culture is sound, whole, and incorruptible and what predictive "markers" exist that may weaken the organization's ability to stand strong.

When one thinks of culture in the case of Enron, one often thinks of the fraud that was committed; however, the corruption was able to manifest because the culture was neither sound nor whole. Applying the Birkinshaw model,[103] Enron failed, not in spite of its talent and mindset, but because of it. Although Enron was named "Most Innovative Company" for six years in a row by *Fortune* magazine[104], Birkinshaw points out, too few boundaries and too much space allowed corruption to ease its way through the firm.[105]

Based upon the premise that financial statements don't create themselves—people do, we begin with the assumption that the integrity of financial statements depends upon a culture that has integrity. Of course, culture has a profound impact on the overall ability of the company to meet its financial numbers. If the leadership and culture lack integrity, however, we will often find that the earnings have been manipulated because most companies realize too late they were unable to meet the key financial projections because they did not have the right human "resources" in place to implement key strategies. Or the lack of communications integrity did not allow for the key elements of execution to filter their way through the organization. The net result means the company risks financial ruin if lack of integrity in the area of leadership, communication, and culture impacts the earnings integrity.

As we are finding, if investors rely solely on traditional financial indicators as their source of information—looking through the rear view mirror—if the company does not have the "right people on the bus" to implement the leadership's strategy, it does not matter how bold the vision is or how revealing the forward-looking statements may be, it will always be from a retrospective view. This places immense pressure on leaders to "hit" their numbers while maintaining a standard of integrity. Unfortunately many leaders are succumbing to the pressure as we find nearly half of CFOs (47 percent) report they are feeling pressured by their bosses to use aggressive accounting to make the results look better.[106] Of course, what's perhaps even more frightening is that only 38 percent think the pressure is less today than it was before Enron's implosion—20 percent think there is more pressure on them to cook the books[107].

Leaders are feeing pressure to perform because they have no tangible understanding of how the culture is impacting their bottom line. The reaction is often to simply lay people off to reduce costs. However, as Dr. Kim Cameron notes less than 10 percent of firms that downsize report improvements in product and service quality, innovation, and organizational climate.[108] Three years after downsizing, the market share prices of downsized companies were an average of 26 percent below the share price of their competitors.[109]

A 2001 study found that "only about 5 percent of the workforce understands the strategy and how their actions link to that strategy. . . . However, only 50 percent of organizations link human capital to strategy and only 25 percent have a consistent way to measure human capital."[110] Even fewer understand the impact this measure of non-financial performance has on the financial performance. These figures become even more important when we realize that a majority of executive teams spend less than one hour per month discussing the achievement of the strategy.

It is important to make the distinction between organizational *culture* and organizational *climate*. "Climate refers to the more temporary attitudes, feelings, and perceptions of individuals," whereas the culture is enduring, slow changing, and encompasses the core characteristics of organizations.[111] Because climate "is based on attitudes, [it] can change quickly and dramatically."[112] This may explain why downsizing, as pointed out by Dr. Cameron, does not have the intended impact on the financial performance; whereas corporate culture can have a significant impact on a firm's long-term economic performance.[113]

In the next decade, corporate culture will probably be an even more important factor in determining the success or failure of firms.[114] Cultures that grow "unadaptive" over time have a tendency to inhibit strategic or tactical changes. Given the importance of innovation and the speed required to be first to market, a restrictive culture could likely jeopardize the integrity of the organization and its ability to respond to change in order to gain or maintain a competitive advantage.

Corporate cultures that actually inhibit strong long-term financial performance are not rare.[115] Like Enron, these inhibiting cultures tend to emerge slowly and quietly over years, and because the firm is performing well, the long-term effect the culture can have on the balance sheet goes unnoticed. These cultures, which often encourage inappropriate behavior and inhibit change to more appropriate strategies, can easily develop. And because they help support the existing power structure in the organization, they can be enormously difficult to change.

The good news is that corporate culture can actually be changed to enhance the performance of the organization. However, absent an assessment as to the structural integrity of the culture, any abscess that may be present and growing can remain unrecognized, leaving even the most qualified leader at a disadvantage to meet the needs of the shareholders. Leaders then find themselves practicing crisis management—rather than responding to the market—they are reacting. This ultimately can provide insight into correlation between the integrity of the leadership and culture, as well as other key components of non-financial performance.

There is no one-size-fits-all culture that works in every situation; therefore, The Integrity Institute uses a competing values framework as the basis for its Cultural Integrity Assessment Model,[116] recognizing that the culture of a high-tech firm will be different than that of a traditional life insurance company. The Competing Values Framework (CVF) Culture Assessment, developed by Kim S. Cameron, Ph.D. and Robert E. Quinn, Ph.D.,[117] has been recognized as "one of the fifty most important models in the history of business."[118]

This framework has been studied and tested in organizations for more than twenty five years by a group of thought leaders from leading business schools and corporations. It has been recognized as one of the 40 most significant contributions to management thought, and it is being applied in several thousand organizations worldwide. The Competing Values Framework emerged from studies of the factors that account for highly effective organizational performance, and it was further developed in response to the need for a broadly applicable method for fostering successful leadership, improving organizational effectiveness, diagnosing and changing organizational culture, and promoting value creation.

The assessment serves primarily as a map, an organizing mechanism, a sense-making device, a source of new ideas, and a learning system. It has been applied to many aspects of organizations such as value outcomes, corporate strategy, organizational culture, core competencies, leadership, communication, decision making, motivation, financial valuation, mergers and acquisitions, human resources practices, quality, and employee selection. From the Competing Values Framework comes a theory about how these various aspects of organizations function in simultaneous harmony and tension with one another. The framework of the assessment helps identify a set of guidelines that can help leaders diagnose and manage the interrelationships, congruencies, and contradictions among these different aspects of organizations. In other words, the framework helps leaders work more comprehensively and more consistently in improving their organizations' performance and value creation.

The culture assessment instrument consists of six items that help cue respondents to describe some of the core dimensions of their organization's culture. Using an ipsative response scale helps eliminate a positive response bias, so the resulting culture profile is a reasonably accurate picture of what the organization's dominant culture really is. Cultural congruence has been found in past research to be predictive of high performance. For example, the extent to which the culture of sub-units in an organization are congruent; the extent to which managerial competencies are congruent with the organization's culture; the extent to which congruence exists among the various dimensions of culture, and; the extent to which an organization's culture is congruent with its environmental dynamics all are predictive of high performance.

Organizational integrity can be at least partially determined on the basis of the extent to which consistency and congruency exist. Unpredictable or incongruent cultures have some probability of being associated with the same pressures that may lead to loss of integrity—e.g., tendencies to overstate earnings or litigation. Predicatively understanding the "markers" or "danger zones" within a culture, helps leaders understand where the "target zones" are to effectively and efficiently build an organization that provides better earnings per share. Absent such an examination and the appropriate weighting in the Model, there is no indication of whether the culture shares the values of the leadership, can uphold the vision, or implement the strategy.

Our cultural integrity assessment is adaptable and thus can be used at a multiple of levels within the organization in order to target problem areas. To do this, the assessment identifies the dominant characteristics of the culture, organizational leadership, management of employees, organizational "glue," strategic emphases, and criteria of success. Through understanding how and to what extent the culture of the organization (1) competes versus collaborates, and (2) creates versus controls, The Integrity Institute can determine what drives the organization and where problems might exist, and perhaps most importantly can predict the success or failure of a merger or acquisition based solely on an assessment of the cultural integrity.

Two cases bear mentioning when it comes to corporate culture: the first is General Electric (GE) and the second is Coca-Cola.

Under Jack Welch, the former Chairman of GE, the company had the uncanny record of hitting its earnings targets during every quarter—something even Warren Buffett found generally suspicious.[119] If Welch's GE was driven by playing the numbers game, Buffett admits candidly, "I not only don't know today what our business will earn *next year*—we don't even know what they will earn *next quarter*."[120] He admits he is "downright incredulous if they [managers] consistently reach their declared targets."[121] Under Welch, GE was known for hard-driving management and a culture, often described as aggressive as Enron's. Today, GE has a very different feel, both for employees, as well as for investors.

As Welch was replaced as Chairman of GE by Jeffrey R. Immelt on September 7, 2001, Immelt issued this statement: "We manage business, not earnings. . . . GE is a company you can trust, delivering excellent earnings achieved with integrity and a transparency unsurpassed in global business."[122] Not only did Immelt acknowledge the reputation that GE had gained as its own accounting practices were called into question after the collapse of Enron, he acknowledged the nature of the culture at GE when he said:

> *One concern that keeps me up at night is that among the 300,000-plus GE employees worldwide, there are a handful who choose to ignore our code of ethics. I would be naïve to assume that a few bad apples don't exist in our midst. We spend billions each year on improving our training, enforcing our compliance to preserve our culture and protect one of our most valuable assets—our reputation.123*

The Chairman of the world's "Most Valuable Company" appears to be well on his way to making his mark—for very different reasons than Welch—as the leader of the "Most Admired Company", for recognizing that the importance of protecting GE's reputation requires the preservation of the culture. An examination of Immelt's view of culture shows that three out of the four things he believes will keep GE on top are predictable: execution, growth, and great people. The fourth, which Immelt listed as the most important, is not predictable but has everything to do with the culture: virtues.[124] Perhaps this is why GE was named the "World's Most Respected Company" and placed "first" in integrity.[125]

The second company, Coca-Cola, during the past decade, faced a number of challenges within its culture that directly impacted its bottom line and shareholder value, including: a commercial investigation in Europe of the company's bottling practices; allegations of tainted Coke in Belgium; allegations of channel-stuffing; and an SEC investigation into a whistle-blower allegation that the company falsified market studies for a product launch at Burger King, for which the company (1) paid $21 million to Burger King to settle the matter; (2) paid $540,000 to the whistle-blower and (3) took a $9 million pre-tax write down.[126]

Although the Company laid off a number of high level executives as a result of the troubles and the general counsel resigned, the troubles for the soft-drink giant did not end there. To add insult to injury, the Company suffered additional scrutiny when it was discovered that their Dasani bottled water was nothing more than tap water.[127] What the Company described as its "highly sophisticated purification process," based on NASA spacecraft technology, was in fact reverse osmosis used in many modest water purification units.[128]

The purpose of these two examples is to demonstrate the power of culture to shape the financial performance of a company. In the instance of GE, there has been a shift in the nature of the culture and its impact on the organization's performance. Coca-Cola on the other hand would be wise to take a lesson from GE.

(6) Earnings Integrity

The extent to which corporate earnings are managed vs. manipulated has long been of interest to analysts, regulators, researchers, and other investment professionals.[129] Earnings manipulation is defined as an instance in which a company's managers violate generally accepted accounting principles (GAAP) to favorably represent the company's financial performance.[130]

There are companies that notably "manage" their earnings within GAAP and as long as accounting treatments fall within GAAP, we do not consider them to be manipulating their earnings, even if a company is forced to change their accounting choices, even if a restatement is required. However, when a company's accounting choices fall outside GAAP and a restatement is required, intentional manipulation is often a key factor.

When knowledge spreads that a company has manipulated its earnings, its stock value plummets. In fact, according to Messod Daniel Beneish, "the typical manipulator loses approximately 40 percent of its market value on a risk-adjusted basis in the quarter containing the discovery of the manipulation."[131] The key is to predict the likelihood of manipulation early so as to alert the company so as to avoid the potential damage that could be caused.

The Integrity Institute's Earnings Integrity Assessment Model[132] determines the likelihood that a firm can sustain current earnings in the future, and whether an accounting risk likely exists that financial statements contain the effects of earnings manipulation. In firms with poor earnings quality, credit and equity investors are exposed to less persistent earnings, which unless recognized, result in lower than expected returns. In more severe cases where the declining performance is alleged to occur as result of a questionable application of accounting rules, the exposure can result in a prompt and substantial decline in wealth. Conversely, failure to recognize firms with good earnings quality results in foregoing the higher than expected returns that are typically associated with more persistent earnings.

The assessment model produces "Earnings Quality Rankings" that are quite successful at delineating future stock returns. The Earnings Quality Rankings are based on a version of the Beneish (1999) Model that distinguishes manipulated from non-manipulated financial reporting. The assessment model relies on financial data to identify firms that have high and low earnings quality.

The Integrity Institute's earnings integrity assessment can capture either the financial statement distortions that result from manipulation or preconditions that might prompt companies to engage in such activity. Perhaps more importantly, the assessment model detects approximately half of the companies involved in earnings manipulation prior to public discovery. As evidence will show, the effectiveness of this assessment model was made public on May 5, 1998, by a group of graduate students from Cornell University[133] by posting their report on the Internet, predicting Enron was manipulating its earnings more than three years before the implosion of the Company.[134] Unfortunately, no one heeded the warnings. Although the graduate students recommended a "sell" on Enron stock,[135] by the time the public became aware of the manipulation investors had billions of dollars.

The indices used to detect earnings manipulation are: days' sales in receivables; gross margin; asset quality; sales growth; depreciation; sales, general, and administrative expense; leverage; total accruals to total assets; and distribution of variables.[136] Because manipulation typically consists of an artificial inflation of revenues or deflation of expenses, variables that take into account simultaneous bloating in asset accounts have predictive content.[137]

One of the many benefits of using the earnings integrity assessment is that it requires only two years of data (one annual report) to evaluate the likelihood of manipulation. The underlying earnings integrity assessment model recognizes two types of errors: classification of a company as a non-manipulator when it manipulates; and classification of a company as a manipulator when it does not manipulate. When the results of the analysis are integrated with the other integrity measures described, the rate of error in either of these two categories will prove to be substantially less.

(7) Governance Integrity

So what is the bottom line when it comes to manipulating the bottom line or paying excessive compensation? Egregious efforts to hide compensation or reward bad behavior ultimately reflect poorly on the quality of the board and its ability to govern. According to a *BusinessWeek* study, which measured the value of board quality in terms of corporate performance, companies with the most highly rated boards averaged 51.7 percent in shareholder returns, while the worst boards dragged their companies down to an average 12.9 percent return over the same period of time.[138] Although according to a recent survey of the Asian markets showed that recent years have proven that "high corporate governance stocks do not necessarily outperform when markets are rising, especially when there are strong liquidity inflows into the markets"[139] "It is only when markets turn ugly that companies and markets with high CG scores outperform as investors abandon risk companies."[140] Assessment of corporate integrity and the predictive nature of the Model equates to "preparedness" for the storm which as we found in the US, in the wake of Hurricane Katrina, the lack of preparedness can be more devastating than the storm itself.

Of course, much of the focus following the passage of SOX has been on corporate governance; however, because compliance with SOX, for the most part, is self-governing, being compliant is simply not enough. Institutional investors are still demanding more transparency when it comes to understanding how the company is governed and who is providing oversight. And as we found at a recent roundtable, any efforts to repeal SOX without an alternative means to ensure shareholder rights are protected, is going to be met with resistance from institutional investors.[141] The position of The Integrity Institute is to transcend the regulation by ending the need for SOX. By offering an alternative of assessment and certification, the law could be amended to establish "guidelines", based on the tenants of SOX, rather than mandatory regulation. Similar to the guidelines established by the King I and II Reports in South Africa, which have been adopted by the South African Stock Exchange, these guidelines and certification by The Integrity Institute could be a requirement for listing on a public exchange.

Absent a broad acceptance of such an alternative, to meet the need for greater understanding and transparency, organizations like Institutional Shareholder Services (ISS)[142] and The Corporate Library[143] are attempting to independently measure and rate the governance aspect of corporate integrity. This leaves organizations on the defense as they attempt to counterbalance the subjective nature of these findings based solely on information in the public domain. And yet, many companies realize these ratings actually impact investment decisions.

Such ratings suggest that a significant minority of companies still face challenges regarding board composition, including a lack of independence, a lack of sufficient financial expertise on the audit committee, and directors who are stretched thin with multiple commitments.[144] Evidence, however, does show that boards and key committees are trying, by holding more frequent and longer meetings,[145] which is a significant improvement from Enron's own audit committee which met once a quarter for one hour; however, board directors are still grappling with the requirements and cost of compliance of SOX.[146]

All of the things discussed thus far are areas of interest to board directors as part of their role as governors and yet too many meetings are being spent trying to assess the risks with little success, as evidenced by the significant increase in whistle-blowing reports. The pressure has perhaps never been greater for boards to have a greater understanding of the business, which requires a broad spectrum assessment that can be used to understand, adjust, and address the risks facing themselves and the companies. The alternative means facing a multitude of class action lawsuits that have become all too common place – or worse face jail time.

The Corporate Governance Integrity Assessment Model[147] is a compilation of a variety of assessment tools, such as the guidelines established in the OCEG Framework, and seeks to incorporate, among other things: an understanding of the possible organizational fraud; internal controls; audit committee oversight; legal assessment; auditor independence; board composition; CEO compensation; shareholder responsiveness; litigation and regulatory problems: takeover defenses; accounting; strategic decision-making; and analyst adjustment. These factors are then compared with a rating of compliance in comparison to "best practices," and a governance risk assessment is then made and compared with the previous rating.

The assessment model is not intended to provide a "rating" and does not seek to replace the ratings of ISS or The Corporate Library. Rather its purpose is to explain the impact the ratings have on overall shareholder value by integrating the assessment of corporate governance ratings into the overall measure of a company's integrity. Additionally, because The Integrity Institute does not perform any consulting services, the conflicts of interest often inherent with the governance rating agencies, or credit rating agencies for that matter, are not present with the independent and objective assessment of The Integrity Institute.

Although figures prepared by ISS indicate the top 10 corporate-governance-rated companies outperformed their industry-adjusted profitability average by 18.98 percent, while the performance of the bottom 10 corporate-governance-rated companies fell below their industry-adjusted profitability average by 4.86 percent, a difference of 23.84 percent[148], these ratings do not necessarily predict the sustainability of the organizations and may focus too much on the "effect" rather than the "cause" of corporate governance integrity. Firms in the bottom decile of industry-adjusted corporate-governance-rated companies have a net profit margin of 6.38 percent above the average while the top rated firms outperform their industry-adjusted average by 21.66 percent, a difference of 15.28 percent[149]. The critics of the ISS rating system point out for a significant fee, ISS will help you raise their governance rating which calls into question the integrity of the rating itself in the opinion of the author.

Some senior executives question whether the policies identified by the "corporate governance rating agencies" actually detract from the bottom-line (in other words, whether a Poison-Pill protects the company for a hostile takeover and is a good thing or whether it is simply a means of protecting senior management with golden parachutes.[150]) To adjust for the argument as to which corporate governance policies may or may not actually add value to the company, The Integrity Institute has expanded the assessment of governance beyond the common single-focus of "corporate governance" to "business governance" which encompasses all ten components.

As studies show a direct correlation between corporate governance in four areas: (1) shareholder returns; (2) profitability; (3) risk; and (4) dividend policies,[151] The Integrity Institute seeks to provide a predictive measure that is a balance of each these factors relative to the other nine components of the Model, rather than myopically focus on governance as the sole indication of whether a company has integrity as implied by the rating agencies. We believe the integrity of a company's governance can *only* be assessed when the board directors have a full understanding of where oversight is needed and whether the board needs assistance in providing such oversight, which is why ratings cannot accurately assess governance integrity. The purpose of The Integrity Institute's integrity assessment is, in large part, to provide a means for companies to counterbalance the impact obscure governance ratings appear to have on shareholder value with no apparent ability to predict the sustainability of the organization.

(8) Leadership Integrity

Key to the success of any organization is the leadership. The Integrity Institute's Leadership Integrity Assessment Model[152] examines two aspects: (1) behavioral complexity in leadership and (2) strategy.

Within the focus of *behavioral complexity*, we examine four aspects of leadership's ability to: (1) provide continuity; (2) lead change; (3) drive for results, and; (4) maintain relationships. Within the focus of *strategy*, we examine four aspects of leadership: (1) discipline, (2) authenticity, (3) transparency, and (4) accountability.

Our behavioral complexity assessment model is designed to understand the leader's ability to address pressing social demands and the ability to play multiple roles that call for diverse or even competing behaviors. Using the CVF, the model is integrated to understand the linkage between cognitive complexity and social behavior. Behavioral complexity is the capacity of a given leader to engage in wide range of behaviors. A leader with a high behavioral complexity is able to engage in a wider array of behaviors than a person with low behavioral complexity is able to do. Specifically, behavioral complexity is "the ability to exhibit contrary or opposing behaviors (as appropriate or necessary) while still retaining some measure of integrity, credibility, and direction"[153] Such a leader maintains continuity while at the same time is capable of leading change. Likewise, a behaviorally complex leader is able to meet the multiple and competing needs of the organization. We find further that the leader who has a high behavioral complexity is able to meet and integrate the paradoxical pressures of life inside the organization. Behavioral complexity does not necessarily guarantee that a leader will "do the right thing" every time but it the manager is more likely to draw on a wider range of behaviors to more effectively meet competing demands.

To demonstrate this, a review of a study of chief executive officers and firm performance found that CEOs with high behavioral complexity were more effective than their counterparts.[154] The firms run by more behaviorally complex CEOs outperformed other firms on three measures of financial performance. Also, studies of middle managers have demonstrated that people with high behavioral complexity are more effective leaders than are those with lower levels of behavioral complexity[155]. This draws us to a better understanding of what managers are more likely to provide for good successors lending to the sustainability of the organization.

There is also a relationship between complexity and effectiveness which causes the model to understand and identify several types of leadership, including laissez-faire, management-by-exception, contingent reward, and transformational leadership. Only two of these types of leaders (contingent reward and transformational leadership) have been found to be active and effective. The result means the leader is better adept at continuity, change, results, and relationships.

The results of the assessment provide us with an understanding that a "contingent reward" leader sets the "tone at the top" for a stable, predictable organizational culture, which provides us with the predictive marker for the correlation between leadership and culture. The "transformational" leader is more like to be creative risk-takers who challenge prevailing assumptions. Transformation leaders are inspiring, enthusiastic people who have a vision for the future, while at the same time illustrate behaviors focused on results and relationships.

Using Quinn's leadership assessment model of behavioral complexity, we are able to recognize the person who uses both styles of leadership to represent all four domains—provide continuity, lead change, drive for results, and maintain relationships—is more effective than leaders who lack such complexity.

To enhance the value of the model, we integrate the results with the leadership assessment of strategy developed by Oren Harari,[156] that quantifiably measures the four qualities a leader of integrity demonstrates—discipline, authenticity, transparency, and accountability

As best stated by Retired General Ronald R. Fogleman, former Chief of Staff of the United States Air Force, "Integrity and leadership are inextricably linked. . . . [T]he main difference between units that perform at their maximum potential and those that fail is usually their leadership."[157] Leaders are either respected or they are not, Fogleman points out. Over time "[t]he more a leader's behavior matches his or her words, the more loyal people will become, both to the leader *and* the organization."[158]

Although experts focus on the characteristics and quality of the leadership, the purpose of our assessment is to quantifiably measure the soundness, wholeness, and incorruptibility of the leadership using a holistic approach never before used to measure leadership integrity. The key to the analysis is to understand the extent to which the leader is adding to or inhibiting the profitable growth of the organization that leads to its financial success. Many leaders believe a strategy of "growth through acquisition" will build shareholder value; however, six out of seven acquisitions actually destroy shareholder value.[159] If most acquisitions actually destroy shareholder value, we assume that 90 percent of the success or failure of an organization is determined by the leadership's design or the cultural integrity, which is just one of the many important reasons why an integrated model that holistically measures the integrity of the organization allows us to assess at a fundamental level the extent to which the leadership is affecting the overall financial performance of the company through profitable growth or whether the culture is predicatively undermining the value the leader brings to the organization.

Great leaders understand that the key to profitable growth is capital stewardship and the integrity of income, cash flow, and asset management. Although there has been a strong emphasis on income, this single-focus fails the integrity test of wholeness. We must include an analysis of the cash flow and asset management (return on assets) to assure a valid measure of integrity; without cash flow, even with strong income and an acceptable return on assets, a company will be out of business. When integrated with our earnings integrity assessment, we are able to find the "markers" of whether the leadership is focused on capital stewardship that requires income, cash flow, and a return on assets all rise at the same time. Achieving this balance necessitates the need for leadership integrity.

As an example of what can happen when cash-flow problems exist, we can examine Enron. Despite showing strong earnings and a reported $1.3 billion in net income (which was actually only $978 million according to Arthur Andersen), the company was using a method of accounting called mark-to-market which was an illusion since it allowed the company to book profits for the entire term of a 20-year contract with no corresponding cash flow. Rather than managing its assets, the company was moving its assets and associated debt, off the balance sheet. The leadership integrity did not pass the test of soundness and therefore, was directly responsible for failing to practice good capital stewardship.

A lack of leadership integrity could be based on a number of factors. Although Ken Lay was considered by many a "transformational" leader he was not an effective leader, perhaps, in part, because he lacked the focus on a "stable, predictable organizational culture" that would represent a "contingent reward" leader. As the leadership integrity at Enron weakened, the cultural integrity weakened, allowing corruption to permeate every aspect of the key areas of non-financial performance, and ultimately the financial performance.

Good leadership begins with a vision, around which a strategy is built. Leadership must be able to relate to, and communicate clearly with managers, who must then implement that strategy. None of this happens without a culture that shares the values of the leadership based on the leader's actions. Leadership must be disciplined to see the vision through to completion, accepting responsibility for the outcome, and exerting a willingness to be held accountable if the result is not what the leadership had either planned or hoped for. And, just as importantly, the leader must be willing to hold others to this same standard, which can only be done if the words and actions of the leader are inline with one another and the shared values of the organization. If the leader fails to hold others in the organization to the same standard, eventually the cultural integrity will weaken as employees no longer respect authority—opening the doors to possible corruption which is the "incorruptibility" test of integrity.

Great leaders recognize that between discipline and accountability there is a "mirror" called *authenticity* and a "window" called *transparency*. Only operating with this level of leadership integrity will the leader be willing to be examined by the organization's stakeholders. Between *discipline* and *accountability* there should be a great deal of self-reflection as to whether the strategy, planning, and implementation are whole, sound, and incorruptible. It is important to point out here that incorruptible does not necessarily mean the leader is corrupt but rather his visions and strategy may become corrupted because the leader lacks the necessary integrity to be successful. Only in the worst of instances will the organization become corrupted because of the leadership's lack of integrity.

Leaders who fail to meet the authenticity and transparency test outlined above generally demonstrate a quiet, or in the case of Enron—a not so quiet, desperation to keep things hidden. One of the many indications that Enron's leadership integrity was weak was Jeff Skilling's letter to shareholders that stated Enron had hit a record $1.3 billion in net income while the audited financials indicated only $978 million.[160] And while Skilling was telling investors and analysts that Enron's strategy in broadband should warrant an additional $40 value to Enron's stock price, inside the company the story was very different as witnessed by the author. In February 2000, at an all-employee meeting, in describing his strategy he revealed his lack of confidence in the soundness of the strategy: "I *think* this will work.

.. there are really only two competitors in this market. One is Duke Energy and the other is Pacific Gas & Electric. Duke is laying people off in this business right now and PG&E announced last week that they were selling the business. So we are in great shape." Meanwhile, inside Enron Broadband Services, when the head of accounts payable asked Skilling where he was getting his numbers, he said, "These are the numbers I was given." The manager retorted, "No you weren't, because I give you those numbers." Towards the end, it was obvious that Skilling could no longer stand the pressure based upon his lack of integrity as he proceeded to used an epithet to describe a "short seller" when they questioned his strategy on an analyst conference call.[161]

In hindsight Enron's leadership integrity failures cost investors $90 billion. But Enron is not alone; Coca-Cola's woes illustrate to what extent leadership integrity impacts the bottom line.

In 1999, in the months following allegations of tainted Coke in Belgium, Coca-Cola experienced a number of problems: the company lost $34 billion in market value;[162] the company's European subsidiary profits fell by more than $205 million;[163] the European Commission rejected Coke's proposed acquisition of Orangina;[164] and the CEO lost his job soon after.[165]

In 2002, Matthew Whitley, a mid-level accounting executive, filed a whistle-blowing suit against Coca-Cola alleging retaliation for revealing fraud in a market study performed on behalf of Burger King.[166] In the three weeks after the lawsuit was filed and the lack of leadership integrity became public, Coca-Cola lost $15 billion in shareholder value. A number of top level executives were fired; as mentioned previously, Coke paid $21 million to Burger King to settle its disputes with the fast-food giant, $540,000 was paid to the whistle-blower, and a $9 million pre-tax write off had to be taken.[167]

Although Coca-Cola disputed and denied the allegations made both in 1999 and 2002, the net result means that shares of Coca-Cola trade today at the same level they were nearly 10 years ago,[168] all because of the weaknesses in the leadership integrity.

To demonstrate that the strength of leadership integrity is interdependent on cultural integrity, one only needs to examine the comment made by one of Westinghouse's corporate relations vice presidents who joined the company in 1995: "There was no real concern about costs;"[169] he was shocked to find people in his department routinely received annual raises of 7-8 percent and up, even as the company was struggling and its stock was falling. "It was just expected."[170]

The culture and leadership at Westinghouse sounds very similar to Enron's. If an independent and objective assessment of the cultural and leadership integrity occurred using the models outlined, the publicly traded stock at both companies probably would not have had to be delisted. By the time the Westinghouse board was willing to admit the organization was heading in the wrong direction, the company, once one of GE's fiercest competitors, simply replaced one bad CEO with another—five times.[171] While removing a leader who lacks integrity is a key to success, simply replacing a leader with another does not necessarily guarantee success. Westinghouse and Coca-Cola have shown, among other things, that a "revolving door" approach to leadership does not ensure integrity.

Replacing the leadership at any organization several times can prove to be very disruptive and further shake investor confidence. Furthermore, leadership instability contributes to the erosion of cultural integrity, which impacts the organization's overall financial success. Attempting to strengthen organizational integrity with a single focus on the leadership, by simply ridding the organization of its leader, negates the entire concept of integrity and the wholeness test required to meet the definition.

Like all other measures in the Model, leadership integrity is weighted to assist the board directors in determining to what extent leadership integrity may jeopardize the organization's overall integrity, and its financial performance. Because 85 percent of executive teams spend less than one hour per month discussing the achievement of strategy,[172] without using the Model, board directors are not likely to know whether their "bus" is heading in the wrong direction, or if the bus needs a new driver. Until a board can obtain this knowledge through an independent leadership integrity assessment, as part of a bigger assessment of the overall organization, directors will have difficulty upholding their fiduciary responsibility to take every precaution to ensure the bus does not crash.

(9) Risk Integrity

Our risk integrity assessment incorporates a number of enterprise risk management tools, including COSO, COBIT, and the OCEG Framework. However, given the emphasis of Section 404 of SOX, we do not attempt to create redundant efforts to assess internal controls or assess whether the organization is managing their risk effectively as we believe this is a strategic decision as independent assessment agents, we are not in a position to do. Rather, the main focus of our Risk Integrity Assessment Model[173] is on the risks associated with intelligence and the sharing of data and related privacy issues. Not because we believe this small piece encompasses all of the risks facing an organization but rather because we believe risk integrity begins and ends with information and the transfer of that information.

However, it is important that we point out our efforts to incorporate what risk management expert James Lam points out in his contribution[174]. Companies have always faced a wide range of risks: business risk, credit risk, market risk, operational risk, and other risks. In the past, companies managed risks in "silos." In other words, different risks were the responsibility of different organizational units. Over time, risk management professionals recognized that risks, by their nature, are highly interdependent. In fact, major corporate disasters are often caused not by a single risk but a confluence of risks. This recognition has led to the development and implementation of integrated approaches to measure and manage risks across the enterprise, also known as Enterprise Risk Management (ERM). A March 2005 survey of global companies by the Corporate Executive Board indicated that an overwhelming 86 percent have established (12 percent), or are in the process of establishing (74 percent), an ERM program.[175]

To assess the integrity of an organization's risk management, the Integrity Institute has adopted the 7-component ERM framework established by James Lam & Associates.[176] The seven components and assessment standards are summarized below:

(1) Corporate Governance

The board of directors and executive management must establish appropriate organizational processes and corporate controls to measure and manage risk across the company. Best practices include establishing risk policies and limits that clearly define the "risk appetite" of the company; setting up board and management risk committees to ensure effective oversight and regulatory compliance; recruiting independent board members with solid finance and risk management skills; establishing an independent ERM function headed by an effective chief risk officer; and paying sufficient attention to the "soft side" of risk management (i.e., culture, values, and incentives).

(2) Line Management

A critical component of ERM is to integrate risk management into the company's revenue generating activities, including business development, product and relationship management, and pricing. Best practices include alignment between business and risk strategies, risk-based pricing models, pre-transaction risk analysis, and integrated business and risk reviews. There are two important reasons why the integration of ERM and line management is so critical. First, as can be seen in the recent problems in the mutual funds and insurance brokerage industries, companies often face their greatest risks and conflicts in providing products and services to their customers. Second, companies must accept risks to generate returns, and pricing is the only point at which they can get appropriately compensated.

(3) Portfolio Management

In order to measure and manage risk aggregations and interdependencies, management must view all key risks within a portfolio context. Best practices include explicit risk limits (e.g. credit exposure limits by obligor and industry, market risk limits by product or exposure, and operational risk limits such as maximum error rates), liquidity management and contingency plans, and the definition of an optimal target risk portfolio based on the underlying risk-return tradeoffs. Management should also understand the inter-risk correlations within its overall risk portfolio, and how these correlations may change over business cycles, or during market stresses.

(4) Risk Transfer

Management should develop hedging, insurance, and securitization strategies for risk exposures that are deemed too high, or are more cost-effective to transfer out to a third party rather than to hold in the company's risk portfolio. In addition to reducing concentrated or inefficient risk exposures, risk transfer strategies also increase the velocity of capital deployment. A company is no longer required to tie up capital to support a "buy and hold" strategy, but can redeploy its capital through a "buy and sell" strategy. Best practices include the ability to execute risk transfer strategies at the portfolio level (versus the transaction level); making consistent economic trade-off decisions between risk retention and risk transfer; and establishing a monitoring process to ensure that the risk transfer strategies are in fact achieving their stated objectives.

(5) Risk Analytics

To support the monitoring and management of enterprise-wide risks requires advanced analytical models and tools.

These models and tools provide the risk measurement, analysis, and reporting of the company's risk exposures as well as track external variables. Best practices include volatility-based models (e.g., value-at-risk, earnings-at-risk, economic capital); risk-adjusted profitability models (e.g., risk-adjusted return on capital or RAROC, shareholder value contribution); and simulation and scenario-based models that stress test the portfolio under pre-determined or computer-generated scenarios. Moreover, a concise ERM report should be developed for senior management and the board that clearly identifies key risks, and facilitates critical business and policy decisions.

(6) Data and Technology Resources

ERM requires significant data management and processing capabilities. Best practices include a detailed loss and incident database that captures all credit, market, and operational events; a mapping algorithm that supports the aggregation of same or similar risk exposures; and real-time tracking of risk exposures that are highly volatile or that have severe consequences. It is difficult, if not impossible, to develop a single system or a single data warehouse for ERM given that risks are dynamic and ever-changing. With the availability of web-based technologies, companies should develop a dashboard technology that supports more flexible data capture, data modeling, executive reporting, and drill-down capabilities.[177]

(7) Stakeholder Management

ERM is not simply a risk measurement and management issue; communications to, and relationships with, key stakeholders drive it. Stakeholders with direct interests in a company's risk management include investors, rating agencies, regulators, and business partners. Beyond meeting the increasing demand for risk transparency from these key stakeholders, it is in the company's best interest to communicate its risk profile more effectively. The losses that cause the most damage to stakeholder confidence, and the company's stock price, are the unexpected ones. Best-practice companies leverage their ERM programs to improve internal control as well as external communication.

Finally, each of the seven components above must work as an integrated whole. For example, the risk management policies and limits established in the Corporate Governance component provide the risk appetite for the board and senior management. The risk measurement and analysis incorporated in the Risk Analytics component provide the risk exposures for the company. Ongoing monitoring of the company's risk exposures against risk management policies and limits is a critical element of an ERM program, and provides the basis for stakeholder communication and reporting under the Stakeholder Management component.

In light of the aftermath of Enron, WorldCom, and Sarbanes-Oxley, the level of interest in risk management has never been greater. According to a 2005 McKinsey & Company survey of 1,000 board members, 75 percent would like to spend more time on risk management.[178] The 7-component ERM framework discussed in this section provides an assessment tool for the integrity of an organization's risk management function.

(10) Stakeholders Perceptions of Organizational Integrity

After analyzing the nine non-financial performance indicators outlined above, The Integrity Institute measures them against the stakeholders' perceptions to make certain that perception and reality are aligned. Warren Buffett points out the need for this measure of integrity in his statement that "Plenty of CEOs don't understand their business as well as a lot of people outside their business or even the people who work for them."[179]

According to the 2003 LRN survey, the public indicated their perceptions of a company's compliance and ethical behavior had a direct influence on their purchasing decisions.[180] Clearly, this appears to be the case with Wal-Mart, as it appears to struggle with the backlash of public perceptions. Rather than maintaining a myopic view of our organizations, employees, customers, vendors, and shareholders may provide insight that business leaders fail to recognize. The board of directors may understand the business from management's perspective. But do they understand its reality from the stakeholders' perspectives?

The Integrity Institute measures stakeholder perceptions using an advanced form of technology developed by Perceptyx[181] that allows measurement and microanalysis of organizational integrity by drilling-down into the context of each aspect of the integrated model described throughout. By using this technology, we begin to see exactly where the impacts are on the organization's financial performance, and what results might be accomplished strengthening its non-financial performance.

Through the analysis of such things as demographics (whether by department, division, region, age, gender, or industry) and responses to questions, a better understanding of organizational integrity and areas for improvement emerges. The technology allows The Integrity Institute to show how respondents answered questions and how long they took to complete the questionnaire. Additionally, a lexical analysis ranks issues by frequency of words and phrases submitted in the comment section of the survey. An opportunity index allows comparisons across demographics to isolate the organizational areas where integrity may be strengthened for better financial performance.

Once the analysis is completed, a gap report prioritizes evaluation of questions, weighted and prioritized by importance ratings or by consensus. The Model dynamically sorts the information by question or by categories to isolate the top integrity issues facing the organization and determines the significance of weaknesses in the overall assessment of integrity. This in-depth analysis demonstrates to what extent the organization has or does not have integrity in its non-financial performance and to what extent it impacts the organization's financial performance. A visual analysis allows a comparison of the results by composite scores to determine the themes that emerge as strengths to leverage improvement, or those that may require immediate attention.

The Integrity Institute performs an assessment to analyze the organization's trends over time; we then benchmark those results against an industry-adjusted average. The composite evaluation scores then determine how whole the organization is by climate dimension, to understand better which operating units are adding to or detracting from the organization's overall integrity.

The Model's Validity

Although the weight of the assessment models outlined above have a specific focus, there is a common thread throughout; thus the data captured in one model reinforces the validity of another. For instance, the shareholder letter can be used to identify integrity weaknesses in environmental and social policies; the cultural assessment can be used to identify weaknesses in the leadership; the earnings assessment can demonstrate problems with the compensation assessment; etc. The integration of these models creates a synergistic effect as the integrated Model allows a comprehensive measure of the organization's non-financial performance strength and its impact on financial performance, and thus the organization's overall integrity (soundness, wholeness, and incorruptibility).

The key to the validity of any model is to understand its relevance, reliability, and comparability. Using the Model to assess an organization's integrity provides executives with the ability to understand what non-financial performance indicators are impacting the organization's financial performance, and to what extent strengthening a measure will create stronger overall financial performance.

The Model's relevance is created by meeting both the organization's need to understand and communicate its ability to withstand market forces, and the stakeholders' needs to trust that communication. The Model's reliability is rooted in the creation of a standardized measure of integrity, which is used solely by The Integrity Institute to provide the independence and objectiveness necessary through assessment and certification. The standardized measure of integrity by an independent and objective institute allows for comparability.

It is important to note, in order to maintain the integrity of the process, The Integrity Institute does not assess the organization but rather licenses the use of its Integria Model to a limited number of authorized and certified assessment agents who run the following assessment models: 1) Citizenship; 2) Compliance and Ethics; 3) Culture; 4) Governance; 5) Leadership; and 6) Risk. The results are then analyzed by The Integrity Institute who independently analyzes the results against the remaining four models: 7) Communication; 8) Compensation; 9) Earnings; and 10) Perceptions and issues a certification of corporate integrity to any company who meets the standards established.

Conclusion

The Model, which integrates widely accepted and acclaimed models, establishes a standardized integrity measure, using non-financial performance indicators for The Integrity Institute to independently assess and certify an organization's soundness, wholeness, incorruptibility, thereby allowing organizations to understand the impact such non-financial performance is having on the firm's financial performance. By providing organizations with a means of independently and objectively certifying their integrity, we establish a standard that allows companies to attract customers, superior talent, and further investments; motivate employees; define its competitive advantage; create a platform for innovation; leverage suppliers; and lower marketing costs, while reducing scrutiny, risk, and impact of a crises, and vulnerability to competitive attacks. The result means a company can capitalize on the value of its integrity while at the same time reduce the risk to investors.

I believe organizations have an obligation to take steps to dispel the fear created by the recent corporate scandals. Without trust, our economy will not sustain itself; it requires investors who trust companies—companies committed to demonstrating and maintaining a commitment to integrity. If assessing, measuring, and certifying integrity is what it takes to rebuild the confidence required to sustain our economy, then the arguments made throughout this are the best chance we have of sustaining the free market society in which we live.

Appendix
C

Chapter 1

[1] *http://www.healthsouth.com/medinfo/home/app/frame?2+article.jsp,0,091505_Scrushy_Press.*

[1b] The terminology and concept of an ethical misconduct disaster (EMD) was first introduced by Dr. Robert C. Chandler in a presentation at the Contingency Planning and Management conference in April 2000. See also, Robert C. Chandler and J. D. Wallace, "Brief Results of the Pepperdine University Ethical Misconduct Disaster Recovery Preparedness Survey," Disaster Recovery Journal, 14 (Summer 2001): 20-24.

[2] Taub, Stephen, (CFO.com). "SEC: 1,300 'Whistles' Blown Each Day: Most Tips Concern Accounting Problems at Public Companies; 'a tremendous source of leads'." *CFO.com*, August 3, 2004, *http://ww.cof.com/article.cfm/3015607.*

[3] Ethics Resource Center; National Business Ethics Survey: How Employees View Ethics in Their Organizations 1994-2005; p. 16.

[4] Ibid at p. 17

[5] *Enron Code of Ethics*, Enron Corporation, 2000, p. 2.

[6] Dave Cook and Helen Shaw, "Scrushy Acquitted on All Counts," *CFO.com*, June 28, 2005, *www.cfo.com/article.cfm/4076776/c_4125234?f=TodayInFinance_Inside.*

[7] *http://www.healthsouth.com/medinof/home/app/frame?2=article.jsp,0,091505+ScrushyPress.*

[8] Caroline E. Mayer, "Blockbuster Sued over Return Policy," *The Washington Post*, February 19, 2005, *www.washingtonpost.com/wp-dyn/articles/A36767-2005Feb18.html.*

[9] Lowe, Jonathan and Cohen Kalafut, Pam (Cap Gemini Ernst & Young, US LLC); *Invisible Advantage: How Intangibles are Driving Business Performance* (Massachusetts: Perseus Publishing, 2002), p. 8.

[10] *Ibid.*

[11] Lawrence, Felicity "Things Get Worse for Coke"; *The Guardian*, [London], March 20, 2004, *http://www.guardian.co.uk/business/story/0,3604,1174127,00.html.*

[12] Daniel McGinn, "Rewinding a Video Giant," *Newsweek*, June 27, 2005, *www.msnbc.msn.com/id/8259044/site/newsweek/.*

[13] "Corporate Scandals," *MSNBC.com*, *www.msnbc.msn.com/id/3032230/* (accessed August 15, 2005).

[14] Steven Taub, "Crisis of Ethics," *CFO.com*, June 19, 2002, *www.cfo.com/article.cfm/ 3005220?f=search*.

[15] *Business Nightly News*, Public Broadcasting Corporation, Interview with Warren Buffett, May 2005.

[16] Mitchell Pacelle, "UPS Loses Citigroup Customer Data," *The Wall Street Journal*, June 7, 2005, p. A3.

[17] Julie Creswell and Julie Schlosser, "Has Coca-Cola Lost its Fizz?", *Fortune*; October 27, 2003.

[18] "Police Call Wendy's Chili Finger Case a Hoax," KTVU News, April 24, 2005, *www.ktvu. com/news/4404295/detail.html*.

[19] "'No More Enrons' Coalition Documents $200 Billion Cost of Corporate Malfeasance, Releases Report, Voter Guides," US Newswire, October 17, 2002, http://static.highbeam. com/u/usnewswire/october172002/nomoreenronscoalitiondocuments200billioncostofc orp/. The complete *The Cost of Corporate Recklessness* report may be found online at *www. americanfamilyvoices.org/pdf/cost.pdf*.

[20] Alan G. Hevesi, "Corporate Corruption Cost New York State's Economy $2.9 Billion, Cut Tax Revenues by $1 Billion and Decreased Pension Fund Value by $9 Billion," New York State Comptroller's office, press release, August 20, 2003, *www.osc.state.ny.us/press/releases/ aug03/082003.htm*; and "Try, Try Again," *Baltimore Business Journal*, May 13, 2005, *www. bizjournals.com/baltimore/stories/2005/05/16/story2.html*.

[21] Hevesi, "Corporate Corruption Cost New York State's Economy."

[22] Carol Graham, Robert E. Litan, and Sandip Sukhtankar, "Cooking the Books: The Cost to the Economy," The Brookings Institute, Policy Brief #106, August 2002, *www.brookings.edu/ comm/policybriefs/pb106.htm*.

[23] Hevesi, "Corporate Corruption Cost New York State's Economy."

[24] "62% of Americans Tell CEOs 'You're Not Doing Enough to Restore Trust and Confidence in American Business,'" Golin/Harris International, press release, June 20, 2002, *www. golinharris.com/pdf/02_summer_trust_survey.pdf*.

[25] Michael Josephson, "The Biennial Report Card: The Ethics of American Youth," Josephson Institute of Ethics, press release, *www.josephsoninstitute.org/Survey2004/* (accessed August 11, 2005).

[26] "Major Survey of America's Workers Finds Substantial Improvements in Ethics," Ethics Resource Center, press release, May 31, 2003, *www.ethics.org/releases/nr_20030521_nbes. html*; "American Workers Say They Expect Their Employers to Do What Is Right, Not Just Profitable—States New National Survey," Ethics Resource Center, press release, June 13, 2000, *www.ethics.org/releases/nr_20000613_nbes.html*.

[27] Ethics Resource Center; 2005 National Business Ethics Survey, p. 32.

[28] "Is Ethical Misconduct Heating up in Your Organization?" PR Newswire, July 11, 2005, via AOL.

[29] Matthew Fordahl, "Lawsuit Accuses Intel of Monopolistic Bullying," *The Coloradoan*, June 29, 2005, p. D7.

[30] Andy Serwer, "Wal-Mart: Bruised in Bentonville," *www.fortune.com/fortune/fortune500/article s/0,15114,1044608,00.html*.

[31] Liz Featherstone, "Wal-Mart's P.R. war", August 2, 2005, *http://www.salon.com/news/ feature/2005/08/02/walmart/print.html*.

[32] Dennis K. Berman, "Qwest Spends Top Dollar to Defend Its Accounting," *The Wall Street Journal*, March 10, 2003, *http://online.wsj.com*.

[33] "Krispy Kreme Problems," *The Coloradoan*, August 11, 2005, p. D7.

[34] Ronald Alsop, "Scandal-Filled Year Takes Toll on Firms' Good Names," *The Wall Street Journal*, February 12, 2003, *http://online.wsj.com*.

[35] "The Effect of Published Reports of Unethical Conduct on Stock Prices," reported in "Business Ethics," Business for Social Responsibility, *www.bsr.org/BSRResources/ WhitePaperDetail.cfm?DocumentID=270* (accessed March 5, 2003).

[36] John Galvin, "The New Business Ethics," *SmartBusinessMag.com*, June 2000, p. 97.

[37] "U.S. Companies Risk Reputations and Finances Due to Broadening Public Concern with all Forms of Corporate Behavior," PRNewswire, August 19, 2002, via *www.findarticles.com*.

[38] R. P. Conaboy, "Corporate Crime in America: Strengthening the 'Good Citizen' Corporation," in *Proceedings of the Second Symposium on Crime and Punishment in the United States* (Washington D.C.: United States Sentencing Commission, 1995).

[39] Conaboy, "Corporate Crime in America," p. 24.

[40] R.L. Johannsen, *Ethics in Human Communication*, 4th ed. (Prospect Heights, IL: Waveland Press, 1996), p. 177.

Chapter 3

[1] O. C. Ferrell, John Fraedrich, and Linda Ferrell, *Business Ethics: Ethical Decision Making and Cases*, 6th ed. (Boston: Houghton Mifflin, 2005), p. 31.

[2] "Ex Ad Agency Execs Sentenced for Fraud," Associated Press Newswire, August 11, 2005.

[3] This section was adapted from O. C. Ferrell, "Nature, Scope and History of Marketing Ethics," in *Marketing and Public Policy, Marketing and Society*, William Wilkie, Greg Gundlach, and Lauren Block, eds. (Mason, OH: Thomson South-Western, forthcoming).

[4] James C. Hyatt, "Birth of the Ethics Industry," *Business Ethics*, Summer 2005, p. 26.

[5] Isabelle Maignon, O. C. Ferrell, and Linda Ferrell, "A Stakeholder Model for Implementing Social Responsibility in Marketing," working paper, University of Wyoming, 2005.

[6] T. M. Jones, "Ethical Decision Making by Individuals in Organizations: An Issue-Contingent Model," *Academy of Management Review*, 16 (1991), pp. 366-395.

[7] D. P. Robin, R. E. Reidenbach, and P. J. Forrest, "The Perceived Importance of an Ethical Issue as an Influence on the Ethical Decision-Marking of Ad Managers," *Journal of Business Research*, 35 (1996), pp. 17-29.

[8] O. C. Ferrell, "A Framework for Understanding Organizational Ethics," in *Business Ethics: New Challenges for Business Schools and Corporate Leaders*, R. A. Peterson and O. C. Ferrell, eds. (Armonk, New York: M.E. Sharpe, 2005), pp. 3-17.

[9] Patrick E. Murphy, Gene R. Laczniak, N. E. Bowie, and T. A. Klein, *Ethical Marketing*, (Upper Saddle River, N.J.: Pearson Prentice-Hall, 2005).

[10] Marjorie Kelly, "The Ethics Revolution," *Business Ethics*, Summer 2005, p. 6.

[11] O. C. Ferrell and Larry G. Gresham, "A Contingency Framework for Understanding Ethical Decision Making in Marketing," *Journal of Marketing*, 49 (Summer 1985), pp. 87-96.

[12] Roselie McDevitt and Joan Van Hise, "Influences in Ethical Dilemmas of Increasing Intensity," *Journal of Business Ethics*, 40 (October 2002), pp. 261-274.

[13] "Ex-WorldCom Comptroller Gets Prison Time," "Ex-WorldCom CFO Gets Five Years," CNN/Money, August 11, 2005, *www.money.cnn.com*; Susan Pullman, "Ordered to Commit Fraud, A Staffer Balked, Then Caved," The Wall Street Journal, June 23, 2003.

[14] Data from O. C. Ferrell, as reported in O. C. Ferrell, John Fraedrich, and Linda Ferrell, *Business Ethics: Ethical Decision Making and Cases*, 6th ed. (Boston: Houghton Mifflin, 2005),

[19] Daniel Goldman, "Leadership that Gets Results," *Harvard Business Review*, March–April 2000, pp. 78-90.

[20] J. M. Burns, *Leadership*, (New York: Harper & Row, 1985).

[21] Royston Greenwood, Roy Suddaby, and C.R. Hinings, "Theorizing Change: The Role of Professional Associations in the Transformation of Institutionalized Fields," *Academy of Management Journal*, 45 (January 2002), pp. 58-80.pp. 144-145.

[22] "WorldCom Chief Outlines Initial Turnaround Strategy," *The Wall Street Journal*, January 14, 2003.

[23] Stephen R. Covey, *The 7 Habits of Highly Effective People*, (New York: Simon & Schuster, 1989).

[24] Archie B. Carroll, "Ethical Leadership: From Moral Managers to Moral Leaders," in *Rights, Relationships and Responsibilities*, O.C. Ferrell, Sheb True, and Lou Pelton, eds, Vol. 1, (Kennesaw, GA: Kennesaw State University, 2003), pp. 7-17.

[25] Andy Serwer, "Wal-Mart: Bruised in Bentonville," *Fortune*, April 4, 2005, *www.fortune.com/fortune/subs/print/0,15935,1044608,00.html*.

[26] Thomas I. White, "Character Development and Business Ethics Education," in *Rights, Relationships and Responsibilities*, O.C. Ferrell, Sheb True, and Lou Pelton, eds, Vol. 1, (Kennesaw, GA: Kennesaw State University, 2003), pp. 137-166.

[27] Carroll, "Ethical Leadership," p. 11.

[28] Keith H. Hammonds, "Harry Kraemer's Moment of Truth," *Fast Company,* November 2002, *www.fastcompany.com/online/64/kraemer.html.*

[29] Carroll, "Ethical Leadership," p. 11.

[30] Chad Terhune, "Pepsi, Vowing Diversity, Isn't Just Image Polish, Seeks Inclusive Culture," *The Wall Street Journal,* April 19, 2005, p. B1.

[31] Carroll, "Ethical Leadership," p. 12.

[32] Steve Quinn, "Wal-Mart Green with Energy," *The Coloradoan,* July 24, 2005, p. E1.

[33] Brent Smith, Michael W. Grojean, Christian Resick, and Marcus Dickson, "Leaders, Values and Organizational Climate: Examining Leadership Strategies for Establishing an Organizational Climate Regarding Ethics," *Journal of Business Ethics,* as reported at "Research @ Rice: Lessons from Enron—Ethical Conduct Begins at the Top," Rice University, June 15, 2005, *www.explore.rice.edu/explore/NewsBot.asp?MODE=VIEW&ID=7478 &SnID=878108660.*

[34] New Belgium Brewing Company, *www.newbelgium.com* (accessed August 25, 2005); "New Belgium Brewing: Environmental and Social Responsibilities," in O. C. Ferrell, John Fraedrich, and Linda Ferrell, *Business Ethics: Ethical Decision Making and Cases,* 6th ed. (Boston: Houghton Mifflin, 2005), pp. 364- 368; Greg Owsley, "The Necessity for Aligning Brand with Corporate Ethics," in Sheb L. True, Linda Ferrell, and O.C. Ferrell, *Fulfilling Our Obligation: Perspectives on Teaching Business Ethics* (Kennesaw, GA: Kennesaw University Press, 2005), pp. 127-139.

[35] Herb Baum and Tammy Kling, "The Transparent Leader," in LeaderPoints, Centerpoints for Leaders, December 2004, *www.centerpointforleaders.org/newsletters/dec04.html.*

[36] Monica Langley, "Course Correction: Behind Citigroup Departures: A Culture Shift by CEO Prince," *The Wall Street Journal,* August 24, 2005, p. A1.

[37] Carroll, "Ethical Leadership," p. 12.

[38] Ibid.

[39] D. L. Swanson and W. C. Frederick, "Denial and Leadership in Business Ethics Education," in *Business Ethics: New Challenges for Business Schools and Corporate Leaders*, R.A. Peterson and O.C. Ferrell, eds., (New York: M.E. Sharpe, 2004).

[40] James C. Hyatt, "Birth of the Ethics Industry," *Business Ethics,* Summer 2005, pp. 20-26.

Chapter 4

[1] John Rosthorn, "Business Ethics Auditing—More than a Stakeholder's Toy," *Journal of Business Ethics,* 27 (September 2000), pp. 9–19.

[2] "Accountability," Business for Social Responsibility, *www.bsr.org/BSRResources/ WhitePaperDetail.cfm?DocumentID=259* (accessed February 13, 2003).

[3] Trey Buchholz, "Auditing Social Responsibility Reports: The Application of Financial Auditing Standards," Colorado State University, professional paper, November 28, 2000, p. 3.

[4] James C. Hyatt, "Birth of the Ethics Industry," *Business Ethics,* Summer 2005, pp. 20–26.

[5] United States Sentencing Commission, Report of the Ad Hoc Advisory Group on the Organizational Sentencing Guidelines, October 7, 2003, *www.ussc.gov/corp/advgrprpt/ advgrppt.htm.*

[6] Marjorie Kelly, "Tyco's Ethical Makeover," *Business Ethics,* Summer 2005, pp. 14–19.

[7] Ibid.

[8] Hyatt, "Birth of the Ethics Industry."

[9] "HCA Ethics and Compliance," HCA Healthcare, http://ec.hcahealthcare.com (accessed September 1, 2005); O.C. Ferrell, John Fraedrich, and Linda Ferrell, *Business Ethics: Ethical*

Decision Making and Cases, 6ᵗʰ ed. (Boston: Houghton Mifflin, 2005), pp. 407–424

¹⁰ "HCA Ethics and Compliance."

¹¹ Kelly, "Tyco's Ethical Makeover."

¹² Janet Wiscombe, "Don't Fear the Whistle-Blowers: with HR's Help, Principled Whistle-Blowers Can Be a Company's Salvation," *Workforce*, July 2002, via *www.findarticles.com*.

¹³ Kelly, "Tyco's Ethical Makeover."

¹⁴ Jeffrey E. Garten, "B-Schools: Only a C+ in Ethics," *Business Week*, September 5, 2005, p. 110.

¹⁵ Susan Pullman, "Ordered to Commit Fraud, A Staffer Balked, Then Caved," *The Wall Street Journal*, June 23, 2003.

¹⁶ "HCA Ethics and Compliance" and Ferrell, Fraedrich, and Ferrell, *Business Ethics*.

¹⁷ The methodology in this section was adapted from Ferrell, Fraedrich, and Ferrell, *Business Ethics*, pp. 198–207.

¹⁸ Lauren Coleman-Lochner; "Independent Look at Wal-Mart shows Both Good and Bad," San Antonio Express-News (November 5, 2005), p. 4D.

¹⁹ "Niagara Mohawk, A National Grid Company," Better Business Bureau, *www.bbb.org/BizEthics/winners/niagara.asp* (accessed May 27, 2005).

²⁰ "Verification," Business for Social Responsibility, *www.bsr.org/BSRResources/WhitePaperDetail.cfm?DocumentID=440* (accessed February 13, 2003).

²¹ Ibid.

²² "HCA Ethics and Compliance."

²³ "Verification."

²⁴ Joseph B. White, "Ford President Faces Inquiry Over Ad-Related Directive," *The Wall Street Journal*, March 10, 2003.

²⁵ Buchholz, "Auditing Social Responsibility Reports," p. 15.

²⁶ Johann Mouton, "Chris Hani Baragwanath Hospital Ethics Audit," Ethics Institute of South Africa, 2001, available at *www.ethicsa.org/report_CHB.html*.

²⁷ Ibid.

²⁸ Dave Cook and Helen Shaw, "Scrushy Acquitted on All Counts," *CFO.com*, June 28, 2005, *www.cfo.com/article.cfm/4076776/c_4125234?f=TodayInFinance_Inside*; Andrew Countryman, "SEC: HealthSouth Earnings Overstated by $1.4 Billion," *Austin American-Statesman*, March 20, 2003, http://austin360.com/statesman/.

²⁹ "Accountability."

³⁰ "Accountability."

³¹ Ethics Officer Association, *www.eoa.org* (accessed September 7, 2005).

³² "Accountability."

³³ See OCEG Benchmarking Survey Summary in Appendix A. For full report go to *www.OCEG.org*.

³⁴ J. C. Collins and J. I. Porras, *Built to Last: Successful Habits of Visionary Companies*, (New York: Harper Collins, 1997).

Chapter 5

¹ Debbie Thorne LeClair, O.C. Ferrell, and John P. Fraedrich, *Integrity Management: a Guide to Managing Legal and Ethical Issues in the Workplace* (Tampa: University of Tampa Press, 1998).

² Stephen Taub, "Crisis of Ethics," *CFO.com*, June 19, 2002, www.cfo.com/article.cfm/3005220?f=search.

³ Robert C. Chandler and J.D. Wallace, "Brief Results of the Pepperdine University Ethical Misconduct Disaster Recovery Preparedness Survey," *Disaster Recovery Journal*, 14 (Summer 2001), pp. 21-22.

⁴ Taub, "Crisis of Ethics."

⁵ Chandler and Wallace, "Brief Results of the Pepperdine University Ethical Misconduct Disaster Recovery Preparedness Survey," 22.

⁶ Grant Ringshaw, "The Judgment of Buffet," *The Telegraph*, August 14, 2005, http://money.

telegraph.co.uk/money/main.jhtml?xml=/money/2005/08/14/ccbuf14.xml.

[7] Robert C. Chandler, "Managing Ethical and Regulatory Compliance Contingencies: Planning and Training Guidelines," *Contingency Planning and Management 2000 Proceedings* (Flemington, NJ: Witter Publishing, 2000), pp. 6-7.

[8] "Ex-Tyco CFO Indicted for Tax Evasion," CNN/Money, February 19, 2003, http://money. cnn.com; "Corporate Scandals," MSNBC, www.msnbc.msn.com/id/3032230/ (accessed September 14, 2005).

[9] R.L. Miller and W.F. Lewis, "A Stakeholder Approach to Marketing Management Using the Value Exchange Models," *European Journal of Marketing,* 25 (8, 1991), pp. 55-68.

[10] Sandra A. Waddock, C. Bodwell, and S.B. Graves, "Responsibility: The New Business Imperative," *Academy of Management Executive,* 16 (2, 2002), pp. 132-149.

[11] R.K. Mitchell, B.R. Agle, and D.J. Wood, "Toward a Theory of Stakeholder Identification and Salience: Defining the Principle of Who and What Really Counts," *Academy of Management Review,* 22 (4, 1997), pp. 853-886.

[12] Mitchell, Agle, and Wood, "Toward a Theory of Stakeholder Identification and Salience."

[13] T. Thomas, J.R. Schermerhorn, and J.W. Dienhart, "Strategic Leadership of Ethical Behavior in Business," *Academy of Management Executive,* 18 (2, 2004), pp. 56-66.

[14] J.S. Harrison and R.E. Freeman, "Stakeholders, Social Responsibility, and Performance: Empirical Evidence and Theoretical Perspectives," *Academy of Management Journal,* 42 (5, 1999), pp. 479-485.

[15] Isabelle Maignan and O.C. Ferrell, "Corporate Social Responsibility and Marketing: An Integrative Framework," *Journal of the Academy of Marketing Science,* 32 (1, 2004), pp. 19-23.

[9] R.L. Miller and W.F. Lewis, "A Stakeholder Approach to Marketing Management Using the Value Exchange Models," *European Journal of Marketing,* 25 (8, 1991), pp. 55-68.

[10] Sandra A. Waddock, C. Bodwell, and S.B. Graves, "Responsibility: The New Business Imperative," *Academy of Management Executive,* 16 (2, 2002), pp. 132-149.

[11] R.K. Mitchell, B.R. Agle, and D.J. Wood, "Toward a Theory of Stakeholder Identification and Salience: Defining the Principle of Who and What Really Counts," *Academy of Management Review,* 22 (4, 1997), pp. 853-886.

[12] Mitchell, Agle, and Wood, "Toward a Theory of Stakeholder Identification and Salience."

[13] T. Thomas, J.R. Schermerhorn, and J.W. Dienhart, "Strategic Leadership of Ethical Behavior in Business," *Academy of Management Executive,* 18 (2, 2004), pp. 56-66.

[14] J.S. Harrison and R.E. Freeman, "Stakeholders, Social Responsibility, and Performance: Empirical Evidence and Theoretical Perspectives," *Academy of Management Journal,* 42 (5, 1999), pp. 479-485.

[15] Isabelle Maignan and O.C. Ferrell, "Corporate Social Responsibility and Marketing: An Integrative Framework," *Journal of the Academy of Marketing Science,* 32 (1, 2004), pp. 19-23.

Chapter 6

[1] This material was adapted from Debbie Thorne, O.C. Ferrell, and John P. Fraedrich, *Integrity Management: A Guide to Legal and Ethical Issues in the Workplace* (Tampa: University of Tampa Press, 1998), pp. 82–100.

[2] Kathryn Tyler, "Do The Right Thing," *HR Magazine,* 50 (February 2005), www.shrm.org/hrmagazine/articles/0205/0205tyler.asp.

[3] Marjorie Kelly, "Tyco's Ethical Makeover," *Business Ethics,* Summer 2005, pp. 14–19.

[4] "About the EOA," Ethics Officer Association, www.eoa.org/AboutEOA.asp, (accessed September 15, 2005).

[5] Kelly, "Tyco's Ethical Makeover."

[6] "HCA Ethics and Compliance," HCA Healthcare, http://ec.hcahealthcare.com (accessed September 1, 2005); O.C. Ferrell, John Fraedrich, and Linda Ferrell, *Business Ethics: Ethical Decision Making and Cases,* 6th ed. (Boston: Houghton Mifflin, 2005), pp. 407–424.

[7] James C. Hyatt, "Birth of the Ethics Industry," *Business Ethics,* Summer 2005, pp. 20–26.

[8] Ibid.

[9] Intercede, www.intercedeservices.com (accessed September 19, 2005).

[10] Ferrell, Fraedrich, and Ferrell, *Business Ethics*, pp. 377–395.

[11] Landon Thomas, Jr., "On Wall Street, a Rise in Dismissals Over Ethics," *The New York Times*, March 29, 2005, http://select.nytimes.com/gst/abstract.html?res=F00D14FC395B0C7A8ED DAA0894DD404482.

[12] Tyler, "Do The Right Thing."

[13] This material was adapted from LeClair, Ferrell, and Fraedrich, *Integrity Management*, pp. 108–114.

[14] Debbie Thorne and Linda Ferrell, "Innovation in Experiential Business Ethics Training," *Journal of Business Ethics*, 23 (February 1999), pp. 313–322.

[15] Tyler, "Do the Right Thing."

[16] Hyatt, "Birth of an Ethics Industry."

Chapter 7

[1] O.C. Ferrell, John Fraedrich, and Linda Ferrell, "Exxon Valdez: Revisited," *Business Ethics: Decision Making and Cases*, 6th ed. (Boston: Houghton Mifflin, 2005), pp. 321-328.

[2] O.C. Ferrell, John Fraedrich, and Linda Ferrell, "Exxon Valdez: Revisited," *Business Ethics: Decision Making and Cases*, 6th ed. (Boston: Houghton Mifflin, 2005), pp. 321-328.

[3] N. Forbes, "Beef up your BCP with Blogs, Podcasts," ZDNet Asia, August 26, 2005 http://www.zdnetasia.com/smb/speicalreports/printfriendly.htm?AT=3925176-39045280t-39000760c

[4] N. Forbes, "Beef up your BCP with Blogs, Podcasts," ZDNet Asia, August 26, 2005 http://www.zdentasia.com/smb/specialrports/printfriendly.htm?AT=39251076-39045280t-39000760c

---

Chapter 8

[1] "Exxon Valdez Revisited," in O.C. Ferrell, John Fraedrich, and Linda Ferrell, (2005) *Business Ethics: Ethical Decision Making and Cases*, 6th ed. (Boston: Houghton Mifflin, 2005), pp. 321–328.

[2] William J. Small, "Exxon Valdez: How to Spend Billions and Still Get a Black Eye, *Public Relations Review*, 17 (Spring 1991), p. 1.

[3] "HCA, Inc.: Learning from Past Mistakes," in O.C. Ferrell, John Fraedrich, and Linda Ferrell, *Business Ethics: Ethical Decision Making and Cases*, 6th ed. (Boston: Houghton Mifflin, 2005), pp. 343–349.

[4] Ibid.

[5] "Disney World Ride Reopened," CBS News, July 13, 2005, www.cbsnews.com/stories/2005/07/13/national/main708906.shtml.

[6] Ibid.

[7] Ibid.

[8] Ibid.

[9] K. Wise, "Attribution Versus Compassion: The City of Chicago's Response to the E2 Crisis," *Public Relations Review*, 30 (2004), pp. 347-357.

[10] I.L. Janis, *Groupthink*, 2nd ed. (Boston: Houghton Mifflin, 1982).

[11] James C. McCroskey, "Oral Communication Apprehension: A Summary of Recent Theory and Research," *Human Communication Research*, 4 (1977), p. 78.

[12] Jerry B. Harvey, *The Abilene Paradox and Other Meditations on Management* (Lexington, Mass: Lexington Books, 1988).

[13] William L. Benoit, *Accounts, Excuses, and Apologies* (Albany, NY: State University of New

York Press, 1995).

[14] William L. Benoit, "Sears Repair of its Auto Service Image: Image Restoration Discourse in the Corporate Sector, *Communication Studies*, 46, (1 & 2) Spring/Summer, (1995), pp.89-105.

[15] S. Brinson and William L. Benoit, "Dow Corning's Image Repair Strategy in the Breast Implant Crisis," *Communication Quarterly*, 44 (1996), pp. 29–41.

[16] Kevin McCoy, "Kozlowski's Trip to the Witness Stand Costs Him Dearly," *USA Today*, June 20, 2005, p. B1.

[17] Greg Farrell, "Against the Odds, Scrushy Walks out of Court a Free Man," *USA Today*, June 29, 2005, p. B1.

[18] Benoit, *Accounts, Excuses, and Apologies*.

[19] James Bandler and Ann Zimmerman, "A Wal-Mart Legend's Trail of Deceit," *The Wall Street Journal*, April 8, 2005, p. A1.

[20] Benoit, *Accounts, Excuses, and Apologies*.

[21] Benoit, "Sears Repair of its Auto Service Image."

[22] Marvin B. Scott and Stanford M. Lyman, "Accounts," *American Sociological Review*, 33, 1 (February, 1968), pp. 46-62.

[23] Farrell, "Against the Odds, Scrushy Walks out of Court a Free Man."

[24] Benoit, *Accounts, Excuses, and Apologies*.

[25] B. L. Ware and Wil A. Linkugel, "They Spoke in Defense of Themselves: On the Generic Criticism of Apologia," *Quarterly Journal of Speech*, 59 (1973), pp. 273-283.

[26] Peter Schonbach, "A Category System for Account Phases," *European Journal of Social Psychology*, 10 (1980), pp. 195-200.

[27] Benoit, *Accounts, Excuses, and Apologies*.

[28] Ibid.

[29] Peter Schonbach, "A Category System for Account Phases," *European Journal of Social Psychology*, 10 (1980), pp. 195-200.

[30] Mike France, "2: The Mea Culpa Defense," *Business Week Online*, August 26, 2002, www.businessweek.com/magazine/content/02_34/b3796604.htm.

[31] Ibid.

[32] Robert C. Chandler, J. D. Wallace, and D. P. Ferguson (2002) *"Corporate Reconciliation with Critical Stakeholders through Communication: An Empirical Assessment of Efficacy, Ethicality, and Utilization Likelihood of Benoit's Image Restoration Strategies in Crisis Management Situational Contingencies,"* unpublished manuscript presented at the International Communication Association, Seoul, Republic of Korea, July 2002.

Appendix A

[1] See OCEG Research Report WP2004.01 –Corporate Governance: Firm and Market Performance Review available to registered users of *www.oceg.org*.

[2] W. Mark Crain and Thomas D. Hopkins, "The Impact of Regulatory Costs on Small Firms," a report for The Office of Advocacy, U. S. Small Business Administration, October 2001. This study is being updated and will be available in the fourth quarter of 2005.

Appendix B

[1] Deloitte and EIU, In the Dark: What Boards and Executives Don't Know About the Health of Their Businesses, 3, (Oct. 13, 2004) (unpublished whitepaper) *available at http://www.deloitte.com/dtt/cda/doc/content/dtt_audit_IntehdarkFINAL2_101304.pdf.*

[2] 15 U.S.C. § 7201 (2003). [hereinafter the Act].

[3] *See id.*

[4] Six Sigma "[l]iterally, refers to the reduction of errors to six standard deviations from the mean value of a process output or task opportunities, i.e. about 1 error in 300,000 opportunities. In modern practice, this terminology has been applied to a quality

improvement methodology for industry." Balanced Scorecard Institute, *Definitions of Terms*, at *http://www.balancedscorecard.org/basics/definitions.html* (last visited July 1, 2005).

[5] A Balanced Scorecard is "a *management system* . . . that enables organizations to clarify their vision and strategy and translate them into action. It provides feedback around both the internal business processes and external outcomes in order to continuously improve strategic performance and results. When fully deployed, the balanced scorecard transforms strategic planning from an academic exercise into the nerve center of an enterprise." Balanced Scorecard Institute, *What is the Balanced Scorecard?*, at *http://www.balancedscorecard. org/basics/bsc1.html* (last visited July 1, 2005).

[6] "The Triple Bottom Line (TBL) focuses corporations not just on the economic value they add, but also on the environmental and social value they add – and destroy. At its narrowest, the term 'triple bottom line' is used as a framework for measuring and reporting corporate performance against economic, social and environmental parameters." Sustainability, What is the Triple Bottom Line?, 1 (unpublished whitepaper) *at http://www. sustainability.com/downloads_public/news/TBL.pdf* (last visited July 1, 2005).

[7] The Underwriters Laboratories Inc. test consumer products for safety. The company has a broad range of exacting standards for its testing. See Underwriters Laboratories, *at http:// www.ul.com* (last visited July 1, 2005).

[8] The Good Housekeeping Seal states that if a product bearing the Seal proves to be defective within two years of purchase, *Good Housekeeping* will replace the product or refund the purchase price. See "What's Behind the Good Housekeeping Seal" at *http://magazines.ivillage. com/goodhousekeeping/consumer/institute/articles/0,,284512_596441,00.html* (last visited Nov. 1, 2005).

[9] The Integria mark has been filed as a "certification" mark with the United States Patent and Trademark Office.

[10] *See* Fair Isaac, Understanding Your Credit Score, 1 (July, 2002) (unpublished whitepaper) available at *http://www.fairisaac.com/NR/rdonlyres/6F127C6D-E5D2-4EB3-B0CC-A0BD3FE00D94/0/UnderstandCreditScoreBklt.pdf* ("The most widely used credit scores are FICO scores. Lenders use FICO scores to make billions of credit decisions every year. Fair Isaac develops FICO scores based solely on information in consumer credit reports maintained at the credit reporting agencies.").

[11] Note: The models outlined below are in alphabetical order. They are not in order of importance or by strength of the weighting in the Integria™ Model.

[12] The Communication Integrity Assessment Model is recognized as a trademark of The Integrity Institute, Inc. and has been integrated into the Integria™ Model. The Integria mark has been filed as a "certification" mark with the United States Patent and Trademark Office. The Communication Integrity Assessment Model was developed by Robert Chandler, Ph.D. (Chair of the Communication Division of Seaver College at Pepperdine University). Professor Chandler is a Founding Member of The Integrity Institute and has contributed his model to The Integrity Institute for integration into the Integria™ Model.

[13] *See* Selena Maranjian, "CEOs Fail Candor Test, THE MOTLEY FOOL", July 21, 2004 available at *http://www.fool.com/news/mft/2004/mft04072106.htm* (citing the studies performed by Laura J. Rittenhouse); Stephen Taub, "Link Found Between Candor, Share Prices: Most CEOs at Large Public Companies Fail to Report Net Income Forthrightly, Survey Finds", CFO MAGAZINE, at *http://www.cfo.com/article.cfm/3014591* (Jun 15. 2004).

[14] *See id.*

[15] *See id.*

[16] Jeffery K. Skilling & Kenneth Lay, Enron Annual Report 2000, Letter to Shareholders, available at *www.enron.com/corp/investors/ annuals/2000/shareholder.html* (last visited June 10, 2005).

[17] The amount of Enron's net income was only $978 million according to the financials audited by Arthur Andersen for the year ended 2000. *www.enron.com/corp/investors/ annuals/2000/shareholder.html*

[18] Patricia and John Stanton, "Researching Corporate Annual Reports: An Analysis of Perspectives Used", 4 in "COLLECTED PAPERS OF APIRA ADLEAIDE 2001: THE THIRD ASIA PACIFIC

INTERDISCIPLINARY RESEARCH IN ACCOUNTING CONFERENCE" (Prof. Lee D. Parker ed. 2001) available at *http://www.commerce.adelaide.edu.au/apira/papers/Stanton51.pdf* (last visited June 10, 2005) (quoting Sam McKinstry, "Designing the Annual Reports of Burton PLC from 1930 to 1994, 21.1 ACCT., ORG. & SOC'Y 89, 109" (1996)).

[19] Id. At 5, In "COLLECTED PAPERS OF APIRA ADLEAIDE 2001: THE THIRD ASIA PACIFIC INTERDISCIPLINARY RESEARCH IN ACCOUNTING CONFERENCE" (Prof. Lee D. Parker ed. 2001) available at *http://www.commerce.adelaide.edu.au/apira/papers/Stanton51.pdf* (last visited June 10, 2005) (quoting Mike Jones, "Accounting Narratives: An Emerging Trend; Management Accounting Management Accounting", Apr., pp. 41-42 (1996).

[20] Id. at 15, in "Collected Papers of Apira Adleaide 2001: The Third Asia Pacific Interdisciplinary Research in Accounting Conference" (Prof. Lee D. Parker ed. 2001) available at *http://www.commerce.adelaide.edu.au/apira/papers/Stanton51.pdf* (last visited June 10, 2005) (citing Daphne Jameson, "Telling the Investment Story: A Narrative Analysis of Shareholder Reports", J. of Bus. Comm., Vol.37 No.1, Jan. 2000, at 7; Carol A. Adams & and George Harte, "The Changing Portrayal of the Employment of Women in British Banks' and Retail Companies' Corporate Annual Reports", Acct., Orgs. & Soc'y, Vol.23 No.8, 1998 at 781; Nola Buhr, "Environmental Performance, Legislation and Annual Report Disclosure: The Case of Acid Rain and Falconbridge", Acct., Auditing & Accountability J. Vol.11 No.2,1998, at 163;Chatham (1978)).

[21] Vivien Beattie & Ken Pratt, "Disclosure Items in a Comprehensive Model of Business Reporting: An Empirical Evaluation", 2 (June 2002) (unpublished white paper) at*http://www.stir.ac.uk/Departments/Management/Accountancy/stfpages/beattie/Disclosureitems.pdf* (citing AICPA, "Improving Business Reporting – A Customer Focus: Meeting the Information Needs of Investors and Creditors", "Comprehensive Report of the Special Committee on Financial Reporting" (The Jenkins Report), American Institute of Certified Public Accountants, New York, NY, at *http://www.aicpa.org/members/div/acctstd/ibr/index.htm* (last visited June 12, 2005)).

[22] Id. at 2.

[23] Id. at 3.

[24] See Forbes.com, "Faces of the Week: March 4 – 8, 2002", Mar. 9, 2002, at *http://www.forbes.com/2002/03/08/0309faceweek.html* (last visited June 12, 2005); IR Magazine, "SEC Seeks Improved Disclosure: Suggestions Offered at the New York Roundtable Discussion", Mar. 4, 2002, at *http://www.ironthenet.com/newsarticle.asp?current=1&articleID=1682* (last visited June 12, 2005).

[25] Beattie & Pratt, supra note 19, at 5 (citing, R.D. Hines "The Usefulness of Annual Reports: The Anomaly Between the Efficient Markets Hypothesis and Shareholder Surveys", ACCT. & BUS. RES., Autumn 1982, at 296).

[26] Khaled Hussainey, Thomas Schleicher & Martin Walker, "The Information Content of the Annual Report Narratives of Loss-Making Firms: Preliminary Evidence", 1 (Aug. 9, 2004) (working draft of unpublished whitepaper) (quoted with permission from authors, copy on file with author).

[27] Jonathan Lowe & Pam Cohen Kalafut, Cap Gemini Ernst & Young, US LLC, "Invisible Advantage: How Intangibles are Driving Business Performance" 62 (Perseus Publishing 2002).

[28] Janet Lowe, "Warren Buffet Speaks" 3 (John Wiley & Sons, Inc. 1997).

[29] Moody's Investors Service, Findings on Corporate Governance in the United States and Canada: August 2003 – September 2004 (Oct. 5, 2004) (on file with author) [hereinafter Findings on Corporate Governance].

[30] California Public Employees Retirement System (CalPERS).

[31] Teachers Indemnity and Annuity Association and College Retirement Equities Fund (TIAA-CREF).

[32] "Pension Plans Pouring Billions Into Hedge Funds"; Riva D. Atlas, The New York Times, Sunday, November 27, 2005

[33] Id.

[34] Fisher Black and Myron Scholes developed the Black and Scholes Option Pricing Model in

1973. The model is widely accepted today as the standard method for expensing options. See Bradley University, "The Black and Scholes Model", at *http://bradley.bradley.edu/~arr/bsm/pg04.html* (last visited June 12, 2005).

[35] U.S.S. Comm. on Commerce, Sci. and Transp. Holds Hearing on the Enron Collapse", 107th Cong. (2002) (Testimony Jeffrey K. Skilling) available at 2002 WL 274631.

[36] Warren Buffett, "Who Really Cooks the Books?", N.Y. TIMES, Jul. 24, 2002, at A19.

[37] Fulcrum Financial Inquiry, "This Corporate Accounting Fraud Is Sanctioned", at *http://www.fulcruminquiry.com/article21.htm* (last revised September 2004).

[38] The Compensation Integrity Assessment Model is recognized as a trademark of The Integrity Institute, Inc. and has been integrated into the Integria™ Model. The Integria mark has been filed as a "certification" mark with the United States Patent and Trademark Office. The Compensation Integrity Assessment Model was developed by compensation expert Fred Whittlesey who is a Founding Member of The Integrity Institute and has contributed his model to The Integrity Institute for integration into the Integria™ Model.

[39] *http://www.fwcook.com/cicreport.pdf*

[40] A rabbi trust is an irrevocable trust used to fund deferred compensation benefits. It is often used as a vehicle for deferring taxable income. A rabbi trust must be both "unfunded" and benefit a select group of employees. The term was created in the 1980s as a result of a synagogue receiving a watershed IRS Letter Ruling that confirmed tax deferral for a rabbi who was the beneficiary of a trust established to pay him retirement benefits. *See* Donald O. Jansen, Fullbright & Jaworski, L.L.P., Nonqualified Deferred Compensation: Securing the Unsecured Promise to Pay (2003) (unpublished paper) at *http://www.fulbright.com/images/publications/NonQualifiedDefered.pdf* (last visited June 13, 2005); *see also* Priv. Ltr. Rul. 9344038, available at 1993 WL 451166.

[41] OCEG Research Report WP2004.01 –Corporate Governance: Firm and Market Performance Review available to registered users of *www.oceg.org*

[42] OCEG 2005 Benchmarking Study sponsored by AON, pg. 4 available at *www.OCEG.org*.

[43] Here It Comes: The Sarbanes-Oxley Backlash; New York Times, April 17, 2005 (Jonathan D. Glater)

[44] Id.

[45] Id.

[46] The Open Compliance and Ethics Group (OCEG) "was formed by a multi-industry, multi-disciplinary coalition that saw the need to integrate the principles of effective governance, compliance, risk management and integrity into the practice of everyday business." OCEG, About OCEG, at *http://oceg.org/about.asp* (last visited July 1, 2005). The Integrity Institute, Inc. is a member of OCEG and the author sat on the Steering Committee that developed the OCEG Framework and is a member of the Leadership Council of OCEG.

[47] The Compliance and Ethics Integrity Assessment Model is recognized as a trademark of The Integrity Institute, Inc. and has been integrated into the Integria™ Model. The Integria mark has been filed as a "certification" mark with the United States Patent and Trademark Office. The Integrity Institute does not claim any proprietary rights to the content of OCEG but only the process of assessment and certification of compliance and ethics and the relative weighting thereto as integrated into the Integria™ Model.

[48] The OCEG Framework is comprised of two broad components: The Foundation and Domains. The Foundation embodies key elements common to all types of compliance and ethics programs. The Domains provide guidelines that are specific to a particular topic, industry, function, geographic location, or size/structure of an organization. See OCEG, Foundation Guidelines "Red Book", B8-9, Apr. 2005, at *http://oceg.org/anonDoc.asp?doc=OCEG.FND.AppDraft.RedBook.pdf* (last visited July 1, 2005).

[49] OCEG, "About OCEG", at *http://oceg.org/about.asp* (last visited July 1, 2005).

[50] See U.S. Sentencing Guidelines Manual, available at *http://www.ussc.gov* (last visited Aug. 3, 2005).

[51] See United States Sentencing Commission, Amendments to the Sentencing Guidelines, May 10, 2004, available at *http://www.ussc.gov/2004guid/RFMay04.pdf*.

[52] Memorandum from Larry D. Thompson, Deputy Attorney General to Heads of Department

Components, United States Attorneys, "Principles of Federal Prosecution of Business Organizations" (Jan. 20, 2003) at *http://www.usdoj.gov/dag/cftf/business_organizations.pdf.* (last visited August 3, 2005).

[53] The Committee of Sponsoring Organizations of the Treadway Commission. "The underlying premise of enterprise risk management is that every entity exists to provide value for its stakeholders. . . . Enterprise risk management helps ensure effective reporting and compliance with laws and regulations, and helps avoid damage to the entity's reputation and associated consequences. In sum, enterprise risk management helps an entity get to where it wants to go and avoid pitfalls and surprises along the way." "COSO, Enterprise Risk Management – Integrated Framework: Executive Summary", 1, Sept. 2004, at *http://www.coso.org/Publications/ERM/COSO_ERM_ExecutiveSummary.pdf.*

[54] See supra, text accompanying note 4.

[55] The Australian Standard for Compliance "covers the structural, operational and maintenance elements to be included in any program. . . . It describes a comprehensive compliance management system, using elements common to systems of management and quality." Gayle Hill, presentation delivered at The 9th International Anti-Corruption Conference, Workshop on Corporate Governance and Business Ethics: How can compliance be promoted and monitored? (available at *http://www.transparency.org/iacc/9th_iacc/papers/ day2/ws3/d2ws3_ghill.html#ref1*) (last visited July 1, 2005).

[56] Sarbanes-Oxley Act of 2002, 15 U.S.C. § 7201 (2003).

[57] Securities and Exchange Commission. The SEC rules may be found in the Code of Federal Regulations.

[58] Public Company Accounting Oversight Board. "The PCAOB is a private-sector, non-profit corporation, created by the Sarbanes-Oxley Act of 2002, to oversee the auditors of public companies in order to protect the interests of investors and further the public interest in the preparation of informative, fair, and independent audit reports." PCAOB, "Our Mission", at *http://www.pcaobus.org/* (last visited July 1, 2005). "PCAOB rules include auditing and related professional practice standards, Forms, and the Board's Bylaws and Ethics Code." PCAOB, Rules, at *http://www.pcaobus.org/Rules_of_the_Board/index.asp* (last visited July 1, 2005). See also PCAOB, "Bylaws and Rules of the Public Company Accounting Oversight Board", Feb. 15, 2005, available at *http://www.pcaobus.org/Rules_of_the_Board/Documents/ Rules_of_the_Board/all.pdf.*

[59] See Practicing Law Institute, PLI Newsletters, The Compliance Counselor, available at *http://www.pli.edu/public/newsletters/default.asp?ptid=000000000000000* (last visited Aug. 3, 2005).

[60] International Organization for Standardization. ISO 9000 and ISO 14000 standards are implemented by some 634 000 organizations in 152 countries. ISO 9000 has become an international reference for quality management requirements in business-to-business dealings, and ISO 14000 is well on the way to achieving as much, if not more, in enabling organizations to meet their environmental challenges. The ISO 9000 family is primarily concerned with "quality management". . . . The ISO 14000 family is primarily concerned with "environmental management." ISO, ISO 9000 and ISO 14000-in brief, at *http://www.iso. org/iso/en/iso9000-14000/understand/inbrief.html* (last visited July 1, 2005).

[61] The Malcolm Baldrige Award was established by Congress on August 20, 1987 to honor former Secretary of Commerce Malcolm Baldrige. See 15 U.S.C. § 3711a.

[62] Health Care Compliance Association. "HCCA exists to champion ethical practice and compliance standards and to provide the necessary resources for ethics and compliance professionals and others who share these principles." HCCA, About HCCA, at *http://www. hcca-info.org/Content/NavigationMenu/About_HCCA/Mission_Statement_and_Bylaws/Mission_ Statement_and_Bylaws.htm* (last visited July 1, 2005).

[63] The Corporate Citizenship Integrity Assessment Model is recognized as a trademark of The Integrity Institute, Inc. and has been integrated into the Integria™ Model. The Integria mark has been filed as a "certification" mark with the United States Patent and Trademark Office. The Corporate Citizenship Integrity Assessment Model is based upon the development of the model of Vasin, Heyn & Company and has been authorized by the

firm for use by The Integrity Institute, Inc. for integration into The Integria Model.

[64] Marc Gunther, "Money and Morals at GE: Jeff Immelt Wants to Instill Values in Everything the Company Does—Without Compromising the Profit Principle", Fortune Magazine, Nov. 15, 2004, at 176, available at *http://www.ge.com/en/company/investor/ge_social_responsibility_and_citizenship.htm* (last visited July 2, 2005) [hereinafter Money and Morals at GE].

[65] Id.

[66] Id.

[67] See CNNMoney, "Business Terror Links Probed: NYC asks Halliburton, G.E. & ConocoPhillips to Review Dealings in Iran and Syria", Feb. 10, 2003, at *http://money.cnn.com/2003/02/10/news/companies/terror_firms* [hereinafter Business Terror Links Probed].

[68] See id.

[69] See Henry Goldman, "Halliburton Won't Seek Iran Work: Company Makes Vow in Response to Shareholder Pressure", Bloomberg News, Mar. 25, 2005, E02, available at *http://www.washingtonpost.com/wp-dyn/articles/A64660-2005Mar24.html*; "Reuters, ConocoPhillips To End Its Business in Iran, Syria", Feb. 10, 2004, available at *http://www.forbes.com/home_europe/newswire/2004/02/10/rtr1253983.html*.

[70] Press Release, William C. Thompson Jr. (NYC Comptroller), "NYC Pension Funds Expand Campaign Urging U.S. Companies To Cease Business with Terrorist Nations: (August 29, 2004) available at *http://www.comptroller.nyc.gov/press/2004_releases/pr04-12-070.shtm*.

[71] See John Christoffersen, "GE Halts New Business Orders in Iran", Pittsburgh Post Gazette, Feb. 03, 2005, available at *http://www.post-gazette.com/pg/05034/452010.stm* (last visited July 2, 2005).

[72] See id.

[73] See AON, "Corporate Reputation: Not Worth Risking", 2, available at *http://www.aon.com/about/publications/pdf/issues/wharton corp rep r040303.pdf* (last visited July 2, 2005).

[74] Arthur Andersen, after nearly 90 years in business and a stellar reputation, imploded after being prosecuted and found guilty for tampering with documents related to its audit of Enron. See id. at 2.

[75] See id. at 5.

[76] See Elliot Blair Smith, "Trader Acquitted; Setback for Spitzer", USA Today, 01B, June 10, 2005, 2005 WLNR 9205035.

[77] See Business Terror Links Probed, supra note 60.

[78] See General Electric, GE 2002 Annual Report, 15 (Feb. 14, 2003) (unpublished report) available at *http://www.ge.com/files/usa/en/ar2002/ge_ar2002_letter.pdf*.

[79] Money and Morals at GE, supra note 57.

[80] See General Electric, Our Actions: GE 2005 Citizenship Report, 64 (unpublished report) available at *http://www.ge.com/files/usa/en/citizenship/pdfs/GE_2005_citizenship.pdf* (last visited July 5, 2005).

[81] See id.

[82] See Who Cares Wins, supra note 75, at 10; Global Environmental Management Initiative, "Clear Advantage: Building Shareholder Value – Environment: Value to the Investor", 1 (Feb. 2004) (unpublished report) available at *http://www.gemi.org/GEMI percent20Clear percent20Advantage.pdf*.

[83] See Innovest Strategic Value Advisors, Inc., "Best Practice Environmental Management: Analysis of Key Practices-Uncovering Hidden Value Potential for Strategic Investors", 23 (Apr. 2002) (unpublished whitepaper) at *http://www.innovestgroup.com/pdfs/ISVA_Best_Practice_Report_2002.pdf*.

[84] GolinHarris, "The State of Corporate Citizenship 2004 — Doing Well By Doing Good" "2004: The Trajectory of Corporate Citizenship in American Business", 2, (unpublished whitepaper) at *http://www.golinharris.com/pdf/CorporateAudit2004.pdf* (surveying 2770 U.S. respondents with margin of sampling error ± 3 percent as of June 2004) (last visited July 2, 2005).

[85] See Martin Langford, Burson-Marsteller London, "Communication in a World of Extremes: How Are We Going to Communicate After 11 September?" (Nov. 11, 2001) at *http://www.kommunikationsforening.dk/d70029*.

[86] Paula B. Thomas & Sara York Kenny, "Environmental Reporting: A Comparison of Annual Report Disclosures and Popular Financial Press Commentary" 1 (Apr. 1997) (unpublished paper) at *http://les.man.ac.uk/ipa97/papers/thomas61.pdf.*

[87] See id.

[88] United Nations Financial Sector Initiative Report, Who Cares Wins, 11 ex. 8, at *http://www. unglobalcompact.org/content/NewsDocs/WhoCaresWins.pdf 11*(Dec. 2004) [hereinafter Who Cares Wins].

[89] See id. at 11, fig 1.

[90] Investor Network on Climate Risk, "Ten Major Investors Issue 10-Point "Call For Action" on Global Warming Risks", Nov. 21, 2003, at *http://www.incr.com/news_release.htm.*

[91] Who Cares Wins, supra note 75, at 25, ex. 16.

[92] See The UN Principles for Responsible Investment, DSJI Newsletter (Dow Jones Sustainability Indexes), Apr. 2004, at 2, available at *http://www.sustainability-indexes.com/ djsi_pdf/news/QuarterlyNewsletter/ DJSI_Newsletter_0404.pdf.*

[93] Id.

[94] See Karen E. Schneitz & Marc Epstein, "Does Corporate Social Responsibility Pay Off?", Garziadio Business Report, Vol. 7, No. 2, at *http://gbr.pepperdine.edu/042/responsibility.html* (Sept. 2004) [hereinafter Does Corporate Social responsibility Pay Off?].

[95] See id.

[96] See id.

[97] See id.

[98] See id.

[99] See id. table 3.

[100] See id. table 4.

[101] "Launched in 1999, the Dow Jones Sustainability Indexes are the first global indexes tracking the financial performance of the leading sustainability-driven companies worldwide." Dow Jones Sustainability Index, at *http://www.sustainability-indexes.com/* (last visited July 5, 2005).

[102] See James F. Orr, "Outsourcing Human Resources: Why You Won't Lose Your Soul, The Chief Executive", June 2004, available at *http://www.findarticles.com/p/articles/mi_m4070/ is_199/ai_n6080645.*

[103] Julian Birkinshaw, "The Paradox of Corporate Entrepreneurship, Strategy + Business", Vol. 30, 46-58 (Spring 2003) (on file with author) [hereinafter The Paradox of Corporate Entrepreneurship]

[104] Press Release, Enron, Enron Named Most Innovative for Sixth Year (Feb. 6, 2001) available at *http://www.enron.com/corp/pressroom/releases/2001/ene/docs/15-MostInnovative-02-06-01-LTR. pdf.*

[105] The Paradox of Corporate Entrepreneurship, supra note 98.

[106] "It's Better (and Worse) Than You Think" Don Durfee, CFO Magazine May 03, 2004

[107] Id.

[108] Id.

[109] Id.

[110] Id. at 3 (citing Balanced Scorecard Collaborative, Aligning HR with Organizational Strategy (2002) (unpublished paper)).

[111] Id.

[112] Id.

[113] John P. Kotter & James L. Heskett, Corporate Culture and Performance, 11 (The Free Press 1992).

[114] Id.

[115] Id.

[116] The Cultural Integrity Assessment Model is recognized as a trademark of The Integrity Institute, Inc. and has been integrated into the Integria™ Model. The Integria mark has been filed as a "certification" mark with the United States Patent and Trademark Office. The Model was developed by Kim Cameron, Ph.D.(Professor of Management and Organization at the University of Michigan Business School and Professor of Higher

Education in the School of Education at the University of Michigan) and Robert E. Quinn, Ph.D. (Margaret Elliott Tracy Collegiate Professor in Business Administration at the Stephen M. Ross School of Business at the University of Michigan). Drs. Cameron and Quinn are Founding Members of The Integrity Institute.

[117] Kim Cameron & Robert E. Quinn, "Diagnosing and Changing Organizational Culture: Based On the Competing Values Framework; Revised Edition" (Jossey Bass 2006).

[118] Competing Values Company, The Competing Values Framework: An Introduction, 1 (unpublished paper) at *http://competingvalues.com/pdf/CVF percent20Introduction percent20Article.pdf* (last visited July 12, 2005). [The Competing Values Framework (CVF)] originally emerged from empirical research on the question of what makes organizations effective. It has since been extended as a framework that makes sense of high performance in regards to numerous topics in the social sciences and organizations. The CVF has been studied and tested in organizations for more than twenty five years by a group of thought leaders from leading business schools and corporations. It has been the topic of many books and papers and it has been employed in the improvement of thousands of organizations. Id. (citations omitted).

[119] See Warren E. Buffett, Berkshire Hathaway, Letter to Shareholders, 21 (Feb. 21, 2003) available at *http://www.berkshirehathaway.com/letters/2002pdf.pdf* ("[W]e become downright incredulous if they consistently reach their declared targets. Managers that always promise to 'make the numbers' will at some point be tempted to make up the numbers.").

[120] Warren E. Buffett, Letter to Shareholders, 21 (Feb. 21, 2003) available at *http://www. berkshirehathaway.com/letters/2002pdf.pdf.*

[121] Id.

[122] General Electric, GE 2001 Annual Report, (Feb. 15, 2005) (unpublished report) available at *http://www.ge.com/annual01/letter/page8.html.*

[123] General Electric, GE 2002 Annual Report, 15 (Feb. 14, 2003) (unpublished report) available at *http://www.ge.com/files/usa/en/ar2002/ge_ar2002_letter.pdf.*

[124] See Money and Morals at GE, supra note 57, at 176.

[125] Press Release, PriceWaterhouseCoopers, General Electric Is The World's Most Respected Company, According to Financial Times / PricewaterhouseCoopers Survey (Nov. 19, 2004) available at *http://www.pwc.com/extweb/ncpressrelease.nsf/docid/A07225F70D526EE085256F5 00053B37B.*

[126] See Sherry Day, "Coca-Cola Settles Whistle-Blower Suit for $540,000", N.Y. Times (Oct. 8, 2003), available at *http://www.agribusinesscenter.org/headlines.cfm?id=245*; Scott Leith, "Coke Apologizes to Burger King",The Atlanta Journal-Constitution (June 6, 2003), available at *http://www.ajc.com/business/content/business/coke/0603/18coke.html.*

[127] See, e.g., BBC News, "Soft Drink is Purified Tap Water", available at *http://news.bbc.co.uk/2/ hi/uk_news/ 3523303.stm* (last updated Mar. 1, 2004).

[128] Felicity Lawrence, "Things Get Worse With Coke", The Guardian (London), Mar. 20, 2004, available at *http://www.guardian.co.uk/business/story/0,3604,1174127,00.html.*

[129] Messod Daniel Beneish, The Detection of Earnings Manipulation, 24 (June 1999, corrected 2004) (unpublished whitepaper) (on file with author).

[130] See id.

[131] Id.

[132] The Earnings Integrity Assessment Model is recognized as a trademark of The Integrity Institute, Inc. and has been integrated into the Integria™ Model. The Integria mark has been filed as a "certification" mark with the United States Patent and Trademark Office. The Model was developed by Messod Daniel Beneish, Ph.D., is a Professor at the Kelly School of Business at Indiana University and a Founding Member of The Integrity Institute, Inc. and has contributed his model to The Integrity Institute for integration into the Integria Model.

[133] Partho Ghosh, Lori Harris, Juan Ocampo, Erik Simpson, Jay Krueger, & Jay Vaidhyanathan, "Stock Analysis of Enron Corporation", 12 (May 5, 1998) (unpublished report) at *http://parkercenter.johnson.cornell.edu/docs/other_research/1998_spring/ene.pdf.*

[134] See id.

[135] See id. at 1.

[136] See Beneish, supra note 122.

[137] See Beneish, supra note 122.

[138] Louis Lavelle, The Best & Worst Boards: "How the Corporate Scandals are Sparking a Revolution in Governance", BusinessWeek, Oct. 7, 2002, available at *http://www.businessweek.com/magazine/content/02_40/b3802001.htm*.

[139] Financial Times, FTfm, pg. 11 November 28, 2005

[140] Id.

[141] "Here It Comes: The Sarbanes-Oxley Backlash"; New York Times, April 17, 2005 (Jonathan D. Glater)

[142] Institutional Shareholder Services is a provider of proxy voting and corporate governance services. See *http://www.issproxy.com/index.jsp*.

[143] The Corporate Library is provider of corporate governance data, analysis, and risk assessment tools. See *http://www.thecorporatelibrary.com*.

[144] Findings on Corporate Governance, supra note 28.

[145] Id.

[146] "Here It Comes: The Sarbanes-Oxley Backlash"; New York Times, April 17, 2005 (Jonathan D. Glater)

[147] The Corporate Governance Integrity Assessment Model is recognized as a trademark of The Integrity Institute, Inc. and has been integrated into the Integria™ Model. The Integria mark has been filed as a "certification" mark with the United States Patent and Trademark Office.

[148] Id. at 1.

[149] Id.

[150] "Poison Pill" is a term commonly used to refer to a "Stockholder Rights Plan" that generally refers to any plan providing for the distribution of preferred stock, rights, warrants, options or debt instruments to the stockholders designed to deter non-negotiated (hostile) takeovers. The plans typically grant certain rights to stockholders, or the board upon the occurrence of a "triggering event," such as a tender offer, a third party acquisition, or a third party's purchase of a specified percentage of stock. See PBS, Wall Street Week With Fortune, at *http://www.pbs.org/wsw/resources/bfglosp.htm* (last visited July 21, 2005).

[151] See Lawrence D. Brown & Marcus L. Caylor, Corporate Governance Study: The Correlation between Corporate Governance and Company Performance, Georgia State University (2004) (unpublished whitepaper) (on file with author).

[152] The Leadership Integrity Assessment Model is recognized as a trademark of The Integrity Institute, Inc. and has been integrated into the Integria™ Model. The Integria mark has been filed as a "certification" mark with the United States Patent and Trademark Office. The Model is a fusion of the Leadership Assessment Model developed by Dr. Robert Quinn, Ph.D. (Margaret Elliott Tracy Collegiate Professor in Business Administration at the Stephen M. Ross School of Business at the University of Michigan) and Oren Harari, Ph.D. (Professor at the Graduate School of Business at the University of San Francisco). Drs. Quinn and Harari are Founding Members of The Integrity Institute, Inc.

[153] Denison, D. R., R. Hooijberg, R. E. Quinn. 1995. Paradox and performance: Toward a theory of behavioral complexity in managerial leadership. Organ. Sci. 6 (5) 524-540.

[154] Hart, S. L., R. E. Quinn. 1993. Roles executives play: CEOs, behavioral complexity, and firm performance. Human Relations. 46 (5) 543-574.

[155] Denison, D. R., R. Hooijberg, R. E. Quinn. 1995. Paradox and performance: Toward a theory of behavioral complexity in managerial leadership. Organ. Sci. 6 (5) 524-540.

[156] Oren Harari studied Colin Powell and wrote The Leadership Secrets of Colin Powell. Oren Harari, The Leadership Secrets of Colin Powell (McGraw-Hill 2002).

[157] Ronald R.Fogleman, Retired General, United States Air Force, The Leadership-Integrity Link, 39 (undated) (unpublished paper) at *http://www.au.af.mil/au/awc/awcgate/au-24/fogleman.pdf* (last visited July 21, 2005).

[158] Id.

[159] Mark W. Sickles, Shareholder Value Assurance: A Cure for Enronitis, 11 (Impact Consulting Group 2002).

[160] Supporting information on file with author.

[161] How to Spot the Next Enron; George Anders; Fast Company; May 2002; Issue 58, Pg. 120

[162] *www.cnn.money.com* (Coca-Cola Ticker: KO)

[163] Low & Cohen Kalafut, supra note 26, at 8.

[164] See Dow Jones, "France Rejects Coke's New Bid for Pernod's Orangina", Nov. 24, 1999, available at *http://www.smartmoney.com/bn/index.cfm?story=19991124115206*.

[165] Low & Cohen Kalafut, supra note 26, at 8.

[166] Leith, supra note 119.

[167] See Leith, supra note 119; Adam Levy & Steve Matthews, Coke's World of Woes, Bloomberg Markets magazine (July 2004), available at *http://www.killercoke.org/cokewoe.htm*.

[168] *www.cnn.money.com* Coca-Cola Ticker (KO)

[169] "Who Killed Westinghouse?"; Post-Gazette; Steve Massey *http://www.post-gazette.com/westinghouse/chapter6.asp* (last visited on November 29, 2005)

[170] Id.

[171] Id.

[172] David Norton, "Managing the Development of Human Capital, Balanced Scorecard Report, Vol. 3 No. 5", (Sep.-Oct. 2001).

[173] The Risk Integrity Assessment Model is recognized as a trademark of The Integrity Institute, Inc. and has been integrated into the Integria™ Model. The Integria mark has been filed as a "certification" mark with the United States Patent and Trademark Office. The Model was developed by Larry Ponemon, Ph.D. (Chairman and Founder of The Ponemon Institute) is a Founding Member of The Integrity Institute.

[174] The rest of the content to the end of this section was contributed by James Lam, who is President of James Lam & Associates, a Wellesley, Massachusetts-based risk consultancy and author of Enterprise Risk Management: From Incentives to Controls (Wiley 2003). He is not associated with The Integrity Institute, Inc. in any other way.

[175] *http://www.corporateleadershipcouncil.com/CLC/1,1283,0-0-Public_Display-105142,00.html*

[176] See James Lam & Associates, at *http://www.jameslam.com* (last visited August 3, 2005). The seven components are: 1) Corporate Governance, 2) Line Management, 3) Portfolio Management, 4) Risk Transfer, 5) Risk Analytics, 6) Data and Technology Resources, and 7) Stakeholder Management.

[177] "Drill Down is a simple technique for breaking complex problems down into progressively smaller parts." Mind Tools, Drill Down-Breaking Problems Down Into Manageable Parts, at *http://www.mindtools.com/pages/article/newTMC_02.htm* (last visited July 22, 2005). It encompasses a chart beginning with the overall, largely complex issue and whittles it down to the fine details involved in the problem. See id.

[178] See Julie Connelly, "CEOs to Boards: Don't You Trust Us?", Corporate Board Member (May/June 2005) at *http://www.boardmember.com/issues/archive.pl?article_id=12197&V=1*.

[179] L.J. Rittenhouse, Leadership, Governance and Breaking the Cycle of Corruption, Address to the Ontario Energy Association (Sept. 24, 2003) (on file with author).

[180] LRN & Wirthlin Worldwide, "Bridging the Divide Between Corporate America and The Public" (Nov. 18, 2003) (unpublished whitepaper) at *http://www.lrn.com/library/whitepapers/wirthlin_2003_print.php*.

[181] Perceptyx *www.perceptyx.com* is a technology provider of The Integrity Institute, Inc.

Index

About TEXERE

Texere, a progressive and authoritative voice in business publishing, brings to the global business community the expertise and insights of leading thinkers. Our books educate, enlighten, and entertain, and provide an intersection where our authors and our readers share cutting edge ideas, practices, and innovative solutions. Texere seeks to cultivate, enhance, and disseminate information that illuminates the global business landscape.

www.thomson.com/learning/texere

About the typeface

This book was set in 11 point Palatino. The original Palatino was designed from 1948-1950 by Hermann Zapf, while he was working at the Stempel AG in Frankfurt. The original font can be recognized by the missing foot serifs of p and q and by the long ascenders.